In the Footsteps of the Buddha

RENÉ GROUSSET

In the Footsteps of the Buddha

TRANSLATED FROM THE FRENCH
BY J. A. UNDERWOOD

AN ORION PRESS BOOK
GROSSMAN PUBLISHERS
NEW YORK   1971

OR 11/77

PREFACE

The theory of the "great ages" is no mere literary fiction. The thousand years of Greco-Roman classicism, not to mention its later "renaissances," undoubtedly had their source in the century and a half between the first Persian War and the battle of Chaeronea. During this short space of time all the potentialities of the Greek genius found their realization; the centuries of Hellenic and Roman civilization that ensued drew their life from this brief period of creative activity. Similarly, were not the greater part of the heart and spirit of France distilled in its glorious thirteenth century? Perhaps the ancient Indian tradition of the *kalpas* or cosmic cycles really does correspond to the hidden nature of things. Every now and again humanity, by dint of infinite gropings, achieves greatness and realizes its *raisons d'être* in a brief period of outstanding success before sinking back once more into an infinitely slow decline.

It would seem that the Buddhist world too enjoyed one of these privileged periods. It occurred in the early Middle Ages, around the seventh century. Our world, the West, lay in a kind of twilight, still unaware of the coming Romanesque dawn; in Byzantium the great "Macedonian" *basileis* had not yet made their appearance. But in the Far East, India and China were experiencing a period of intense political, intellectual, religious and artistic life. Buddhism, by drawing them into contact, had created a vast current of humanism flowing from Ceylon to the northernmost islands of the Japanese archipelago. The desiccation of Islam, the impoverishment brought about by Neo-Confucianism, and the retrogressive effects of Hinduism, though unfortunately at hand, had not yet made their presence felt. Buddhist mysticism, bred through a thousand years of meditation, had reached hitherto

1. Portrait of Hiuan Tsang, from Touen-
   Houang. (*Musée Guimet*)

undreamed-of regions of the soul, and the Indian aesthetic had been thereby renewed. China—receptive, open to innovation and then at the height of its strength—allowed itself to be touched by this sweetness. And there the human spirit lived out one of its privileged hours, an hour worthy of Athens and Alexandria. This was the period of the Chinese epic in central Asia and of the great pilgrimages to the holy land of the Ganges, the period of Mahayana idealism and of Gupta sculpture.

It is this period of high culture that I should like to try to evoke in this book. I should like to sketch the portraits of some of the leading characters of the period, the founders of Chinese imperialism and of the T'ang dynasty and their contemporaries Hiuan Tsang and Yi Tsing, those pious pilgrims whose journeys across the Gobi Desert and the Pamirs or down through the southern seas are as fascinating as those of the most intrepid explorers of our day; and finally the philosophers and sages whose speculations in the realm of metaphysics reached horizons even more vast. And our background, as we cross the Himalayas and sail down through Malaysia, shall be the whole glorious heyday of Buddhist art, from the "Romanesque" statues of the Wei dynasty at Yun-kang to the supernatural apparitions of Ajanta, Horyuji and Borobudur.

I need hardly add that it is not my intention here to indulge in tendentious dogmatizing. Where I have had occasion to expound the philosophical or religious theories of Buddhism I have done so without bias whether in one direction or in another, without bias but in all sincerity of heart. For whatever our private opinions may be, how can we refuse our common human assent to this immense endeavor of goodness and beauty? Without repudiating any of our own personal convictions but simply in all piety and admiration.

Note. For the chronology of Hiuan Tsang's travels in India I have adopted Vincent Smith's solution (see T. Watters, *On Yuan Chwang's Travels in India,* vol. 2, p. 335) which, despite its high content of hypothesis, remains in my opinion the most plausible.

CONTENTS

ILLUSTRATIONS

In the Footsteps of the Buddha

CHAPTER I

China in the Age of the Epics

Rᴀʀᴇʟʏ ʜᴀs the stuff of humanity entered such a melting-pot as it did in the Far East in the early Middle Ages following the collapse of the national empire of the Han dynasty, the Chinese equivalent of our Roman Empire. During the next two centuries, the fourth and the fifth, successive waves of Turco-Mongol hordes, more or less related to our European Huns, overran the provinces of northern China. The spectacle was analogous to that which the West was to witness during the fifth and sixth centuries. Morally, too, it was similar enough, the Tatar "Sons of Heaven" wedding their primitive bestiality to the vices of ancient civilizations in decay. Did not Charles Vignier point out to us the legacy of this retrogression in the sumptuous barbarism of contemporary bronzes?

I

Finally, at the beginning of the fifth century, one of these Tatar dynasties, more politically minded than the others, the dynasty of the T'o-pa Turks who styled themselves "Kings of Wei," eliminated the consanguineous hordes, adopted Chinese culture and for almost a hundred and fifty years held glorious, powerful and on the whole relatively peaceful sway over northern China.

In A.D. 453 the sovereign of these Sino-Tatars of Wei, T'o-pa Siun, was converted to Buddhism.

Buddhism, let us not forget, was no newcomer to China, having already been preached there for almost four centuries. Its fortunes had been various; long reckoned to be a negligible quantity by the national emperors of antiquity it had subsequently been adopted by several of the barbarian invaders of northern China, benefiting from their ephemeral power but also, by the same token, meeting with the conservative opposition of the literate classes. The conversion of the T'o-pa kings of Wei was an event of quite another order of importance. Although of barbarian origin these lords were sufficiently assimilated for the northern Chinese to consider them indigenous sovereigns. With them Buddhism received its naturalization papers. And since the southern emperors of Nanking took the same religious course as their rivals in the North, Buddhism became almost overnight the official religion throughout the whole of China.

In the realm of art, as we shall see, this triumph was to leave an immortal legacy: the crypts of Yun-kang and Lung-men with their carved reliefs and statuary which in their vitality and burning sincerity anticipated the art of our Western cathedrals. This mighty renaissance, so analogous to our own Romanesque renaissance of the ninth century, reached even greater heights when a brilliant national dynasty, that of the Sui, united the two Chinas and re-established the great empire of former days. During its brief dominion (589–617) the Sino-Buddhist workshops increased their output even further, and we need only leaf through the albums of Oswald Sirén[1] to realize what a wealth of mas-

---

[1] Oswald Sirén, *Chinese Sculpture from the Fifth to the Fourteenth Century*, 4 vols., 1925.

terpieces stem from this short period of time. Then, as a result of the follies of the second Sui emperor Yang-ti, the "Xerxes" or "Sardanapalus" of China, everything suddenly collapsed once more; the praetorians and legionary commanders rebelled and war broke out between *condottiere* and *condottiere*. We have seen it again in the early years of this century and we are familiar with the rhythm of these Chinese civil wars and their wake of misery, at that time inevitably capped by the reappearance of the barbarians on the fringes of the Gobi and at all the passes of the Great Wall.

Yang K'iung, a T'ang dynasty poet, tells us of his despair at this recurrence of the millenary convulsions after the ephemeral unity of the Sui period:

"Ch'ang-an is lighted by the fires of war. None today is at ease in his heart of hearts. Iron-clad horsemen surround the imperial capital. The snow lies heavy on the frozen standards. The furious voice of the wind mingles with the sound of the drums. And once again the man who commands a hundred soldiers is held in higher esteem than the learned and gifted scholar."

Another contemporary poet, Wei Cheng (d. 643), left his writing-desk to go and sign up with one of the combatant armies:

"The Empire having once more become the subject of dispute I throw aside my brushes to dream henceforth only of the chariots of war. Though many projects have been disappointed and many hopes deceived my energy at least is unabated. With a stick for climbing and a whip for galloping I set spurs to my horse, for I am going to join the Son of Heaven. I want him to give me a rope to bind the leader of the rebels. I wish my victorious arms to shatter the boldness of our enemies. By twisting paths I reach the tops of mountains and descend again toward the plain. On ancient, stunted trees sings the bird all a-glitter with hoar-frost. In the solitude of the mountains I hear monkeys calling at night. After the excitement of bottomless precipices come the roads without end. Other spirits would weaken before this ordeal but not the man of war who nurtures in his heart a harsh and ruthless will."

The chief whom Wei Cheng was going to join was the young general Li Shih-min, later Emperor T'ai-tsung the Great. The warrior of genius who was to restore the empire almost single-handed and set Chinese history and civilization for three centuries on a new course had just then made his appearance.

Li Shih-min's father, Li Yuan, Count of T'ang and governor of a military district in Shansi province, was a gentleman of noble birth, a respected general and as honest an administrator as was possible for someone of his importance; he was also a timorous man who lived in constant fear of compromising himself and who retained sufficient loyalty not to break his oath until the very last extremity. Moreover he was saturated with Confucian wisdom and learned maxims. Li Shih-min too, in spite of his youth (he was born in 597 and was consequently little more than twenty at this time), had been brought up on a diet of historical reminiscences and fine phrases. But his experience of camplife—for his father's fief, being in the nature of a march, was in a perpetual state of alert against Turkish raiders—as well as of courtlife (and the Sui court was the most magnificent, the most corrupt and the most fickle ever to have existed in the Far East) had taught the young man to make use of the wisdom of Confucianism rather than be its slave. Whatever he was to do in the future, and we shall see some singular blots upon his conduct, he always contrived to have morality on his side. Added to which he possessed extraordinary dynamism and an almost infallible knack of making sound decisions; a perfect balance of cunning and bravery, boldness and good sense, he was for the China of his day the epitome of the complete man.

The empire, meanwhile, was a scene of total military anarchy. Emperor Yang-ti had retired to Yang-chu in the shelter of the Blue River (Yang-tse) estuary and was living a life of resignation and debauchery while his generals squabbled over the various provinces. The young Li Shih-min, assured of a solid military following in his Shansi domains, strengthened by his relations of personal friendship with several Turkish khans, and having furthermore established valuable links with various palace officials, fretted and chafed before his father's anachronistic loyalism. To force the latter's hand he resorted to a method that was utterly Chinese. According to the *T'ang Shu* or *History of the T'ang Dynasty* he had struck up an alliance with a eunuch of the imperial harem. This eunuch, at Li Shih-min's instigation, offered Li Yuan one of the girls intended for the emperor. The young recluse must have been attractive because the worthy Li Yuan accepted this dangerous "gift" without a moment's reflection. Li Shih-min then promptly pointed out to his father that their family had now placed itself under the imperial ban, the abduction of a palace girl being, at law, punishable by death. Li Yuan was horror-struck but what could he do? It was too late to retreat. He summoned his followers and mobilized his official troops at T'ai-yuan (Yangku), his residence and the capital of present-day Shansi—not without first having calmed his own scruples by announcing that his only motive for taking up arms was in order loyally to deliver the emperor from the hands of the other claimants.

This was all Li Shih-min wanted. His army was ready. Just as he had contrived to elicit favors from the very harem of the imperial court, so he had succeeded, by his soldierly plain-speaking, in obtaining the sympathy of the Turks, and these dangerous neighbors had placed at his disposal five hundred crack mercenaries and two thousand horses. At the same time his sister Li Shih, a young heroine who sat a horse as well as he did, had sold her jewelry and used the cash to raise ten thousand men whom she brought to join him. Li Shih-min soon had an army of sixty thousand men under his command—men whose fatigues he shared, whom he was capable of spurring to fanaticism by his own example, and who were ready to lay down their lives for him. For more than four years (618-622) he led them from province to province against one army after another, putting order into the chaos that was China.

Circumstances removed his father's qualms at an early stage: down on the Blue River certain members of the imperial guard had taken advantage of the general unrest to assassinate Yang-ti, the rightful emperor. The Count of T'ang thereupon declared himself the dynasty's avenger and assumed in the name of the last member of the Sui the general lieutenancy of the empire; a few months later, at the instigation of Li Shih-min, he deposed this phantom ruler and proclaimed himself emperor (618).

The imperial capital Ch'ang-an (Sian), which played somewhat the same role in ancient Chinese history as Rome in the history of the West, was the first to open its doors (618). The T'ang after all were natives of this province of Shensi which, ever since the days of the T'sin of old, had been the birthplace of all the great dynasties. Li Shih-min then set out to lay siege to the second capital, Lo-yang, which was commanded by one of his father's most redoubtable rivals. It was a difficult undertaking for the town was particularly well defended, and furthermore the other claimants, whom the success of the T'ang was beginning to disturb, were not slow in coming to its assistance. The young hero took with him Yu-che King-te, a man who until recently had been his enemy but whom he had won over to his cause after taking him prisoner and to whom, despite the misgivings of his advisers, he had entrusted a position of command.

According to his biographer, when Li Shih-min arrived within sight of the town he took a party of eight hundred horsemen on a tour of reconnaissance. The garrison spotted them, however, made a sortie and soon the little troop was completely surrounded. As he was trying to cut a way through with his sword an enemy officer recognized him and made a rush for him with pike at the ready. The future emperor was on the point of paying for his temerity with his life when King-te, who had not once taken his eyes off him, struck down the assailant. The T'ang battalions arrived on the scene at that moment and rescued their chief from a tight spot. Meanwhile an enemy army under the command of one of the claimants was on its way down from Pe-chi-li to relieve Lo-yang. When it was still several miles from the town, Li Shih-min set out at dawn with the pick of his cavalry, rode at the gallop to

2. T'ang Dynasty soldiers, from Touen-Houang. (*Archives photographiques*)

the enemy camp, took it by surprise and laid everything to the sword, including the general's tent. The general himself, with his troops in disarray, received a pike-wound and was taken prisoner. Lo-yang capitulated a few days later. Li Shih-min burned down the imperial palace, still full of the art treasures of the Sui, and returned in triumph to Ch'ang-an (621).

The Chinese chroniclers portray with quite unwonted colorfulness this return of the young conqueror, depicting him riding slowly through the streets of the capital mounted on a richly caparisoned charger, dressed in his battle tunic and golden breast-plate, his helmet on his head, his bow slung across his chest, a quiver full of arrows at his shoulder and a sword in his hand. The defeated claimants marched at his stirrups. And this description from the *T'ang Shu* takes on an extraordinary relief for us now that the discoveries of archeologists have allowed us to visualize it almost exactly as it was. Funerary statuettes have made us familiar with every swaggering caracole of that T'ang cavalry. We even know by their portraits, names and service records, Li Shih-

3. One of the horses of T'ai-tsung. (*Archives photographiques*)

min's favorite mounts, those sturdy horses with plaited manes which he had carved on his tombstones at Li-ts'iuan Hien. To be even more precise, the charger which took part in the triumphal procession through Ch'ang-an was very likely the "Autumn Rose" who is celebrated as having been a faithful companion to his master during the conquest of Honan. As for the conqueror's armor, we can see its exact replica any day on the broad shoulders of the warriors or *lokapalas* in the funerary portraits or Buddhist statues of our museums.

Chinese unity had, by fire and the sword, once more become a reality. It was high time, too, for the Turks were already at the borders.

From the middle of the sixth century, when they had replaced the Avars as lords of the steppes, the Turks had dominated all northern Asia from the forests of Manchuria to the banks of the Oxus. They had set up one khanate in the Mongolian pasturelands to the south of Lake Baikal and another on the plains of Russian Turkistan. During the long years in which they had been contained to the southwest by the Persian Sassanian Empire and to the east by the Wei and Sui dynasties of China, and thus confined to the deserts and the steppes, they had incessantly cast eyes upon these ancient civilized empires and their wealth. Already the grey eyes of these semi-nomadic herdsmen held the dream of the Seljuks and Jenghis Khan, the vision of the hordes pouring into the imperial cities on the Euphrates and the Huang-ho. The state of military anarchy in which China still appeared to be toiling seemed to them an excellent opportunity. Kie-li, khan of the northern Turks who reigned from the Orkhon in northern Mongolia, and Tu-li his nephew together led a tremendous ride which swept past the frontierposts and on across Shensi to the outskirts of Ch'ang-an itself. Old Li Yuan panicked and spoke of evacuating the capital. Li Shih-min said nothing but took a party of a hundred picked horsemen and went out to meet the Turkish challenge. Taking an enormous risk he went up to them, entered their ranks and began haranguing them: "The T'ang dynasty owes nothing to the Turks! Why do you invade our realms? I, the king of T'sin, have come to pit my strength against your khan!" At the same time he made a personal appeal to those of their leaders such as Tu-li Khan with whom he had formerly been on terms of military comradeship, reawakening in them a feeling of the brotherhood of arms. His firmness of bearing together with his deep knowledge of the Turkish soul intimidated the fickle spirits of the barbarians. The leaders of the horde conferred together for a while and then, without a blow having been struck, reined their horses round and departed. Several hours later a torrential rainstorm burst over the region. Li Shih-min immediately summoned his captains. "Comrades," his chronicler has him say, "this is the time to show our mettle. The whole steppe is one great flood. Night is about to fall and it will be one of the darkest. We must march. The Turks are to be feared only when they can fire their arrows. Let us have at them with saber and pike and we shall put them to rout before they have had time to prepare their defense!"

And so it was. The Turkish camp was roused at dawn and everything laid to the sword, even the tent of the khan who, asking for terms, withdrew to Mongolia (624).

It was becoming increasingly apparent that the young hero was the mainstay of the empire, and his two brothers, jealous of his fame, resolved to do away with him. Even his father, who owed his throne to him, gradually came to resent his popularity and kept him at a distance from affairs of state. Then began one of those savage dramas which were almost as frequent in the Forbidden City as they were in the Sacred Palace of Constantinople; indeed we might almost, as we follow the record of those tragic days in the *T'ang Shu,* be reading a page from the epic of Byzantium. At a banquet which they offered him in celebration of his victories, Li Shih-min's brothers had him poisoned. He took an antidote. They then posted some hired assassins to lie in wait for him at one of the doors of the palace. A traitor warned him, however (the whole story is as full of treachery as it is of blood and of protestations of virtue) and Li Shih-min switched to the initiative. His faithful followers, anticipating their adversaries' plans, posted spies in all the suitable places, and as the ambush against him was being prepared he marched out to meet the enemy, the same man in this war of assassins as he was on the field of battle. "He donned his breast-plate and helmet, took his quiver and his arrows and set forth for the palace." As soon as his two brothers saw him coming they let off a volley of arrows. They missed, but Li Shih-min killed one of them with his very first arrow. The second brother was killed by Li Shih-min's lieutenant. At this point the soldiers who had been placed in ambush for him emerged and, according to the *T'ang Shu,* "none dared make another movement." Meanwhile, continues the chronicler, as the palace servants and even the populace of the town were beginning to flock to the scene, Li Shih-min took off his helmet and made himself known to them; standing before the bleeding corpses of his brothers, he shouted to the crowd: "Fear not for me, my children. Those who would assassinate me are dead!" Whereupon his faithful follower King-te cut off the two young men's heads and held them up before the people.

It remained only to announce the execution to the emperor, whose partiality for the side of the two victims had never been a secret. With this duty Li Shih-min charged King-te. In defiance of all the sacred rules of etiquette King-te burst into the emperor's apartments fully armed, perhaps even with his hands still red with the princes' blood.

We catch a glimpse, through the language of the official records, of what must have taken place—one of those beautiful scenes of Confucian hypocrisy in which the murderers, still glowing with battle, indulged in a spate of moralistic saws with the sole aim of achieving a return to legality without losing face.

The old emperor, however, hearing the news, had at first been unable to suppress his anger and grief. His first reaction was to order a searching inquiry. It had not yet dawned on him that he was no longer the master. One of his courtiers discreetly brought him back to reality: "There is no longer any inquiry to be held . . . Whatever form the event took, your two dead sons are guilty and Li Shih-min is innocent." The words are worthy of Tacitus and put just the right finishing touch to this Neronian drama. Furthermore those very same courtiers now revealed monstrous crimes to be laid to the victims' charge: had not the two murdered princes been conspiring with a number of their father's wives? What more was needed to justify their execution!

Li Shih-min then had himself announced. When the fratricide presented himself, showing moreover every sign of the most moving filial piety, the old monarch fell on his neck and wept, even congratulating him on having saved the dynasty. It was a touching scene. "The emperor," writes the official chronicler imperturbably, "had always hesitated between his sons. The death of the two elder put an end to his perplexity and his old affection for Li Shih-min resumed its rightful place in his heart. Seeing him kneeling at his feet in the posture of a criminal seeming to beg for mercy he was unable to restrain his tears. He raised him up, kissed him and assured him that, far from believing him guilty, he was convinced that Li Shih-min had acted only in legitimate self-defense." Having said which the emperor promptly abdicated in favor of his son, though not without further edifying scenes, for in conformity with the demands of etiquette Li Shih-min refused the throne. In vain did the assembled nobles declare themselves unanimously in favor of the hero of the hour; again he refused and, "kneeling before his father, begged him with tears in his eyes to remain in power until his death." However, the old man then made it an order and Li Shih-min, as a loyal subject, was obliged to obey. Having allowed his hand to be forced, he at last mounted the throne. The date: 4 September 626. To remove all possibility of vendetta and to complete the pacification of the empire the new emperor promptly had his sisters-in-law and all his nephews put to death. As for old Li Yuan, he retired to one of his palaces where according to the *T'ang Shu* "he lived on in the enjoyment of all honor and tranquil pleasure, his son giving him never the least occasion to regret the step he had taken in abdicating."

This palace drama, however, had renewed the hopes of the Turks. Hardly was the new emperor on the throne than the hordes from Mongolia descended on the empire. A hundred thousand horsemen galloped across the Gobi in a daring raid, invaded Kansu and Shensi and swept down the Wei valley as far as Ch'ang-an. On 23 September 626 their squadrons appeared before the Pen-kiao bridge opposite the city gate. On this occasion too the courtiers begged their young sovereign to abandon his dangerously exposed capital. But Li Shih-min, whom we shall henceforth call by his canonical name of Emperor T'ai-tsung, was not the sort of man to let himself be intimidated. Kie-li Khan insolently sent one of his men to demand tribute, failing which a million nomads would pour in and sack the capital. T'ai-tsung's reply was to threaten to cut off the emissary's head. He was taking a considerable risk as he appears to have had a very limited number of troops in Ch'ang-an at this time. However, in order to mislead the enemy he gave orders that these troops should emerge from a number of different gates and form up at the foot of the walls. He himself, switching to the initiative, took a small party of horsemen and went off in his usual way to reconnoiter the enemy army. Ignoring the protests of his companions he made his way up the course of the Wei River in full view of the Turkish squadrons and at the mercy of the first arrow. The fact is that he had a better idea than his men of the psychology of the nomads: "The Turks know me," his biographer has him say. "They have learned to fear me. The mere sight of me will fill them with terror. And when they see my troops file out they will believe them to be far more numerous than they really are." He rode on toward the enemy "as confidently as if he had been going to visit his own camp." At the sight of him the Turks, "struck by the air of fearlessness and grandeur that emanated from his entire person, dismounted from their horses and saluted him after the custom of their country." Furthermore the Chinese army was at that moment forming up on the flat ground behind him, its armor and its standards gleaming and glinting in the sun. T'ai-tsung advanced even closer to the Turkish camp and then, holding his horse by the bridle, made a sign for the Chinese army to draw off and remain in battle formation.

Raising his voice the emperor summoned the two Turkish khans,

Kie-li and Tu-li, and proposed meeting them in single combat, after the manner of the warriors of the steppes. "Li Shih-min, though he be now emperor, has not forgotten the use of his weapons!" And in the name of soldierly honor, addressing them in their language and appealing to their feelings as men of war, he reproached them severely with having violated the truce and been false to their oath. Thus challenged, over-whelmed as they were by such courage and taken aback by the deploy-ment of the Chinese cavalry, the Turkish khans sued for peace. This was concluded next day before the very gates of Ch'ang-an, on the bridge over the Wei, following the sacrifice of the traditional white horse. This time the Turks had learned their lesson. They were not to return again.

Several weeks later three thousand horses and ten thousand sheep arrived at the frontier, representing the nomads first tribute. T'ai-tsung refused to accept them until all the Chinese who had been taken pris-oner in the recent wars had returned from Mongolia. As soon as this condition was fulfilled, however, he invited the emissaries of the Turks into his presence "and treated them as if they had been ambassadors of the very greatest powers."

To avoid a recurrence of similar alarms T'ai-tsung's counselors ad-vised him to rebuild or at least reinforce the Great Wall. He smiled: "What need is there to fortify the frontiers?" Indeed by clever en-couragement of internal dissent and even rebellion he progressively un-dermined the authority of the Orkhon khans. Then, following an un-wise act of provocation by Kie-li Khan he threw his cavalry columns right across the Gobi Desert into the very heart of the Mongolian steppe. The startled nomads were cut to pieces and the khan and all his vassals taken prisoner (630).

The *T'ang Shu* gives a complacent description of the awe-inspiring spectacle of the Turkish leaders prostrated at the feet of T'ai-tsung. The emperor had expressed the desire to see them all together in public au-dience, both the recently conquered enemies and the khans who had long been won round. "Arriving in the audience chamber they proceeded ceremonially to show their respect by striking the floor with their foreheads on three separate occasions, and three times at each occasion." The Grand Khan Kie-li was treated as a prisoner-of-war and as such all the leaders of the loyalist Turks were given precedence over him. After this humiliation, however, it was the emperor's subtle policy to grant him a pardon and, while still keeping him captive, give him a palace at the court.

The whole of the former khanate of the northern Turks, that is to say the whole of what is now Inner Mongolia and the Mongolian Peoples' Republic, was annexed to the empire (630). The Turkish inscription at Kosho Tsaidam dramatically summarizes this demise of an entire nation: "The sons of the noble Turks became slaves of the Chinese people, their spotless daughters bondwomen. The Turkish nobles gave up their Turkish titles and, receiving the titles of Chinese dignitaries, placed themselves under the Chinese *qagan* and pledged to him for fifty years their work and their strength."

The Turks indeed found in T'ai-tsung a warrior entirely to their taste. Having lived among their mercenaries from his early youth he could, as we have seen, speak a language they understood. They loved this emperor who was always on horseback, so unlike the timorous Sons of Heaven of the olden days; in him they found a war leader resembling their own former *qagan* to lead them to battle and plunder. As the Kosho Tsaidam inscription deplores, they vowed him an unshakable loyalty and were bound to him by that military oath which was the foundation of Turkish society.

With the help of such allies T'ai-tsung, having crushed the Mongolian Turks, was during the next twenty years to extend his suzerainty over the Turks of Turkistan, the Indo-European oases of the Gobi and even the various central Asian states as far as the Caspian and the borders of India. Under him a quite unexpected China, a China of epic proportions, revealed itself to an astonished Asia. Far from treating with the barbarians and buying them off with gold, this China made them tremble in its turn. The realistic art of this period—that powerful animalist and military art of reliefs, statues and funerary terra cottas with its almost exaggerated vigor (the athletic *lokapala* of Lung-men) and its taste for emphasis which went as far as an almost caricatured violence—perfectly expresses this state of mind. Even the ceramics of

4. Life in China at the time of Hiuan Tsang. Lacquered folding-screen. (*Archives photographiques*)

the T'ang period, with their somewhat savage colors, orange-yellows and pure greens, bear witness to the spirit of this time.

Comparing his achievement one day with those of the great conquerors of former times, T'ai-tsung was to evoke the name of the most illustrious emperor of Chinese antiquity, Han Wu-ti. And indeed, across the gulf of the barbarian invasions of the fourth century, it was the China of the Han dynasty that had been resuscitated, and the epic now beginning was destined to surpass even that of the Han emperors. Pan Ch'ao himself, contemporary and emulator of our Trajan and conqueror of old Kashgharia, could not number so many plundered herds, so many routed hordes and so many thousands of severed heads to his credit as the generals of the house of T'ang. For since that time, in the three centuries during which she had given way before the invading barbarians, China had absorbed the blood of the victorious hordes; she had nourished and strengthened herself with it and now directed back against the people of the steppes, coupled with the vast superiority of her millennial civilization, the force she had derived from them.

We can see them in our collections of funerary statuettes, these horsemen and foot-soldiers wearing the caftan of the Turkish auxiliary or the helmet of the T'ang legionary, their rude faces invariably half-Tatar, with their features hardened into grimaces; harsh figures standing there in their armor of boiled leather reinforced at chest and back by metal plates, with their pauncers of leather or metal plates and their great round or rectangular shields decorated with monsters, ready for the crossing of the Gobi or the ascent of the Altai. Even in Buddhist works like the statues or paintings depicting the *lokapalas* Vajrapani or Vaisravana we find that shell-like armor, that gruff and formidable bearing. There in the silence of the tomb we encounter the whole T'ang cavalry still pawing and snorting and whinnying in its impatience to be off on that promised raid to Kashghar or Kucha. We need hardly be surprised that the Tokharian cities of the Gobi, so proud of their delicate Indo-Persian culture, were unable to resist the onslaught of those galloping squadrons. For were not all the adventurers of Upper

5. Two riders in a Chinese landscape, from Touen-Houang. (*Musée Guimet*)

Asia, from Turkish khans like A-she-na Sho-eul and A-she-na Ta-nai to Korean war-lords such as Kao Sien-che, admitted to positions of command in the imperial army on condition only that they show themselves bold and eager? Even the western Turks themselves, who made the Sassanian Empire tremble and were later to cause the rising Arab power such anxiety, even they gave ground before this cavalry that was so like their own. Down it swept like a whirlwind on their encampments, scattering their *yurts* as far as the gorges of the Tarbagatai and throwing them right back to the flat Kirhiz steppe.

The hero of the hour was henceforth the "frontiersman," as celebrated in the lines written by Li T'ai-po during the following century, lines which breathe something of the T'ang epic:

"The frontiersman never so much as opens a book his whole life long. But he knows how to hunt, being skillful, strong and bold. In the autumn his horse is plump, for the grass of the prairies suits it excellently; when he gallops he leaves no shadow. . . . How proud and disdainful he looks! His ringing whip strikes the snow or resounds in the gilded holster. Quickened by generous wine he summons his falcon and rides deep into the countryside. His bow is rounded by his mighty arm; it never straightens without a victim. Often two birds fall together, both struck out of the air by the same whistling arrow. All move aside at his coming for his valor and war-like humor are well known throughout the Gobi."

The advent of the T'ang dynasty once again raised the problem of religion. With his education, the sort of tastes and interests we have seen him to have had, and the entourage which we have just described, it was only natural that Emperor T'ai-tsung should at the time of his accession have had very little sympathy indeed for the religion of peace, idealism and renunciation represented by Buddhism. "Emperor Leang Wu-ti," he remarked on one occasion, "preached Buddhism to his officers to such effect that they were incapable of taking horse to defend him against the rebels. Emperor Yuan-ti expounded to his officers the texts of Lao-tse instead of ordering them to march against the Huns who were ravaging his empire. Such things speak volumes to him who takes their meaning!" His confidant in these matters, the aged Confucian scholar Fu Yi, had a suitable horror of Buddhism. It was Fu Yi who in 626 had submitted to Emperor Li Yuan a petition listing all the grievances of Confucian positivism against Buddhist monachism:

"The teaching of the Buddha is full of follies and absurdities. The loyalty of subjects toward their prince and filial piety are duties to which this sect gives no recognition whatever. Its disciples spend their lives in idleness, never making the slightest effort. If they dress differently from ourselves it is merely in order to influence the public authorities or to spare themselves trouble. By their musings they persuade the simple to pursue an illusory happiness and fill them with mistrust for our laws and the wise judgments of the ancients."

The positivism of the scholar was here wedded to the instinctive anticlericalism of the old soldier. And sure enough Fu Yi himself in his appeal to Li Yuan and Li Shih-min, argued against the Buddhists on the grounds of their pacifism and celibacy: "This sect," he protested, "today comprises a hundred thousand bonzes and as many bonzesses living in a state of celibacy. It would be in the interests of the state to oblige them to marry. The resultant hundred thousand families would provide citizens to be enrolled in the army for forthcoming wars. At present these people constitute by their idleness a burden upon the society at whose expense they live. Reintegrated within that society, they would contribute to the general good and would no longer be depriving the state of the arms whose duty it is to serve in its defence."

This curious brand of military anticlericalism was quite in harmony with the inclinations of the T'ang. Shortly after receiving this petition from his minister, Li Yuan ordered a census of all monasteries and religious throughout the empire. He followed this up with a program of almost total secularization, leaving only three authorized monasteries in Ch'ang-an, his capital, and one in each of the largest cities. These "official" monasteries were moreover kept under strict surveillance by the authorities. We shall see from the story of Hiuan Tsang the difficulties with which every new ordinand had to contend from this quarter.

T'ai-tsung, when he acceded to the throne, continued the same policy. In 631 for example, acting on the advice of Fu Yi, he issued an edict obliging all monks to perform the Confucian rites of filial piety. This was pure chicanery, but evidence nonetheless of a systematic ill-will.

An era of anticlericalism coupled with brutal militarism appeared to be dawning over the Far East. Yet how could the conqueror reverse the flow of Chinese development? He might change the face of Asia and draw his people into an epic worthy of Macedonia and Rome, but whatever the force of his personality, and it was to loom majestically over three centuries of history, it did not lie within his power to stem the tide of mysticism that was rising in the Chinese soul.

CHAPTER 2

The Call
of Buddhism

THE AGE of the sword is often an age of faith. In the West in the early Middle Ages, amid the ruins of the Germanic invasions, sensitive souls turned in upon themselves and found in their belief the consolation they could not do without. It was exactly the same in fifth-century China. There is no need to turn to the texts to be persuaded of the intensity of religious feeling at this time. We need only glance at the art of the Wei dynasty, steles, reliefs or statues, in our museums and collections.

Here, however, we must add a word of clarification. Notwithstanding their fashionable popularity, these Wei works are by no means uniformly or necessarily beautiful in themselves. Indeed it is our opinion that the sculptural quality of the majority of these pieces is quite mediocre. It is not in that respect, then, that they interest us. The quality that draws our attention in the votive steles of the period—the great stele of 554 in the Boston Museum, for instance—is the total subordination of sculpture to religious sentiment. The pre-Buddhist or at least sensual origins of this art undoubtedly remain clearly discernible, yet how deeply they have been transformed by the mighty current of the new idealism. There are obvious reminiscences of the "Confucian" funerary reliefs of ancient China, but without the fantastic movement that informs men, spirits and animals in the burial chambers of Shantung, dating from the Han dynasty; divinities and other figures are here depicted motionless in the great peace of Buddhism. There are reminiscences too of the Greek art of Gandhara or the Indian art of the Gupta period, but with no trace, or hardly any, of Greek sculptural technique or of Hindu grace and sensuality; nothing but stiffly reclin-

6. Chinese stele, Fifth Century.
(*Archives photographiques*)

7. Painting from Qyzil,
typical of Chinese influ-
ence. (*Musée Guimet*)

ing figures with fixed smiles, forming the ritual gesture of trust or the
appeal for mercy, their robes crudely broken into great angular folds or
treated with a childish calm in little rounded waves. In reality they are
no longer material beings beneath these enormous pointed haloes surrounding and crowning them with their tall flames: this is the styliza-
tion, fleshless and incorporeal, of the mantle of monasticism.

What transcendent idealism, what miracle of ardent faith accomplished this transformation of the insipid Apollonian Buddhas of
Gandhara and the Indian Buddhas of the Gupta schools, nude figures
of a tropical sensuality, into these tall, benedictory statues? But then

how was it that the reliefs of Christian sarcophagi were able to give birth to the deeply affecting figures of the Romanesque period? For early French sculpture does indeed make a most appropriate comparison here; Alfred Salmony is entirely justified in drawing a parallel between Wei art and the reliefs of the great French cathedrals—S.Sernin, Toulouse; S.Pierre, Moissac; S.Pierre, Angoulême; Vézelay; S.Lazare, Autun; even the Romanesque portal of Chartres Cathedral. However, the tympana of Vézelay, Moissac and Autun display a liveliness which is quite unknown in Wei art. On the other hand a touch of Gothic tenderness is already apparent in the great reliefs of Yun-kang and in a number of contemporary statues and stele figures. A smile has softened the severity of the old Sino-Buddhist imagery; the rehabilitation of realism which during the T'ang period was to rob art of almost all its fervor and mystery still lies in the future. One or two of the Yun-kang Buddhas and various steles such as the stele with three characters in the Guakino (ex-Vignier) Collection present in the caress of their peaceful lines an impression of calm, freshness, candor and relaxing simplicity which is possibly unique in Far Eastern art. It is the idealism of the Mahayana itself translated into artistic form. Later, under the T'ang dynasty, there were to be works which perhaps, like those of Lung-men, came closer to our own classicism, and which were also, like those of T'ien-lung-shan, closer to the Indian art from which they originally derived. But the exquisite simplicity of Wei art was never to be equalled.

We must bear these great works constantly in mind if we are truly to enter the soul of Buddhist China in the early Middle Ages. They will make the vocation of a man like Hiuan Tsang abundantly clear to us.

In 618, the very year in which the future emperor launched the series of campaigns that was to win him control of the empire, a young Buddhist monk, fleeing from the civil wars that were laying waste the northern districts, arrived in Ssu-ch'uan. This sequestered province of sheltered alpine valleys was to provide him with a relatively calm asylum while awaiting the passing of the storm.

The fugitive was only about fifteen years of age, having been born in Lo-yang probably in 602. The name we know him by, his monastic name of Hiuan Tsang, was to become, together with that of T'ai-tsung, the most renowned of this century, for history was one day to associate the conqueror and the pilgrim in a common celebrity. Yet can there ever have been two more contrasted spirits? We have already pictured this Chinese Caesar, standing on the threshold of the epoch he was so majestically to dominate. The figure who now confronts us is a young monk for whom the world literally did not exist, a young man afire with metaphysical concern and mysticism and yet as deeply Chinese as the other; for this fervent Buddhist was the heir of a long line of scholars and mandarins mellowed in the observance of Confucian wisdom and the age-old etiquette, that courtesy of the Chinese heart. He himself had been brought up in the pure Confucian tradition. At the age of eight he was already astounding his father with his observance of the rites; everything about him appeared to point to his becoming the most illustrious scholar of his day, when the example of his brother, who had just taken Buddhist orders, determined his vocation. The youngster too went and knocked "at the Black Door," in the monastery of Tseng-t'ussu at Lo-yang, and his precocious wisdom so impressed one of the heads of the community that he was admitted in spite of his youth. He took his vows in that same monastery in Lo-yang. He was then not yet thirteen years old.

Hiuan Tsang had found his life's path. He plunged into the study of Indian philosophy. The schools of Buddhism, as we shall see later, were as numerous as they were diverse, ranging from the positivistic sects of what was known as the Little Vehicle (the Hinayana) to the mystical doctrines of the Great Vehicle (the Mahayana). It was toward the latter that Hiuan Tsang was immediately drawn. The mystical "nihilism" of the *Nirvana Sutra* and the absolute idealism of the *Maha-yana Samparigraha Sastra* fired him with such a passion that he forgot even sleep and sustenance.

However, as we have seen, Lo-yang was hardly a propitious site for such meditations. In the anarchy that followed the collapse of the Sui and in the midst of the civil wars between the T'ang and their rivals "the imperial city had become a haunt of brigands and Honan a den of wild beasts; the streets of Lo-yang were littered with corpses. The magistrates were massacred. As for the many Children of the Buddhist Law, they were obliged to flee or perish." [1]

But where could they flee? Virtually the entire empire was wallow-ing in anarchy. It was a terrible time for a scholar and sensitive soul like Hiuan Tsang. "At that time," writes his disciple and biographer Hwui-li plaintively, "the T'ang dynasty was only just beginning to establish itself. All troops were still under arms. No one was concerned about anything but the craft of war. People had no time to devote to the teachings of Confucius or the Buddha. . . ." It was then the Hiuan Tsang and his brother went off to seek asylum in the mountains of Ssu-ch'uan.

At Ch'eng-tu, the capital of Ssu-ch'uan, the fugitives found a tiny group of religious and philosophers exiled like them by the civil wars. Hiuan Tsang spent two or three years there in the monastery of Kung-huei-ssu studying in depth the various Buddhist systems. It is interest-ing to note that it was at this time that his philosophical opinions began to become more pronounced, for though he also studied the works of the positivist and realist school such as the *Abhidharma Kosa Sastra* it was toward the idealism of the *Mahayana Samparigraha Sastra* that his preferences more and more inclined. However, no trace of exclusivity could be detected in Hiuan Tsang at this or at any future time, and it was precisely this that was to be his strength. His familiarity with the teaching of the most opposing schools, at a time when so many other

---

[1] From *Hsi yu chi* (*Descriptions of the Western Lands*), Hiuan Tsang's account of his trav-els written in 648.

monks limited themselves to the doctrines of their own sect, was to ensure his superiority in debate. We shall see how in the course of his metaphysical discussions with the doctors of central Asia and India he was able on every occasion to overwhelm them by the weight of his erudition and the appositeness of his quotations. In the pages of his biography we see him traveling throughout the vast Sanskrit world, which at that time stretched from the tip of the Deccan to Nara and from the southernmost point of Sumatra to Turfan, no sooner arriving in a place than he gathered together all the learned men of the locality and began to debate with them. The picture is exactly that of the great scholars who carried in their memory the double treasure of the sacred and secular scriptures and journeyed six centuries later throughout the Latin world from Salerno to Uppsala and from Santiago de Compostela to the abbey of Fulda.

And when one day Hiuan Tsang took up his brush to write his own treatise on metaphysics, it was that same breadth of knowledge that gave his *Vijñapti Matrata Siddhi* its richness.

Reaching his twentieth year, this man whom from now on we shall refer to as the "Master of the Law" received at Ch'eng-tu the complement of the monastic "rules." The date was 622. The civil wars were drawing to their close with the emergence of the victorious T'ang, and consequently Hiuan Tsang left Ssu-ch'uan and proceeded to the capital city of the new dynasty, Ch'ang-an, in the province of Shensi. This famous city, the Rome of ancient China, had been one of the first centers of Buddhism in the Far East. Missionaries from India and Kashgharia had arrived there five centuries earlier and set up monasteries whose monks had continued untiringly ever since the work of translating from Sanskrit into Chinese the vast literature of the two Buddhist Vehicles. In Hiuan Tsang's time the city contained many masters professing the teachings of the Buddha Sakyamuni. Unfortunately they were far from agreeing among themselves; they were split into as many schools as Buddhism had sects and their teachings offered strange discrepancies. We can get some idea of the situation from the gulf which today separates a "minimalist" from Ceylon and a "maximalist" theologian from Tibet.

These discrepancies were considerable. Without going into detail about the various Buddhist sects let us simply recall that the most diverse interpretations had, over the centuries, been erected upon the teachings of the Buddha. For some, the adherents of the Little Vehicle of Salvation or the Hinayana, Buddhism more or less came down to the practice of the monastic rules for the religious and the practice of charity for the layman; in the realm of philosophy to a sort of realist positivism and, as the final aim, a theory of individual salvation by "waning away," the "nirvana" of the human being. The Great Vehicle of Salvation or Mahayana offered a more elaborate series of ideas and for its believers the Buddhist theory of salvation was crowned with a metaphysic. Some of them, the masters of the Middle Path or Madhyamika arrived by means of a curious and radical critical method at a conception of "universal void" which was itself later to result in the most tender pietism. Others, following the school of Idealism (Vijñanavada), also called the school of Mysticism (Yogachara), professed as their names suggest an absolute idealism in conjunction with a theory of mystical union.

As we have seen, Hiuan Tsang's intellectual sympathies lay rather with this latter school. He was nevertheless disturbed by the mutual opposition of the various masters and by the unfortunate existence of what appeared at least to be contradictions in the sacred books. "The Master of the Law," as his biographer very nicely puts it, "recognized that all these learned men were of most eminent worth. But when he came to check their teachings against the holy books he realized that the latter contained grave discrepancies and as a result he knew not what system to follow. He then made a vow he would travel through the countries of the West to question the sages upon those points which had so disturbed his spirit."

His decision once taken, Hiuan Tsang together with a number of other monks presented to the emperor a request for permission to leave

China. The answer took the form of an imperial decree. It was a refusal. T'ai-tsung, whose authority at home was as yet far from secure and whose diplomacy abroad had come up against the hostility or treachery of several of the peoples of central Asia, had no intention of allowing his subjects to go venturing into these dangerous regions on any but official missions. Nor, let it be said, did Hiuan Tsang have any illusions as to the difficulties which he could expect. "Knowing that the roads of the West were full of perils and looking deep into his heart, he felt that, since he had been able to break free from the life of his century, he would be able to face every obstacle without retreating so much as a step." The emperor forbade him to cross the frontier. His companions left him. What did any of that matter to him? "He desired to walk in the steps of the wise men and saints, to restore the laws of religion and convert the foreign peoples. He would have faced wind and wave without blenching and, in the presence of the emperor himself, the firmness of his character would but have become more strong." Scorning the assistance of men, he went into retreat in a sacred tower "in order to lay his intentions before the multitude of the saints and pray that they would encompass with their invisible protection his voyage and his return."

The apostle was confirmed in his resolution by a dream. One night in 629 he dreamed he saw the holy mountain Sumeru rising up out of the sea. Desiring to reach the sacred summit he had no hesitation in throwing himself upon the bosom of the waves. At that moment a mystic lotus appeared beneath him and transported him effortlessly to the foot of the mountain. This, however, was so precipitous that he would not have been able to climb it. But a mysterious whirlwind lifted him up and he suddenly found himself at the top. There he discovered a vast horizon clearly visible in every part, a symbol of the countless countries which his faith was to conquer. He was filled with a joyful ecstasy and woke up.

A few days later he left for the Great West.

CHAPTER 3

Across the Great West

At the time of his departure the pilgrim was about twenty-six years of age. He was an extremely handsome man, tall like many of the northern Chinese. "His complexion was lightly touched with color and his eyes shone brightly. His bearing was grave and majestic and his face seemed to be filled with light and grace." His powerful personality, a compound of strength and gentleness, obviously radiated a deep charm, as so many episodes during his voyage testify. "The timbre of his voice was pure and carried well and his language was a brilliant blend of nobility, elegance and harmony so that his listeners never tired of hearing him speak. . . . He liked to wear ample robes of fine cotton with a broad belt which gave him the looks and appearance of a scholar."

Possibly the secret of his superior genius really lay in this intimate partnership of the ancient wisdom of Confucianism with the tenderness of Buddhism. He had all the qualities of the Confucian, not only those formal qualities which go to make up the charm of Chinese or Japanese society, that hereditary politeness which can extend, when called for, to actual heroism, but also the profound virtues: good sense, circumspection, moderation, discretion in one's daily affairs, infinite delicacy in friendship, tranquillity of heart. "A strict observer of discipline, he was always the same. Nothing could equal his moving kindness and tender piety, the firmness of his zeal and his unshakable attachment to the

8. Bazaklik painting, typical of Iranian influence. (*Musée Guimet*)

practice of the Buddhist Law. Furthermore he was reserved in friendship and never lightly gave his trust." And, underlying all this, there was the radiance, the inner joy of all great mystics: "His bearing was gentle and relaxed. He always looked straight ahead of him and never glanced to one side or to the other. He was as majestic as the great rivers that surround the earth, as calm and brilliant as the lotus that rises in the midst of the waters. . . ."

Resolved at whatever cost to carry out his vow, Hiuan Tsang made his way into the deep valleys and gorges of what is now Kansu, the province that thrusts toward the northwest like a finger between the sands of the Gobi and the wild plateau of the Koko Nor. Liang-chou (the present-day Wuwei), the last important town of Kansu, was then as now the head of the caravan trails to Mongolia and the Tarim Basin. It was also a market town frequented by all the peoples of the Great West from the loop of the Yellow River to the Pamirs, and we can picture that cosmopolitan crowd with the help of some of the frescoes of Bazaklik, near Turfan: perhaps a scene depicting a *pranidhi* in which we see a succession of bearded donors filing past, a great mixture of types, some of them looking Turkish, others clearly Persian, yet others wearing a sort of flat helmet, all followed by their camels and their mules, "Buddhist magi" no doubt drawn from Turkistani or Sogdian caravaneers whom the silk trade attracted as far as the borders of China.

Arriving in Liang-chou Hiuan Tsang took advantage of one of these fairs at which different tribes were gathered to begin his preaching. As we know, the good caravaneers whom he evangelized here insisted in their gratitude on loading him with gifts of gold and silver and white horses. He passed on almost all of these gifts to the Buddhist monasteries of the district "to provide for the upkeep of the lamps" and for the other needs of the Order.

Beyond Kansu China stopped and the Great West began with the Ala Shan steppe and the sands of the Gobi. It was appallingly inhospitable country. A century later, in spite of the intervening conquests of the T'ang armies, the poets of the court of Emperor Ming Huang still revealed in their verses the age-old terror of the Chinese soul before these hostile wastes:

"In the autumn," wrote Li T'ai-po, "our frontier neighbors come down from their mountains. We must pass outside the Great Wall and go forth to meet them. The bamboo tiger is divided and the general orders the march to begin; the soldiers of the empire will not stop until they reach the sands of the Gobi. The crescent moon hanging in an empty sky is all that can be seen in that cruel desert where the dew is distilled on the polished metal of swords and breast-plates. Many a day will pass before the day of return. So sigh not, young woman; you would have to keep sighing too long."

Still farther on lay the snowy crests of the T'ien Shan, the K'un Lun Shan and the Pamirs where even greater perils awaited the soldier and the pilgrim:

"In the fifth month the snow has still not melted in the T'ien Shan. Not a flower lifts its head in such a harsh climate. The flute can be heard playing the spring-like melody of the song of the willows but the gay colors of spring are nowhere to be seen" (Li T'ai-po).

In this borderland between two worlds even the T'ang armies themselves were never safe:

"Dawn appears. The soldiers must fight, alert to the voice of bell and drum. Night falls and they sleep in the saddle, each with his arms flung around his horse's neck. . . ." (Li T'ai-po). What then of the pilgrim who was about to venture into these wastes, and without even the support of his government since he must, on the contrary, keep himself hidden from the last Chinese outposts?

Beyond Liang-chou the frontier was closed and no one was allowed to cross without authorization from the emperor. Learning of Hiuan Tsang's intentions the governor of Liang-chou summoned him and ordered him to return to China. The pilgrim's only reaction was to display a greater degree of prudence; he left in secret for the West, hiding by day and traveling by night. Thus he reached Kua-chou in the southern part of the Anhsi oasis about eight miles south of the Sulo Ho or Bulunghir River. To get on to the trail for Hami, the first oasis of eastern Turkistan, he had first to cross the river. This was a difficult undertaking for the Sulo Ho was a steeply embanked and violent torrent for part of its course and quite unnavigable; and though farther on it widened out it was only to become a swamp at the Qara Nor. Moreover the crossing was guarded by the Chinese fortress of the Jade Gate or Yü-men Kuan which commanded the entire valley. Once on the north bank and following the only trail across the desert in a northwesterly direction toward Hami, the traveler still had to pass within sight of five more Chinese guard towers, the last sentinels on the threshold of another world.

Realizing his situation, so his biographer tells us, Hiuan Tsang was filled with anguish. His horse had just died and to cap his misfortune his departure had been noticed and mounted orderlies had just arrived at the frontier with instructions to arrest him. Luckily for him the governor of the region turned out to be a pious Buddhist who, instead of carrying out the orders he had received, disposed of the official rescript, warned the person concerned and invited him to make as much haste as he could. But the two novices who had accompanied the pilgrim thus far now felt their courage failing. The first fled in fear to Tun-huang. Hiuan Tsang dismissed the second himself, judging him incapable of supporting the hardships of the journey.

And so the Master of the Law found himself alone. He purchased a new horse and beseeched the Bodhisattva Maitreya to send him a guide to lead him past the last frontier posts. Shortly afterward a young barbarian, a Buddhist by religion, introduced himself and offered to serve as his guide. Trusting to the man's protestations of piety the pilgrim joyfully accepted his offer, and with this impromptu guide set out before sunset across a steppe which was covered with grassy scrub. Meeting there an old man who was a native of this border country, Hiuan Tsang found his courage put severely to the test. Speaking with great force, the old man laid before him the full extent of his imprudence:

"The roads to the West are bad and dangerous. The traveler is brought to a halt now by moving sands, now by burning winds; and when they blow, no man can escape their fury. Often large caravans are lost and perish utterly. How much more impossible for you, venerable master, who are alone, to complete the voyage? Take care, and do not gamble thus with your life!" Since Hiuan Tsang persisted in his unshakable resolution, however, the old man made him accept his horse, an aged red bay which had already done the journey to Hami more than fifteen times.

Eventually Hiuan Tsang and his guide came within sight of Yü-men Kuan. It was night. Cutting down a number of trees, the guide threw an improvised footbridge across the Sulo Ho and whipped the master's horse across. Once on the northern bank the Master of the Law laid his sleeping-mat out on the ground and collapsed upon it exhausted. Suddenly he witnessed a strange spectacle: his enigmatic companion, who had lain down a hundred or so feet away, now drew his sword, got up and began slowly to approach him; then, less than ten paces from him, he appeared to hesitate and began retracing his steps. When Hiuan Tsang, realizing the danger he was in, leapt to his feet commending his soul to the Bodhisattva Avalokitesvara, his disturbing companion beat a final retreat and, returning to his mat, lay down and went back to sleep. Clearly the guide's fickle and greedy spirit had for a moment been seized with thoughts of crime; then, whether from superstitious fear or from a remnant of piety, the man had changed his mind. But never was any man's company less secure. . . .

At first light Hiuan Tsang, without alluding to the curious adventure of that night, commanded the guide to go in search of water. The young man obeyed with the greatest reluctance. Whether because he was secretly ashamed at having been found out or because he was genuinely afraid of the Chinese outposts, he began to plead the difficulties of the journey: "This trail is extremely long and full of perils. It has neither water nor grazing. The only water is right below the fifth signal tower, and that is excellent water. It will be necessary to go and draw it at night, in secret, and to be quick about it, for if they see us from the tower we are lost. The safest thing would be for us to turn back." The Master of the Law having categorically rejected this latter course, they continued on their way across the steppe, concealing themselves as best as they could, walking in a crouching position and looking up every now and then to get their bearings. Suddenly the young man drew his sword, strung his bow and asked Hiuan Tsang to walk in front. Hiuan Tsang, to whom the man's intentions were now clear beyond any shadow of doubt, refused. Intimidated by his firm bearing the guide agreed once more to act as his scout, but after a few more miles, on the pretext of his reluctance to violate the orders of the emperor, he abandoned the pilgrim and disappeared.

Hiuan Tsang continued alone into the sandy desert, the endless Gobi, murderer of whole herds and caravans. Guiding himself by the heaps of bones and piles of camel-dung which dotted the desert trail, he trudged slowly and painfully on. Suddenly he saw the whole horizon filled as it were with hundreds of armed troops. "He could see them now marching, now at the halt." All the soldiers were dressed in felts and furs in the style of the barbarians of the Gobi and the Altai. "Here were camels and horses with splendid harnesses, there glittering lances and gleaming standards. Soon these became new shapes, new figures; each instant it changed, this teeming scene, offering one by one a thousand metamorphoses. But as soon as he approached, everything vanished. . . ." The pilgrim believed he was in the presence of the army of Mara, the demon of Buddhism. In fact he had been the victim of a desert mirage.

There was a more real danger, however; he was drawing near the first of the signal towers, the furthermost guardians of the Chinese frontier.[1] In order to escape the eyes of the watchman he hid in a ditch

---

[1] The reader who wishes to follow Hiuan Tsang's journey across central Asia in detail is recommended to use the atlas which constitutes Volume 4 of Sir Aurel Stein's last publication, *Innermost Asia*, Oxford, 1928. This first tower Stein locates at the halt of Pei-tan-tau, as shown on Map 38 of the atlas. See also Aurel Stein, *Hiuan Tsang's Journey Across the Desert*, T'ung-pao, 1921–22, p. 350.

that was choked with sand and came out only when night had fallen. He found the spring he had been told about lying to the west of the tower and climbed down to drink at it and fill his water-skins. But at that very moment he heard the whirr of an arrow which narrowly missed wounding him in the knee. Then a second arrow buried itself in the sand beside him. Realizing he had been spotted he cried out at the top of his voice: "I am a religious come from the capital. Do not shoot!" And leading his horse by the bridle he walked up to the tower. The guards let him in and took him to their commander. This man, who came from the town of Tun-huang, was a professed Buddhist. He too pointed out to Hiuan Tsang the perilous nature of his undertaking and attempted at first to dissuade him from it.

The good man advised our pilgrim to terminate his voyage at Tun-huang where lived a most learned religious. Hiuan Tsang's spirited reply still carries its impact in his biographer's account of the interview: "Ever since my childhood I have had a passionate fondness for the religion of the Buddha. In both capitals (Ch'ang-an and Lo-yang) men learned in the Buddhist Law and the most zealous monks hurried without fail to my lectures in order to study them and reap their fruits. I spoke, I preached and I debated before them. I confess, not without blushing, that I am the most renowned religious of our time. If I wished to make further progress in virtue and develop my reputation, do you think I would remain in subjection to the monks of Tun-huang?"

After this heated diatribe in which the famous preacher from the capital crushed the simple provincial officer tucked away in his colonial fortress, Hiuan Tsang appealed to his interlocutor's religious feelings: "I was deeply grieved to find that the books were incomplete and that their interpretation was obstructed by annoying lacunae. Forgetting all concern for my life and daring every obstacle and danger I have vowed to go to India to seek the law which the Buddha bequeathed to the world. And you, my man, though you mean well, instead of fanning my zeal, exhort me to retrace my steps! Will you dare afterward to say that you share my compassion for the world's unhappiness and that you wish like me to help men attain Nirvana? If you absolutely insist on detaining me you have my permission to take my life. Hiuan Tsang will not take one step of the way back to China! "

The commander of the frontier-post had very likely never heard such eloquence in his life. Crushed by this reprimand and with his piety aroused, he resolved to assist the pilgrim. He renewed his provisions and gave him a letter of recommendation for the next frontier-post. The fifth and last guard tower[2] he advised him to avoid, the commanding officer there being hostile to Buddhism.

And so Hiuan Tsang, leaving the Hami trail and taking a parallel course toward the northwest in order to by-pass this last frontier-post, plunged right into the desert proper, the Gashun Gobi which the Chinese call the river of sand: "There are to be found neither birds nor four-footed beasts nor water nor grazing." And his chronicler adds this marvelous sentence: "To guide his steps he set himself to observe the direction of his shadow as he walked, and he read fervently the book of the *Prajña Paramita* (Holy Buddhist Wisdom)." Can we picture the scene to ourselves—the desert and that lonely figure, trudging through every danger and in the face of the unknown, going to India to look for a few texts and to debate systems of metaphysics? That pilgrim whose only guide was his shadow, the shadow of his faith thrown on the limitless sand, and whose only solace beneath the flaming sun was the mystical flame of the Holy Wisdom?

He searched vainly for the watering-place he had been told about, the "Spring of the Dziggetai." "Dogged by thirst he lifted his water-skin to his lips, but the water-skin was very heavy and fell from his hands and his whole water supply ran out upon the ground. Moreover, the trail being extremely circuitous, he no longer knew which direction to follow." In desperation he took the road back to the Chinese frontier. It was the pilgrim's one and only moment of doubt. After having covered seven or eight miles of the return journey he pulled himself to-

2 This post is identified by Sir Aurel Stein as Sing-sing-hia.

gether again: "At the beginning I swore that if I could not reach India I would never take a step back toward China. I would rather die on the road to the West than return to the East and live." "Whereupon," says his biographer, "he reined his horse round and, uttering fervent prayers to the Bodhisattva Avalokitesvara, set off toward the northwest. Looking around him in every direction he could see only a limitless plain with no trace of either men or horses. During the night evil spirits shone torches as numerous as the stars; during the day terrible winds lifted the sand and scattered it like torrents of rain. Amidst all these cruel assaults his heart remained a stranger to fear, but he suffered greatly from lack of water and at last was so tortured with thirst that he could not take another step. For four nights and five days not one drop of water had passed his lips. A devouring fire was burning at his entrails and he was almost expiring. Unable to continue, he lay down in the sand where he was, and, albeit prostrate with exhaustion, ceaselessly invoked the name of Avalokitesvara.

" 'I covet from this journey neither wealth nor praise nor reputation,' he prayed. 'My sole aim is to discover the Higher Understanding and the Right Law. Your heart, oh Bodhisattva, applies itself ceaselessly to delivering poor creatures from the bitterness of life. Was there ever more cruel bitterness than mine? How can you ignore it?'

"Thus he prayed with untiring ardor until the middle of the fifth night when suddenly a delicious breeze came up and, suffusing his every limb, made them as supple and fresh as if he had just bathed in cooling water. Immediately his lusterless eyes recovered their sight and even his horse had the strength to stand up. Thus revived he was able to enjoy some sleep. But as he slept there appeared to him in a dream a mighty spirit of the height of several *chang* who held a lance and a standard and cried out to him in a terrible voice: 'Why do you go on sleeping instead of eagerly continuing your march?'

"Waking up with a start, the Master of the Law set out once more on his way. When he had gone about four miles his horse suddenly changed direction and nothing he could do would hold it back or keep it on the original path." Letting himself thus be guided by the animal's instinct, he soon found himself approaching an area of several acres of green pasturage where he dismounted and allowed his horse to graze at its leisure. Nearby gleamed the surface of a pond whose water was as clear and pure as a mirror. The pilgrim drank long and deep. Having recovered his strength he filled his water-skin, cut some grass for his horse and set out again.[3]

After two days' march Hiuan Tsang finally left the sands behind and came to Yi-wu, known today as Hami. This oasis, which had for a long time been occupied by a Chinese military colony, had during the period of the Empire's troubles accepted the suzerainty of the Turks. Several months after Hiuan Tsang's visit it was to fall once more to China (630). There were still three Chinese religious living in a monastery and there Hiuan Tsang stayed. One of them, a poor and very old man, came up to the Master of the Law and embraced him with tears in his eyes. After pressing him to his bosom for a long time with much weeping and exclaiming he said to him: "How could I have hoped to meet today a man from my own village?" The Master of the Law, himself overcome with tender emotion, was unable to restrain his tears.

Meanwhile the king of Kao-ch'ang, the modern Turfan and the nearest oasis to the west, had received word of Hiuan Tsang's presence at Hami. He dispatched ten of his officers to the town, mounted on the finest horses, to invite the pilgrim to continue his journey by way of Turfan. This invitation rather upset Hiuan Tsang's plans for he had intended to continue in a more northerly direction and visit the Turkish city of Beshbaligh or Pei-t'ing, lying to the west of present-day Guchen, because of the Buddhist stupa there which had earned it its other name of Quaghan Stupa. But the king of Turfan was a devout Buddhist and a powerful monarch whose influence was great throughout the whole of the Gobi. Hiuan Tsang bowed to his wish and after six days' journey through the Shar Nor Desert arrived in Turfan.

[3] Sir Aurel Stein located this waterhole at the post of Chang-liu-Shuei, thirty-five miles southeast of Hami (see Map 34 of his *Innermost Asia*).

CHAPTER 4

Persian Paintings
in the Heart
of the Gobi

THE KINGDOM of Turfan (Kao-ch'ang, as the Chinese called it) was one of the most important states in central Asia in the seventh century, not only politically but also in terms of civilization.

Situated in the central Gobi and protected by two ranges of mountains, the Bogdo Ola and Edemen Daba to the north and the Chol Tagh to the south, the Turfan basin forms an arc around the northern shore of the partially dried-up lake of Aidin Kol, still fed today from the west by the Daban-tshing-su River. At this period a whole collection of prosperous localities was grouped around this cool depression, localities corresponding to the present sites of Toqsun, Yar, Bazaklik,

Murtuq, Sangim, Subashi, Idiqut-Shahri, Khotsho or Qara-Khoja, and Tuyoq, the capital itself being at Qara-Khoja, twenty-six miles to the east of present-day Turfan; all celebrated names in archeological history since the discoveries made by the German expedition led by von Le Coq and Grünwedel. Indeed this whole country, which today is virtually dead, once enjoyed an intense economic, political and cultural life, as witness the magnificent stuccoes and the marvelous frescoes which von Le Coq brought back to the Museum für Völkerkunde, Berlin. Curiously enough the population which, as late as the seventh century, still inhabited this region in such close proximity to the Celestial Empire and more particularly to the Turkish hordes of the Altai was neither Chinese nor Turco-Mongol. It was an Indo-European population, speaking a dialect of that Tokharian language which, among the languages of the same family, showed surprising affinities not only with Armenian and Slav but also with Italo-Celtic. The Turfan frescoes moreover depict numerous characters with blue-grey eyes and red hair who bear a marked resemblance to certain European types.

At the same time the people of Turfan, like all the peoples of central Asia at this period, professed the Buddhist religion, which meant that the literate classes were entirely steeped in Sanskrit culture. Hundreds of monks, as recent discoveries have shown, were occupied in translating the sacred books of India from Sanskrit into Tokharian. In its material aspect, on the other hand, their civilization was in large part borrowed from China and also from Persia. Sassanian Persia, through the intermediary of the Sogdian caravaneers, had already taught the people of Turfan a part of its art, and the process was to become more intense during the next century with the great Buddhist frescoes and the Manichean miniatures of the Uigur era.

Although the majority of the archeological finds from the Turfan region appear to date from the period of Uigur rule, between 750 and 850 approximately, Hiuan Tsang must surely have come across some of these famous works in the sanctuaries and palaces of the late Tokharian period: the stucco figurines and frescoes of Bazaklik with their Buddhas and Bodhisattvas, the most easterly occurrence of the Greco-Buddhist art of Gandhara; the frescoes of Idiqut-Shahri in which we find the occasional female divinity with a Greek headdress and draped in the Greek *palla* and *peplos;* the lunar divinities of Sangim in their Indian scarves, a most successful blend of Indian suppleness, Hellenic elegance and Chinese prettiness. We find that the Hellenic figures of the Gandharan Buddhas, so insipid everywhere else, here have the power to move us. We delight in the purity and still Apollonian gentleness of their oval form. The reason is that, to use von Le Coq's happy expression, these are the last "belated antiquities," belated in time until right into the Middle Ages, lost in space as far as the heart of the Gobi. Products of a quite different inspiration, this time curiously Persian, the fine horsemen of the Bazaklik frescoes discovered by von Le Coq were very likely the contemporaries or at most the grandsons of the lords of Turfan whom Hiuan Tsang met; the "Parsifal of Bazaklik" in the Berlin Museum, a pleasant-looking young knight being ordained with the tonsure by a religious, was certainly a compatriot of King K'iu Wen-t'ai who, as we shall see, was to show such zeal for the faith that he stayed up all night listening to Hiuan Tsang. And at Murtuq a little farther on we find faithfully depicted with their camels and their mules those Tokharian and Sogdian caravaneers who must on more than one occasion have been our philosopher's traveling companions, for the pilgrim route was also the route used by the silk trade.

China for her part had given the people of Turfan their dynasty, that of the K'iu, which had occupied the throne since 507. The then reigning monarch, K'iu Wen-t'ai (c. 620–640), who is in fact the best-known representative of the dynasty, appears to have been a fairly powerful personality. Mindful of his Chinese descent, or perhaps just sensing which way the wind was blowing, he had presented Emperor T'ai-tsung with a black fox fur as soon as he learned of his accession to the imperial throne. Whereupon T'ai-tsung gave the queen, his wife, an ornament of gold flowers. Whereupon K'iu Wen-t'ai made T'ai-tsung a present of a little table with a jade top. In December 630, shortly after Hiuan Tsang's visit, he paid a visit to the Chinese court in person, and there received the signal honor of being adopted into the imperial clan. It was not until later, toward the end of his life, that these honors and the prosperity of his realm went to his head and, placing his trust in the Turkish hordes, he was rash enough to contract an alliance with them to refuse to pay homage to the Empire and cut off the caravan route between China and Kashgharia. He was to die of shock on learning of the approach of the imperial armies (640).

Hiuan Tsang's description of K'iu Wen-t'ai corresponds to the arrogant and domineering prince whom we glimpse through the pages of the T'ang chronicles. Hearing that Hiuan Tsang was staying at Hami, he had sent for him there and, in spite of the protests of the pilgrim who would have preferred to take a different route, had practically had him carried off by force. Hiuan Tsang arrived at Turfan after sundown, and the king was in such a hurry to see him that he did not even wait for day. Emerging from his palace then and there he went by torchlight to meet the pilgrim and install him in a magnificently equipped pavilion in the middle of a tent of costly materials.

King K'iu Wen-t'ai was in fact, his impetuosity notwithstanding, extremely devout. His speech of welcome to Hiuan Tsang revealed the ardor of his Buddhist faith: "Master," the biographer reports him as saying, "from the moment when your disciple heard tell of the imminence of your arrival, he has been filled with such delight as to have forgotten even to eat and sleep. My reckoning of the distance you had to travel made me certain that you would be here tonight. For this reason I and my wife and children, renouncing all thought of sleep, have been occupied in reading the sacred books while respectfully awaiting your arrival." And indeed a few moments later the queen too, accompanied by several dozen servants, came to visit the Master of the Law. It is an irresistible temptation to conjure up this royal retinue by evoking all the princely donors and all the beautiful ladies of Bazaklik and Sangim as they appear out of the depths of the past in the pages of von Le Coq's volumes.[1]

So great was the king of Turfan's zeal that Hiuan Tsang was obliged to grant him an immediate interview. This lasted for the rest of the night and by the time dawn began to show in the sky the pilgrim was utterly exhausted. He had gently to recall the monarch to a degree of discretion and was at last able to enjoy a little rest.

This first encounter was symptomatic. In fact the piety of the king of Turfan was to turn out to be singularly demanding and his protection somewhat tyrannical. He did indeed heap gifts and honors upon the Master of the Law and place under his orders the most prominent religious of his realm. But in his joy at being visited by such a learned man he conceived the idea of keeping him as his family's spiritual guide and as the head of the Buddhist community of Turfan. In vain did the Master of the Law explain to him the reasons for his journey: "I did not undertake this journey in order to receive honors! I was grieved to see that in my country we had only an incomplete understanding of the Buddhist Law and that the holy texts had become few and defective. Moved by painful doubts I resolved to go myself and search for the pure and authentic monuments of the Law. For that reason I set off at the risk of my life toward the countries of the West in order to hear unknown teachings. I desire that by my efforts the divine ambrosia shall moisten not only the soil of India but that it shall spread throughout all the length and breadth of China. How could you stop me when I am but halfway? I beseech you, oh king, give up your plans and honor me no further with such an excess of friendship!"

The king's reply showed him to be unbending: "Your disciple loves you with a tenderness that is without limit. I am determined to keep you here so that I may offer you my homage. It would be easier to move the Pamir Mountains than to move me in my resolve."

Hiuan Tsang was crushed with dismay but his decision was no less irrevocable. He persisted in his refusal. "At which the king turned red

[1] Von Le Coq, *Die buddhistische Spätantike in Mittelasien.*

with anger, and extending a threatening arm, cried out in a loud voice: 'Your disciple will now treat you in a different manner and you shall see if you are free to leave at will. I have decided either to keep you here by force or to have you escorted back to your country. I advise you to think about it; the best thing would still be for you to give in.' " The discussion began to take a dramatic turn: " 'It is for the sublime Law that I have come,' replied Hiuan Tsang heroically. 'The king will be able to keep no more than my bones; he has no power over my spirit or my will.' "

King K'iu Wen-t'ai remained obdurate. At the same time he showered the pilgrim with quite extraordinary honors, even going so far as waiting on him at table. Hiuan Tsang, seeing that he would never persuade him to yield, threatened to let himself die of hunger. "He sat motionless in an erect posture and for three days not even so much as a drop of water passed his lips. On the fourth day the king became aware that the breathing of the Master of the Law was becoming progressively weaker. Ashamed and alarmed at the consequences of his severity, he prostrated himself on the ground and respectfully offered his apologies." He swore before the statue of the Buddha that he would allow his guest to leave. Then and then only did Hiuan Tsang consent to take some nourishment.

At the request of K'iu Wen-t'ai, however, Hiuan Tsang agreed to remain for another month in Turfan in order to expound his teachings to the court and to the people. "The king had a tent erected in which three hundred people could be seated at once. The queen-mother, the king, the superior of the religious houses of the country and the high officials were arranged in separate groups and listened to him with respect. Each day, as the lecture began, the king went before him with an incense burner and led him to the foot of the rostrum. There, humbly kneeling, he insisted on serving as the step by which he must mount to his chair."

Having been unable to keep Hiuan Tsang by him, King K'iu Wen-t'ai now showed the same touching zeal and the same unbounded enthusiasm in putting everything in motion to facilitate his journey. He had made for him all the clothes he would need against the cold— protective masks, gloves, boots, etc., while crossing the T'ien Shan and Pamir Mountains. He showered him with gifts of gold, silver, satins and silks with which he might purchase everything he needed on his projected pilgrimage. He gave him thirty horses and twenty-five servants. Above all he gave him one of his officers to escort him as far as the residence of the Grand Khan of the western Turks with whom he was on terms of close friendship and almost of vassalage. This last was, as we shall see, an inestimable service, for the empire of the western Turks, then at the height of their power, extended from the Altai to Bactriana and the success of Hiuan Tsang's pilgrimage depended upon their goodwill. To the same end K'iu Wen-t'ai gave Hiuan Tsang twenty-four letters of recommendation, each accompanied by a gift, addressed to the princes of central Asia beginning with his neighbor, the king of Kucha. But clearly at this period the most important thing was the protection of the Turks, for that would answer for everything else. So K'iu Wen-t'ai, in order to gain for the pilgrim the goodwill of the Grand Khan, sent the latter by the same occasion what amounted to a veritable tribute. "He had two wagons loaded with five hundred pieces of satin for the khan. These gifts were accompanied by a letter which read: 'The Master of the Law is your slave's younger brother; it is his intention to go and seek the Buddhist Law in the land of the Brahmins. It is my most fervent desire that the khan treat the Master of the Law with the same benevolence as he does the slave who pens these respectful lines.' "

From that point on Hiuan Tsang was to continue his journey in quite different circumstances from those which had obtained hitherto. Leaving China without the consent of the court and lacking any political support or help of any kind, he had been at the mercy of the smallest obstacle. Now, however, as a result of the personal protection and diplomatic intervention of the king of Turfan, his mission took on an official character. It meant an entrée to all the little courts of the Gobi.

It meant above all that the power of the western Turks was at his service, for the king of Turfan's letter to the khan can leave us in no doubt as to the relationship between the two princes: the former was the vassal of the latter and it was by virtue of this vassaldom that he had the right to demand aid and protection for his friend. This protection, moreover, was to bring the pilgrim to the very gates of India, for the monarch who held sway over Bactriana was at once the son of the khan and the son-in-law of K'iu Wen-t'ai.

Hiuan Tsang, from having narrowly missed seeing his journey come to an abrupt end in Turfan, had ultimately found there quite unexpected possibilities of seeing it successful. On the day of the pilgrim's departure K'iu Wen-t'ai, together with his whole court, all the country's religious and the whole multitude of his people, accompanied him out of the city. He wept as he took his leave of the Master of the Law. The latter promised that on his return he would come and spend three years at Turfan, and we know that such indeed was Hiuan Tsang's first thought as he re-entered Kashgharia from India fourteen years later. But his benefactor's tragic death, occurring in the interval, was to make the pilgrim's gesture a fruitless one.

Leaving Turfan and crossing a mountainous spur which was famous for its silver mines, Hiuan Tsang made his way toward the city of Yen-k'i or Qarashahr. Although at this time both Turfan and Qarashahr were civilized states of long standing and important stations for the caravan trade, or precisely because of this reason, the trails between them were frequently cut off by gangs of brigands. Hiuan Tsang saw the corpses of several wealthy foreign merchants who had separated themselves from the rest of their caravan in order to steal a march on their competitors. He himself ran into a band of brigands who demanded a ransom before releasing him.

These dangers once passed, the pilgrim arrived in a quite remarkably prosperous part of the country. He describes Qarashahr as a fertile oasis which, by reason of its surrounding belt of mountains and the narrow gorges which gave access to it, could easily be defended. "Several rivers coming together here provide it with a kind of girdle"; the oasis is in fact watered by the picturesque Qaidu Gol or Yulduz River which flows down from the Boro Khoro chain of mountains in a narrow valley running in a northwesterly direction known as the Lesser Yulduz, and then suddenly turns and flows in the opposite direction, toward the southeast, parallel to its former course, the valley here being known as the Greater Yulduz; until, downstream from Qarashahr, it empties into the Bagrash Kol, the lake on whose western shore the city is situated. An irrigation system, now fallen into disuse, made the oasis extremely fertile and permitted the cultivation of rice, millet, wheat, grapes, pears, plums, jujubes and mangoes.

At this date Qarashahr was, like Turfan, an Indo-European city speaking a Tokharian dialect, and as at Turfan the archeological researches of von Le Coq on the site of the city itself and slightly to the south at Shorshuq have revealed a rich, Buddhist-inspired civilization with a mixed art borrowed partly from India and partly from Sassanian Persia. We learn from Hiuan Tsang's report that it possesesed ten or so monasteries numbering almost two thousand religious affiliated to the Hinayana sect of the Sarvastivadins. After the example of the king of Turfan, the King of Qarashahr proved to be a most pious Buddhist; he too came out with his ministers to meet Hiuan Tsang and led him to the palace where he placed at his disposal everything that the traveler might need. Hiuan Tsang owed this welcome entirely to his fame as a religious, for the diplomatic recommendations furnished by the people of Turfan could here do him nothing but harm; the inhabitants of Qarashahr, as immediate neighbors of the Turfanians, had always had to put up with abuse and encroachments on the part of the latter. Thus, while giving Hiuan Tsang personally the very best of welcomes, they refused all hospitality to his Turfanian escort, not even allowing them relay horses. Hiuan Tsang consequently spent no more than one night at Qarashahr, and next morning left for Kucha.

Qarashahr and Kucha, though appearing on small-scale maps to be twin cities, are in actual fact separated by high mountains coming down from the north from the principal chain of the T'ien Shan. Hiuan Tsang had first to cross "a great river" (the Qaidu Gol or Yulduz) and then take the trail which ran along at the foot of the mountains through Korla and Ya‑ ‑issar, entering the kingdom of Kucha probably by way of the oases of Bugur and Kirish or Yaqa Ariq.

Kucha (which in Chinese was called Kiu-che or better K'iu-tsiu or K'iou-tsiu, and in Sanskrit Kuci) was possibly the most important city in central Asia. Hiuan Tsang was struck by its material prosperity and the brilliance of its civilization. "The kingdom measures approximately a thousand *li* from east to west and six hundred *li* from south to north" —one *li* being the equivalent of 633 yards—"and the capital is between seventeen and eighteen *li* in circumference. The soil lends itself to the cultivation of red millet and wheat. Rice is also grown, of the type known as keng-t'ao, as well as grapes, pomegranates and large quantities of pears, plums, peaches and apricots. The country possesses gold, copper, iron, lead and tin mines. The climate is mild and the customs of the people pure and honest. Their writing is borrowed from India, but with certain modifications. The musicians of this land surpass those of all other kingdoms by their skill upon the flute and the guitar."

The lay historians of China complete this picture. As early as the fourth century the official chronicler of the *Tsin Shu* was writing with wonder that "the palace of the king of Kucha has the splendor of an abode of geniuses." For the following period and the period of Hiuan Tsang the *Wei Shu* and the *T'ang Shu,* more interested than the pious pilgrim in the things of their century, give us a glimpse of the life of pleasure which the caravaneer emerging from the desert could find in this fertile oasis. The charm of the women of Kucha was as celebrated as the Persian perfumes and cosmetics which they used and of which Kucha was the repository. Kucha was also famous for its carpets, and men spoke of the beauty of its peacocks, which were found wild in a mountainous valley to the north of the city. However, as Hiuan Tsang says and as we know also from the *T'ang Shu,* the city was above all else renowned for the excellence of its musicians. "These musicians were at that time so skillful that they could, after a little practice, reproduce an air which they had heard only once. Attached to this orchestra were four dancers. The dance known as the Five Lions which enjoyed great success in China was introduced into the country by musicians from Kucha." Indeed a Kuchean orchestra had been adopted by the Chinese court and took part in imperial festivals throughout the T'ang period. The musicians, according to the *T'ang Shu,* wore turbans of black silk, robes of purple silk with embroidered sleeves and purple trousers. Even the names of their airs have been handed down to us— "The Meeting of the Seventh Evening," "The Jade Woman Passes Round the Cup," "The Flower Contest," "The Game of Hide-the-Clasp," and so on—and these old titles, florid and poetic, convey to us something of the spirit of the music of long ago, there in that lost oasis of the Gobi which still, at the height of the Middle Ages and on the very eve of Turkicization, preserved the ancient cultures of India and Iran.[2]

The population of Kucha, like those of Turfan and Qarashahr, was still Indo-European at this period. The language spoken there, "Kuchean," is one of the two known dialects of those Tokharian languages which are related not only to Iranian and Sanskrit but also, and perhaps even more closely, to our ancient Western languages such as Latin and Celtic. Indeed certain scholars have even gone so far as to describe Kucha as "an Italo-Celtic oasis tucked away in the middle of the Gobi."

From the cultural point of view however, Kucha was steeped in Indian and Iranian influences. In respect to its religion and art Kucha was Indian. One name is sufficient to remind us of the importance which, thanks to Buddhism, Sanskrit studies had assumed there: the name of Kumarajiva. This religious, who according to Sylvain Lévi

---

[2] The pilgrim Wu-k'ung (790) relates a charming legend according to which the airs of Tokharian music were derived from the songs of waterfalls: "In those mountains there is a spring which falls drop by drop producing musical sounds. Once a year on a certain date these sounds are gathered together to make a musical air" (*Journal asiatique*, 1895, vol. II, p. 364).

was "possibly the greatest of all the translators who passed on to China the spirit and the works of Indian Buddhism," had in fact consecrated his life (he lived from 344 to 413) to the same task as was to occupy the Master of the Law Hiuan Tsang two and a half centuries later. The son of an Indian who had settled at Kucha and of the daughter of the king of the country, Kumarajiva had gone at an early age to Kashmir where he took orders and perfected his knowledge of Sanskrit literature from the *Vedas* to the texts of Hinayana Buddhism. Returning to Kucha before the age of twenty, he was converted to the Mahayana doctrine by a son of the king of Yarkand. He remained in his native city until 383, when a Chinese army of invasion took him back with it to northern China. In China he continued the work he had begun in Kucha, translating a vast quantity of Buddhist texts including notably *The Lotus of the Good Law*, various metaphysical works of the Madhyamika school and the delightful *Sutralamkara*. Indeed it is no exaggeration to say that Kucha was instrumental in bringing about the transmission of a great part of Sanskrit literature to the Far East.

Together with the religion of Sakyamuni, Indian art in both its Greco-Buddhist and Gupta forms, found in Kucha a fertile soil. Among the stuccoes of Qizil, Qumtura and Duldur-Agur we see portraits of Brahmins, *mlecchas* and *yakshas* whose foreign aspect must have struck Hiuan Tsang, for as at Gandhara these are figures of Zeus, Heracles and Silenus adapted to Buddhist iconography. We also find classical draperies, nude ephebes worthy of Greek vases, erotic scenes conjuring up some Greco-Roman banquet, figurines reminiscent of Alexandria and charming female statuettes of an elegance which might derive either from Ch'ang-an or from Myrina. And that series of stucco heads, delightful "belated antiquities" which Pelliot discovered at Tumshuq on the road between Kucha and Kashghar and which today can be seen at the Musée Guimet, Paris—the head of a bearded stranger which in its genial delicacy might be that of some Athenian philosopher of the golden age, another like the Roman head of a monk, thin, sharp and cunning, or a fat Roman head like some Vitellius, *mlecchas* which are like so many satyrs or Socrateses. It was through works such as these that Chinese pilgrims like Hiuan Tsang could, without being aware of it, come into contact at Kucha with the art of the Greco-Roman world, the far-off "Ta-t'sin" and "Fu-lin" (Rome and Roman Asia) of which the Chinese already had some idea. Moreover these stuccoes are virtually contemporary with Hiuan Tsang, dating for the most part from the sixth century. As far as the West was concerned, at Byzantium by this time Greek art was no more than a memory; yet in this belated and as it were posthumous flowering its presence could still be felt in Kashgharia. In the same way does the light from a star which has been dead for centuries continue to reach us across space and time.

Simultaneously with Indo-Greek art the genuinely Indian art of

9. Head of a Bearded Stranger, Tumshuq. (*Musée Guimet*)

the Gupta workshops had a direct influence upon the Kucha region. In this respect we need only call to mind one of the frescoes of the Maya cave at Qizil, a pre-eighth-century representation of the Four Great Miracles which includes, in the posture of a dancer before the Tree of the Nativity, a Queen Maya who is directly related to the most supple female figures of Ajanta.

Persian influences were no less marked. If, from the point of view of literature and religion, Kucha formed an integral part of "Greater India," from the point of view of material civilization it was at the same time a province of "Greater Iran." Nothing is more revealing on this score than the paintings brought back by von Le Coq to the Berlin Museum.[3] Here we find corroboration both of the ethnic type of the Tokharian population which still controlled the city in the seventh century and of the extent to which that population was attracted by Persian culture.

The frescoes of Qizil and Qumtura (most of which probably date from this very seventh century) do indeed give us an unusually precise picture of the brilliant Kuchean society encountered by Hiuan Tsang. And it is a real surpirse, for here in this dead oasis of the Gobi we find coming to life in all their freshness a whole company of brilliant horsemen and heroes who might have stepped out of some Persian miniature. Indeed there is nothing Chinese, nothing Indian about them at all. Nothing but an artistic province of Iran tucked away on the threshold of the Far East which, by escaping the Moslem catastrophe, formed a link between the Sassanian painting of Bamian and Dokhtar-e, Noshirwan and Timurid or Safavid painting. Now, by a curious circumstance this little Persia in the heart of the Gobi was in terms of its artistic conceptions and its material culture extremely close to our medieval West; in outward appearance, general style and even atmosphere, the chivalrous society depicted at Qizil and Qumtura is the sister of our own.

---

[3] There are excellent color reproductions in von Le Coq's *Die buddhistische Spätantike in Mittelasien.*

Here we see before us in all his youthful grace—he could be the work of Benozzo Gozzoli or of Behzad!—the brilliant artist who painted his self-portrait in the cave at Qizil named after him "the Cave of the Painter." Holding his pot of colors delicately in his left hand he is tracing on the wall with all the joy and fervor of a Fra Angelico the image of some Bodhisattva, some scene of the "previous lives" or some paradise of purity. This Kuchean, however, is only of the middle rank, as witness the fact that the weapon at his belt is not the sword of the noble but the broad dagger with the rectangular or lilied hilt. But what elegance there is in his short jerkin belted at the waist and decorated on the right of the collar with the large rectangular or triangular lapel so characteristic of Kuchean costume. In his high boots he reminds us that in this tiny, isolated Indo-European community of Kucha, a true ethnic oasis where the entire people constituted as it were an aristocracy, even the artist was a knight.

Here, too, we see the aristocracy proper, depicted for us on the walls of Qizil and Qumtura by our artist and his emulators. We find in the "Cave of the Sixteen Sword-bearers" a whole company of knights who might have formed part of Hiuan Tsang's escort, for we know they date from the seventh century. What a surprise to discover here people of a Western race with pure oval faces, long straight noses and strongly arched eyebrows. Unless the effect was achieved by means of henna, most of them had red hair, and there was nothing Persian about that at all. What elegance in these delicate faces, clean-shaven except for a tiny moustache, the hair done according to the local fashion and divided into two locks in the middle of the forehead with the rest thrown back on the neck and tied with a ribbon. Just as Hiuan Tsang could admire them that day in 629, just so can we admire them today on the walls of the Berlin Museum to which von Le Coq brought them, these svelte "dandies" in their full-dress clothes with their well-turned waists and dancing gait.

For we know them right down to the last detail of their fashions in dress, right down to their favorite colors. We see them file past in their long, straight "frock-coats," gathered at the waist by a metal belt and then falling in a flare about the knees. And whether it is on the right side only as with the "Painter" or whether it is on both sides of the collar as with the lords of more noble lineage, we notice the large, very ornate and extremely stylish lapel which was the hallmark of Kuchean elegance. Knowing as much as we do, we can take great delight in detailing all the flowerets and braid and embroidery and gaudy trimmings with which not only these lapels but also the broad edgings of the tunics are decorated. And to complete the evocation we have the colors, barely subdued at all by time and in any case in no need of being so for this whole Kuchean aristocracy appears to have had a predilection for neutral tones and delicate pale tints. Those white tunics, for example, with their edgings of milky blue, or those pale blue tunics edged with white, or the brown jerkins decorated with flowerets and with edgings of a very soft olive green set off by medallions of white beading—do they not reveal precisely that Persian taste for symphonies of gentle hues which we know from the frescoes of Cehel Sutun and the porcelain of the Great Mosque of Isfahan?

Occasionally the luxury of Kuchean costume reached almost unparalleled heights of splendor, for this European city which lay in a commanding position on the Silk Route had by this time, shortly before it was to disappear, accumulated enormous wealth. Consider the dress of a group of donors at Kirish, those "Buddhist Magi" kneeling before the Buddha: blue caps set off with trimmings of fur and pearls, the olive green, ermine-lined coat with the collar of brown fur, the long grey jacket with large white lapels edged with blue, gathered at the waist by a belt of garnet red from which hangs the bourde of the wealthy caravaneer; bell-shaped sleeves and protruding from them a kind of blue undersleeve edged with green; and the whole thing studded with passementerie, flowerets and stars. It might be a page from a fifteenth-century Western manuscript depicting a costume from some ceremony of the Order of the Golden Fleece.

For all its civilized refinement, however, Kucha was a mere oasis in the Gobi Desert surrounded and coveted by all the Turco-Mongol hordes, and on pain of being swept away these elegant Kuchean lords had also to remain warriors. Even at the foot of the Buddhist altars, even in their portraits as supplicants and donors, it is always in the guise of an iron-clad cavalry that we see them. For even in this the pious Buddhist painters of Qizil have not left us in ignorance of a single detail. Sometimes the coats of mail reach down to the knees in the Sassanian style; more often they cover only the shoulders and thorax, the abdomen being protected by a corslet of flexible strips. As for the Kuchean sword, the long straight sword with the slender cruciform hilt and the spherical, mushroom-shaped or lilied pommel, that is no stranger to our eyes: it is the great sword of our Western knights, the weapon of cut and thrust designed to be brandished with both hands. Sheath and hilt are worked with great magnificence and decorated with stars, rosettes, coffers and flowerets revealing the exquisite taste of these noble lords.

As with our Western medieval armies we find streaming above the ranks of the Kuchean cavalry splendid serrated oriflammes (with generally three pennants per banner) attached to the tips of their lances and occasionally decorated near the shaft with some heraldic animal, a tiger or a dragon. Further heraldic beasts appear on the crests of their helmets, conical helmets reminiscent of our Bayeux Tapestry, and even the foreheads of the horses are adorned with plumes flying in the wind. In this gorgeous cavalcade in the "Cave of Maya" at Qizil we see the escort of the king of Kucha as it rode out to meet Hiuan Tsang. . . .

Finally we are introduced to the ladies of Kucha, those same beautiful creatures of whom the *T'ang Shu* has already given us an inkling. We meet them all at Qizil, at Qumtura, donors and zealots, crowding around the altars of the Buddha in all their worldly elegance. We see them pass before us in their sumptuous bodices that hug the bosom and waist and open on either side of the throat in the large triangle of the characteristic Kuchean lapel; in their long trailing dresses which it was the fashion to wear very full and with a broad flare at the hem; and with lapels, belts and the edging of bodice and dress adorned with that passementerie of medallions, beading and flowerets so dear to Tokharian taste.

Around this general theme, of course, the caprices of fashion wove a thousand fantasies. The ladies of Kucha appear sometimes in long narrow sleeves, sometimes in bell-shaped sleeves beneath which can be seen the sleeve of some undergarment. Occasionally the bodice ends in a frill of sharp points to which tassels or little bells are attached. In terms of color the costumes of the female sex follow more or less the same tones as those of the male: jackets of a milky white with lapels of a soft warm blue and edging of purple-brown, and white dresses with violet stripes; olive green bodices with white edging, black bodices trimmed with white and green, white bodices trimmed with black, blue bodices trimmed with gold edging, green or pale blue dresses with yellow stripes. . . . Colors and costumes of a by-gone age, worn by the lovely women of a forgotten race in the heart of the Gobi Desert thirteen hundred years ago. . . .

Most of these female donors are holding things of value which they have come to offer to the Buddha: multicolored scarves or jeweled necklaces, goblets and candelabra. Often too they are holding a flower by the stem with a mannered gesture which was to recur in the Uiguro-Buddhist and Uiguro-Manichean paintings of Turfan as also in classical Persian painting.

For the person who is interested in Hiuan Tsang's epoch the frescoes of Qizil hold an even more precious surprise: the "Cave of Maya" which appears to date from this very century or possibly from the one after, provides us indeed with the authentic portraits of a king and queen of Kucha. Like the majority of his subjects, the king has reddish-brown hair divided into locks by a central parting. He is wearing a green garment, open at the top and edged with a broad strip of brown material decorated with gold passementerie. Beneath the bell-shaped sleeves which stop at the elbow with a band of embroidery is a long, narrow, green undersleeve which is in turn terminated with white, brown and gold passementerie. The trousers are brown and the shoes white. The queen is wearing a green jacket-bodice which also has bell-shaped sleeves; in conformity with Kuchean fashion this bodice has a narrow waist and is flared over the hips, and it has the usual large lapels which are here navy blue with brown edging and white and gold stippling. Emerging from the bell-shaped sleeves are long under-sleeves with blue and brown stripes. The dress, which is extremely flared, is white and sewn with blue and brown flowerets. The queen's costume is completed by a rounded hair-style.

Such was quite certainly the appearance of the people who wel-comed the Chinese pilgrims of the seventh century to this great Tokhar-ian city. And it is one of the most moving visions of history to think that we have here before our eyes the last representatives of that Indo-European population of the Gobi, so curiously similar to ourselves in race and appearance and who, only a few decades later, were to disap-pear forever before the onslaught of the Turks. . . .

At the time if Hiuan Tsang's visit, however, there was still a Tokharian dynasty on the throne of Kucha. The names of several of the princes of this dynasty include a root translated in Chinese by the words Su-fa, corresponding to the Sanskrit "Suvarna" and implying an idea of a "Golden Dynasty." Thus the king of Hiuan Tsang's day was called in Chinese Su-fa Tie, in Sanskrit Suvarna Deva and in the indigenous Tokharian language Swarnatep, which is to say "Golden God." He was the son and successor of King Su-fa Pu-she, or in Sanskrit Suvarna Pushpa, "Golden Flower." Like all the minor Tokharian princes of the Gobi he was an extremely devout Buddhist. His kingdom contained no less than five thousand monks under his active patronage, of whom the most senior, a venerable old man named Mokshagupta, acted as his spiritual advisor. Moreover Swarnatep was at this period on very friendly terms with China. As soon as T'ang had acceded to the throne in 618 his father Suvarna Pushpa had sent an ambassador to pay homage at the court of Ch'ang-an. In 630, shortly after Hiuan Tsang's visit, Swarnatep himself was to send Emperor T'ai-tsung a tribute of horses and receive in return an imperial warrant of investiture.

As a zealous Buddhist and one who was bent upon securing the good graces of the Chinese, Swarnatep very naturally accorded Hiuan Tsang an excellent welcome. Indeed as soon as he learned of the pilgrim's approach he went out to meet him accompanied by the principal court officials and the monks of the country. As the returning procession entered the city a religious brought Hiuan Tsang a basket of fresh-grown flowers which the pilgrim proceeded to scatter before the statue of the Buddha. The Master of the Law paid a visit to each of the religious houses in Kucha (numbering about ten in all) one after another and to each he presented gifts of flowers and wine to be offered to the Buddhist images.

Unfortunately the Buddhism practiced at Kucha was that of the Little Vehicle or Hinayana. Kumarajiva's conversion to the Great Vehicle had not had any lasting effect. The Master of the Law refused King Swarnatep's invitation to dine with him since the meal included certain special dishes peculiar to Hinayana prohibitionism, whereas followers of the Mahayana attached no importance to such dietary restraints. The disagreement between the Master of the Law and the local religious was further aggravated by considerations of a philosophical nature. Their doctrine was taken from the ancient schools of the Vaibhashika and the Sautranktika, of which the first was sharply realist and even atomist and the second more phenomenist though its phenomenism was still purely positivist. An idealist metaphysician such as Hiuan Tsang had nothing but scorn for these intellectual positions. It was in vain that Mokshagupta, the most revered scholar in all Kucha, quoted references from the basic texts of the *Vibhasha Sastra* and the *Abhidharma Kosa Sastra.* "We in China," replied Hiuan Tsang, "have also these two works, but since I found to my regret that their content was banal and superficial I left my fatherland behind me in order to study above all else the texts of the Mahayana such as the *Yoga Sastra* (the doctrine of mystical idealism)." Mokshagupta reiterated the accusation leveled by followers of the Little Vehicle against the doctrine of the Mahayana, to the effect that it was a new doctrine which had been arbitrarily superimposed upon the teachings of Sakyamuni and stood in opposition to them: "What is the use of inquiring into these books which contain only erroneous views?" he asked. "The true disciples of the Buddha never study such works!" This time Hiuan Tsang was unable to control his indignation: "The *Yoga Sastra*," he protested, "was expounded by a sage who was an incarnation of the Bodhisattva Maitreya. In calling it today an erroneous book have you no fear of being cast into a bottomless pit?"

The discussion between the two philosophers began to take on the bitter tone of a monkish quarrel. However, Hiuan Tsang, while continuing to raise vehement objection to the doctrines professed by the religious of Kucha, loyally acknowledged their erudition in the scriptures of the Little Vehicle and the saintliness of their lives. Old Mokshagupta, for his part, in spite of Hiuan Tsang's reproof, remained on speaking terms with him. Fortunately enough, we might add, for the snow covering the T'ien Shan in the direction of the Muzart obliged the pilgrim to remain at Kucha for sixty days. Furthermore, and this shows that the doctrinal discussions had not left too much bad feeling, on the day when the temperature allowed Hiuan Tsang to leave Kucha at last, King Swarnatep presented him with a veritable caravan of servants, camels and horses and accompanied him right to the outskirts of the city, followed by a crowd of monks and pious laymen.

CHAPTER 5

On the Eve of
the Convulsion

LEAVING KUCHA by the Qizil trail Hiuan Tsang crossed the Muzart River probably to the southwest of Bai and continued by way of Yaqa Ariq, which he calls Po-lu-k'ia and the *T'ang Shu* calls Ku-mo, toward the present-day town of Aqsu. This region was under the control of the western Turks whose khan had his summer residence on nearby Mount Aqtagh, the "White Mountain," to the north of Kucha. But the existence of this Turkish kingdom straddling the T'ien Shan and embracing on the one side part of the present-day Sinkiang Uigur Autonomous Region and on the other part of the Kirgiz and Kasakh Republics —a veritable empire of the steppes enjoying regular diplomatic relations with China, the Tokharian oases, the Sassanian Empire and Byzantium—did nothing to improve the safety of the roads. Very likely its organization was somewhat weak. At any rate, two days after leaving Kucha Hiuan Tsang came across a party of two thousand Turkish horsemen who had just pillaged a caravan of its treasures and provisions and were still arguing over the spoils. "Fierce disputes had arisen between them over this, which they settled with much brandishing of weapons, and afterward dispersed." The pillaged caravan and then the scuffle between the marauders—an ever-recurring tableau of the deserts and steppes . . .

After this encounter the pilgrim left the Tokharian valleys behind him, proceeded up the Aqsu River and then, passing to the south of the almost twenty-four thousand feet high Khan Tengri Massif, crossed the T'ien Shan chain at the Bedal Col, which links the Tarim Basin with the upper valley of the Naryn and the Syr Darya Basin. This face of the T'ien Shan is covered with glaciers of which Hiuan Tsang, anticipating the great explorers of modern times, gives an extremely picturesque description: "This mountain of ice constitutes the northern part of the Pamirs. It is extremely dangerous and its peak reaches to the sky. Ever since the world began snow has collected there and has changed into ice which melts neither in spring nor in summer. Sheets of this ice, hard and gleaming, stretch as far as the eye can see and mingle with the clouds. Looking at them one is blinded by their brightness. The road is strewn with cliffs and pinnacles of ice some of which are up to a hundred feet high and others several tens of feet across. One cannot cross the latter without great difficulty nor climb the former without great peril. Added to this the traveler is constantly assailed by blasts of wind and by snowstorms so that, even with shoes and garments lined and trimmed with fur, he cannot help shivering with the cold. When it comes to eating or sleeping he can find no dry place to lie down. He has no alternative but to hang up the cooking-pot to prepare his food and lay out his mat upon the ice." The crossing of the T'ien Shan cost Hiuan Tsang's caravan thirteen or fourteen men dead of hunger and cold and a great many more cattle and horses.

Descending the northern face of the T'ien Shan Hiuan Tsang

made his way toward the Issyk-kul and followed its southern shore. The Issyk-kul, the "Warm Lake" (Yo-lai in Chinese), is so named because it never freezes. "This lake," remarks Hiuan Tsang, "is approximately one thousand *li* in circumference. It is longest in the east-west direction and narrow from south to north. Surrounded by mountains on all sides, it is fed by a multitude of rivers. Its water is a greenish black color and has a bitter, salty taste. Sometimes its vast expanse lies still in huge calm sheets, sometimes it swells and rolls furiously." The relative warmth of the water and the fact that around its shores the snow rarely attained any great depth had made this the winter abode of the Turkish chieftain. It was to the northwest of the lake, near the city of Suei-ye, the modern Tokmak, that Hiuan Tsang met the grand khan of the western Turks, the *yabgu* T'ung (T'ung Shih-hu in Chinese) who was out hunting. That was at the beginning of 630.

The empire of the Western Turks was then at the height of its power. From the middle of the sixth century when their khan Ishtämi had crushed the last of the Hephthalite Huns they had dominated central Asia from the Altai to the Oxus and Badakhshan. For a time even greater dreams had haunted the imagination of the Turkish rulers. Ishtämi had drawn up, to his profit and to the detriment of Sassanian Persia, a vast project of political alliance and commercial exchange between the Far East and Byzantium. A Turkish ambassador named Maniach, of Sogdian extraction, had gone to Byzantium to solicit the alliance (567-8), and in the following year a Byzantine ambassador, Zemarque, had visited the khan's summer residence near Kucha (568-9). The Turco-Byzantine military alliance against the Persians never came to fruition but we would do well, if we are surprised at the Mediterranean influences evident in the frescoes of Kucha, to bear in mind the ease with which an ambassador from the emperor could, at the height of the Turkish hegemony, make the journey from Constantinople to Tokharia. Nor should we overlook the fact that this original Turkey was itself not entirely without culture. Around 580 Khan T'o-po had, by the offices of the Gandharan monk Jinagupta, been converted to Buddhism, and his successor *yabgu* T'ung was to evince the same religious sympathies on the occasion of Hiuan Tsang's visit.

He was a powerful ruler, this nomad prince whose frontiers touched both Persia and the Chinese Empire. "He was bold and prudent," wrote the T'ang chroniclers of him, "magnificent in battle and attack." No doubt taking advantage of the terrible war which had just broken out in the West between the Persian king Khosrau II and the Byzantine emperor Heraclius, he had added a number of fresh encroachments toward Bactriana to those of his predecessors and established his hegemony as far as Gandhara. In order to keep a closer watch on Persia he had moved his capital to Chash, or She as the Chinese called it, corresponding to the modern Tashkent. To the northeast, as we know from Hiuan Tsang's report, he had as a dependent and virtual vassal the king of Turfan. To the south one of his sons ruled over Bactriana. "His hegemony," says the *T'ang Shu,* "covered all the countries of the West. To the kings of those countries he sent his *tudun* (Turkish dignitaries) to keep them under surveillance and to raise taxes and levies. Never had the barbarians of the West been so powerful." But with all that he was prudent too and continued his flirtation with the T'ang court in order to keep his hands free on the Persian front. In 620 he had even asked for the hand of a Chinese princess, and a few years later in 627 he had presented to the court at Ch'ang-an a belt of pure gold studded with ten thousand jewels and a gift of five thousand horses. Emperor T'ai-tsung, for his part, still at grips with the Turks of Mongolia and thinking that it would be "better to join with those who are far off against those who are nigh," had been careful not to reject these overtures, and although he had avoided dispatching any princesses he was for the time being treating the Khan of the West as a loyal friend.

Hiuan Tsang's description of the Turkish ruler conjures up some Attila or Jenghis Khan figure. "The horses possessed by these barbarians were extremely numerous. The khan wore a coat of green satin and had his hair quite free; only his forehead was bound round several times with a strip of silk ten feet long, the rest of it trailing behind him. He was surrounded by some two hundred officers in brocade coats and all wearing their hair in plaits. The rest of the troops consisted of riders mounted on camels or horses, dressed in furs and fine woolen cloth and carrying long lances, banners and straight bows. Their multitude stretched for so far that the eye could not tell where it ended. . . ." [1]

The sight of this nomad cavalry clearly impressed Hiuan Tsang, and indeed the vision that he evokes here is that of a piece of history in the making; in these mountainous valleys of Kirgiz the pilgrim from China had just discovered the extent of the barbarian reserves.

Can we indeed really imagine those assembled hordes, awaiting the moment when they would begin their onslaught? The place: that wild Issyk-kul region high up on the flank of the T'ien Shan chain which on one side faced the Chinese world and on the other the Persian. The time: an historic moment in the destiny of Asia, the decisive seventh century that was to see the Tokharian lands, crushed by T'ang China, thenceforth exposed and defenseless against the occupation of the Uigur tribes; that was to see Emperor Harsha's united India replaced by a feudality that was to be swept away before the first Ghaznevid onslaught, and that was to see the Sassanian Empire, that barrier to Turkish expansion, smashed by the power of Islam and replaced by a Moslem Persia which was to be the fortune of the Turkish *condottiere* and was eventually to have a Turkish sultan; and finally, beyond Per-

---

[1] Compare this picture with the one drawn by the Chinese pilgrim Sung Yun in 518 of another barbarian people, the Hephthalite Huns, who had dominated the western steppes before the Turks destroyed them between 563 and 567: "The Hephthalites do not live in walled cities; their seat of government is a movable camp. Their dwellings are of felt. They move about in search of water and pasture, spending the summer in places where it is cool and repairing to more temperate districts in the winter . . . For himself the king has a great tent of felt erected which stands forty feet square; the walls all around it are tapestries of wool. He wears garments of embroidered silk; he sits upon a gold couch with four feet in the form of four gold phoenixes. His chief wife also dresses in a garment of embroidered silk which trails upon the ground behind her to a length of three feet. On her head she wears a horn-shaped headdress eight feet long. This horn is decorated with precious stones in five colors . . . Of all the barbarians the Hephthalites are the most powerful. They do not believe in the Buddhist Law and worship a large number of divinities. They kill living creatures and are eaters of bloody meat. The various neighboring kingdoms give them large quantities of jewels and precious objects."

sia, Byzantium, the fabled "Rum," wounded by Islam with a wound
that was not to heal before 1453.

That assembly of nomads around the khan in 630 was not unlike a
farewell muster by the old Turkish Empire of its member tribes, still
for a while united. For the Turkish Empire, the ancient empire of the
"Tu-kiu," as the Chinese called them, was about to break up. A few
years more and T'ai-tsung, who had already subjugated their brothers
in Mongolia, would also overthrow the Turks of Turkistan. Only in
appearance, however, for the tribes, left once more to their own devices
by the collapse of the last unified khanate, were about to resume with
regard to their imperial neighbors their terrifying freedom of action;
and their onslaught, which could be stopped by money or by the sword
when it had been under the command of a single chief, became irresistible as soon as it was a matter of anonymous hordes, scattered clans and
anarchic *condottieri* looming up over every horizon in the steppes. Indeed the *kuriltai* of that winter of 630, the gathering of the "Tu-kiu"
squadrons witnessed by Hiuan Tsang, was indeed the final gathering
of all the Turks on their native soil before the bannners went their
separate ways to meet their various destinies and weave their various
epics. What Hiuan Tsang saw there was the last meeting between the
ancestors of Seljuk and Mahmud of Ghazni, of Mohammed of Khwa-
rizm and of the Turks of the great army of Jenghis Khan, the forebears
of Timur and of Mohammed II. And it is this terrible sense of anticipa-
tion, the fearsome unknownness about these squadrons hidden in a fold
of the Ala-tau that makes the pilgrim's account so thrilling for us.

For a moment, however, these wild horsemen, contained to the
east by the T'ang Empire and to the southwest by the great Sassanid
kings, seemed to be in a fairly good-natured mood. Moreover they
showed great respect for questions of religion. Not that they themselves
professed any religion in particular; Hiuan Tsang credits them with no
more than a kind of fire cult which was no doubt derived from Persian
Zoroastrianism. But they had a great respect for Buddhism. T'ung had
even been host for a time to an Indian missionary named Prabhakara-

mitra, who had taken upon himself the task of converting the Turks. Prabhakaramitra had arrived at the khan's court with ten companions and made such a favorable impression upon his host that the latter would only grudgingly agree to their departure when in 626 the missionaries decided to continue their apostolate in China. So when, four years later, Hiuan Tsang's arrival reminded him of his former spiritual master, he must have been greatly moved.

When the hunting was over the khan invited the pilgrim to his Tokmak residence. "The khan lived in a great tent adorned with flowers of gold so bright they were blinding to look upon. His officers had had long mats laid out on the ground in front of it and were seated upon them in two rows. All wore gorgeous costumes of figured silk. The khan's guard were standing behind them. Although this was a

10. The life of the Buddha. Tibetan painting. (*Musée Guimet*)

barbarian prince and his palace a tent of felt, it was impossible to look upon him without being inspired to admiration and respect." It is interesting to compare these lines with the accounts of Western travelers of the thirteenth and fourteenth centuries which express in almost exactly the same terms the impression of majesty conveyed by Jenghis Khan's princes.

A further scene also portrayed by William of Rubruquis, for example, was the banquet which took place whenever foreign ambassadors were received. During Hiuan Tsang's visit the khan had occasion to receive some Chinese envoys and ambassadors from the king of Turfan. He invited these envoys to be seated and gave orders that they should be served wine to the accompaniment of musical instruments. "The khan drank together with the foreign envoys, and he commanded a separate

11. The life of the Buddha. Tibetan painting. (*Musée Guinet*)

jug of grape wine to be brought for the Master of the Law. The guests became increasingly animated and began to vie with each other in calling for toasts, clinking their cups together, filling them up and emptying them over and over again; and all this time the air was full of the music of the barbarians of the South and of the North, of the East and of the West, ringing out its sonorous chords. The airs they played, though half-savage, were pleasing to the ear and gladdened both heart and mind. Shortly afterward fresh dishes were brought; boiled quarters of sheep and veal were piled in large quantities before the guests. . . ."

The respect in which the khan held religion was proved by the consideration which he displayed toward Hiuan Tsang during the course of this feast. The Master of the Law was given an armchair of solid iron; "pure foods" were specially prepared for him—rice cakes,

12. The life of the Buddha. Tibetan painting. (*Musée Guimet*)

cream, milk, crystallized sugar, honeycomb, and grapes, and at the end of the banquet the khan begged him to expound the Buddhist Law. Before this assembly of tribal chieftains the Master of the Law proceeded to explain the essential principles of his faith: love for all living creatures and the means of reaching the Other Shore and of obtaining the Final Deliverance. When the preacher had finished "the khan lifted up his hands and prostrated himself upon the ground; then with radiant face he announced that he received these teachings with faith." Conceiving a great fondness for the pilgrim he tried, as the king of Turfan had done before, to dissuade him from continuing his voyage. "Master," he told him, "you must not go to India. It is an excessively hot country, so hot indeed that the temperature is the same in winter as in summer. I fear lest your countenance should melt as soon as you

13. The life of the Buddha. Tibetan painting. (*Musée Guimet*)

arrive. The natives are black-skinned. The majority of them go naked without any respect for propriety; they are quite unworthy that you should visit them." Hiuan Tsang retorted: "I stand before you consumed with desire to go in search of the Law of Buddha and to consult the monuments of antiquity in order to follow with love in his footsteps."

The khan yielded. He had an interpreter draw up letters of recommendation to the minor princes of the Gandhara region, his vassals. He then ordered the interpreter to take these letters and accompany the pilgrim as far as Kapisa in the Kabul Valley. It was largely thanks to this official protection by the powerful Turkish sovereign that Hiuan Tsang was able to negotiate so easily the passes of the Pamirs and Bactriana. Incidentally this must have been one of the *yabgu* T'ung's last political acts. In the same year, 630, shortly after Hiuan Tsang's departure, he died at the hand of an assassin and the ten tribes of the western Turks divided themselves into two khanates on either side of the Issykkul which lasted until the final collapse.

Hiuan Tsang took his leave of the khan and continued his journey toward the West. Passing to the north of the Alexander Mountains he crossed the plain in which rise the nine rivers which feed the Chu and the ten rivers which feed its tributary the Kuragati. The region is known to this day as the "Land of a Thousand Springs" (Ming bulak in Mongol, Bing göl in Turkish). "This region is approximately two hundred *li* square. To the south it is bordered by snow-clad mountains and on the other three sides by flat plains. The land is plentifully watered and the trees of its forests are as remarkable for their height as for the abundance of their foliage. In the last month of spring flowers of the most various sorts adorn the ground like rich embroidery. A multitude of lakes and ponds have earned it the name of Thousand Springs. The humidity of the climate gives it a cool sweetness. It is there that the khan repairs each year to escape the heat of summer. Large quantities of deer are to be seen. They are adorned with collars and little bells and are used to men and do not flee at their approach. The khan is fond of them and takes great delight in seeing them there. He has issued a decree to his subjects to the effect that whoever dares kill a single one of them shall be punished with death. All these deer, therefore, may live out their days in peace."

The pilgrim then crossed the Talass River, passing through the town of the same name (in Chinese Ta-lo-ssu and today known as Aulieata) and afterward turning southwest to Chash, the modern Tashkent which the Chinese called the city of She. He crossed the Syr Darya, formerly the Yaxartes and called by him the Ye-ye, probably at the point now occupied by the little town of Chinaz. From there, in order to reach Samarkand, he had to cross the eastern arm of the Red Sand Desert, the Qizil Qum, which lies between the lower courses of the Syr Darya and that of the Amu Darya or Oxus. "This is a great sandy desert in which are to be found neither water nor grass. The road stretches away as far as the eye can see and it is impossible to discern its limits. Only the sight of some high mountain in the distance and the discovery of some abandoned skeleton will show one the direction to be taken and indicate the road one must follow." After some hundred and fifty miles of this empty solitude he came to the Qara Darya or Zaraf-shan, the river of Samarkand.

Samarkand, which the Chinese called Sa-mo-kien (or simply K'ang, their name for the whole of Sogdiana), was already at this time a city of great antiquity, for we find it mentioned nine centuries earlier, under the name of Marakanda, on the occasion of Alexander the Great's expedition. An outpost of Persian culture in the northeastern marches, it had preserved its Iranian character even in the ethnic sphere. The language spoken there was an eastern Iranian dialect known as "Sogdian," rediscovered early in this century by the Pelliot and Gauthiot expeditions and which the caravaneers of Samarkand had carried with them across the Gobi trails as far as Tun-huang. "The peoples of this country," the *T'ang Shu* informs us, "excel at trade and adore profit. As soon as a man reaches the age of twenty he departs for the neighboring kingdoms. . . . Everywhere where profit is to be had, they have been there." It was during this very period with which we are concerned, between 627 and 649, that a Sogdian colony settled at the western gate of the Gobi in the vicinity of Lop Nor Lake where Pelliot uncovered its traces.

Hiuan Tsang was well aware of the economic importance of Sogdiana. As a trail-head for caravans plying between Persia and China, Samarkand, as he tells us, "possessed vast quantities of rare and precious merchandise." It was also one of the best cultivated oases of the Persian East. "The soil is rich and fertile; all types of seed grow there in abundance, the forests are magnificent in their vegetation and prodigious quantities of flowers and fruit are to be found in the country." And we may add, with the Chinese pilgrim, that the pasturelands of the Qara Darya produced a highly reputed breed of horse: even before they bore the Seljuk cavalry to the Sea of Marmara and the Timurid squadrons to the Aegean and the Jumma, these Transoxianan stallions were famous on every marketplace from the Near East to the Far East.

The culture of Transoxiana—Hiuan Tsang himself conveys this impression very clearly—was still completely orientated towards Sassanian Persia. The alphabet of the country, the so-called "Sogdian" alphabet, was derived from Aramaic script, as was also that of Sassanian Persia. The prevailing religion was still Zoroastrianism, the national religion of the Iranian people and most particularly of the Sassanid dynasty. The Sogdians, however, as the caravaneers of central Asia, also came into daily contact with Buddhism. And from the political point of view Transoxiana had long ago (at the time of the fall of the Achaemenids) ceased to be part of the Persian Empire. Belonging first to the Macedonians and then to the Greco-Bactrians (fourth to second centuries B.C.), it had passed into the hands of the Indo-European Scythians, (second century B.C. to fifth century A.D.), before being overrun by a Mongol horde, the wild Hephthalite Huns (fifth century), from whose clutches it was delivered in the middle of the sixth century by the appreciably more civilized Turks from the Altai. At the time of Hiuan Tsang's visit in 630 it constituted a Turco-Iranian kingdom centered on its capital, Samarkand. Indeed, notwithstanding the indubitably Iranian character of the culture of the country, its king, who prided himself upon his Turkish nobiliary title of *tarkhan,* was a virtual vassal of the Grand Khan of the western Turks, to whom he was also bound by family ties.

For this population of farmers and merchants, however, the suzerainty of semi-nomad hordes was not without a certain risk. The Iranian Sogdians were to feel themselves threatened by the prodigious expansion of these Tu-kiu peoples who before four centuries had passed were to have turned this part of the Persian world into Turkistan. Consequently in 631, shortly after Hiuan Tsang's visit, a Transoxianan delegation arrived at the court of China to request that the T'ang extend their protectorate to cover Sogdiana. (Remember that there was no question at this period of the Sogdians having to defend themselves against the Arabs for the Arab conquest had not yet reached Persia; the delegation's purpose was thus clearly to throw off the Turkish yoke.) Emperor T'ai-tsung, however, despite his taste for conquest, was gifted with sound good sense. Samarkand seemed to him to be altogether too far away from the Great Wall. Satisfied with having subdued the Gobi, he refused to extend his military concern as far as Persia: "I am averse to adorning myself with vain titles at the expense of the people. If I took Sogdiana into subjection I would have to send troops to defend it and those troops, in order to reach it, would have to travel ten thousand *li!*" He declined their offer. Instead, rather than annexing their territory, he established diplomatic and commercial relations with the Sogdians, as confirmed by the dispatch of regular embassies by both parties.

Hiuan Tsang appears to have felt, arriving at Samarkand, that he had entered another world. For this was already Persia, the world of Zoroastrianism, in instinctive opposition to Sino-Indian beliefs. Although the city contained a number of ancient Buddhist monasteries dating very likely from the period of Indo-Scythian domination, these had long been abandoned as a consequence of the Zoroastrian reaction which had obviously spread from Sassanian Persia. "The king and peo-

ple do not believe in the Law of the Buddha. Their religion consists in
the cult of fire." When he arrived Hiuan Tsang found himself greeted
by the king "with a certain disdain." Next day, however, the pilgrim
having undertaken to expound to him the Doctrine of Salvation, the
Sogdian monarch declared himself to be in receipt of grace. Was this
through admiration of the missionary's zeal and the radiance of his
powerful personality? Or was it perhaps that this wily Transoxianan
was keen to humor the might of a renascent China in order to counter
the double pull of the Turks and the Sassanids? Indeed in the following year, as we have seen, the king of Samarkand sent emissaries to
Emperor T'ai-tsung to offer him vassalage. Whatever the reason for this
change of attitude the king took Hiuan Tsang under his protection,
and the Zoroastrian populace having gone so far as to pursue the pilgrim with flaming brands, he had the attackers arrested and would
have had their hands and feet cut off had not Hiuan Tsang, with true
Buddhist charity, obtained a reduction of their sentence.

Basically this border country of Transoxiana was unshakably Iranian only with respect to its material civilization. In the matter of
religion it resembled its neighbors the Turks in oscillating between
Zoroastrianism and Buddhism according to the dictates of commerce
and political interest. More or less Zoroastrian under the Achaemenids
and more or less Buddhist under the Indo-Scythians, it had undergone a
Zoroastrian reaction during the Sassanian period. To judge from Hiuan
Tsang's account his visit there marked the beginning of a partial restoration of the Buddhist faith. Indeed, as his biographer rather curiously
relates, when the king of Samarkand had had his persecutors beaten
with rods, "men of all ranks of society were struck with fear and respect and came in crowds to ask to be instructed in the Law." Hiuan
Tsang called an assembly at which he ordained a number of religious
and restored the old abandoned monasteries to the service of the cult.

Leaving Samarkand and proceeding due south Hiuan Tsang
passed through Shebr-e Sabz or Kesh, which he calls Kieshuang-na
(Kasanna?), and entered the Kotin Koh Mountains, a chain of the

Pamir Massif. "The paths through these mountains," we read in his biography, "are deep and dangerous. Once engaged upon them the traveler finds neither water nor vegetation. After a journey of three hundred *li* through the middle of these mountains he enters the Gates of Iron." The caravan trail from Samarkand to the Oxus still passes through this famous defile even today. "These are the gorges," Hiuan Tsang tells us, "between two mountain masses which rise to right and left to a prodigious height. They are separated only by a path which besides being extremely narrow is fraught with precipices. On either side these mountains form huge walls of rock the color of iron. The rocks in fact contain iron ore. At the entrance a double door has been erected and above are hung a multitude of little bells of cast or wrought iron. And because the passage is difficult and well defended it received the name which it still has to this day." At that time the Gates of Iron constituted the southern frontier of the empire of the western Turks. By this means the Turks controlled all the traffic between central Asia and India.

CHAPTER 6

The Greco-Buddhist World

Continuing south from the Gates of Iron and crossing the Oxus, now known as the Amu Darya, by the Pata Kesar ferry, opposite Tirmidh, Hiuan Tsang entered the old kingdom of Bactriana.[1]

An ancient Iranian land since the very dawn of history, Bactriana had subsequently become Greek. After Alexander the Great had conquered it by force it became for two centuries, from 329 to 135 B.C. approximately, the bulwark of Hellenism in this region. Under Dio-

[1] Hiuan Tsang's itinerary through the Greco-Buddhist region was worked out by Alfred Foucher in the following two articles: 1) For the different districts of modern Afghanistan: *Notes sur l'itinéraire de Hiuan-tsang en Afghanistan* in "Études asiatiques pour le vingt-cinquième anniversaire de l'École française d'Extrême-Orient (1925)," vol. I, pp. 257–284; 2) For the Peshawar district, *Notes sur la géographie ancienne du Gandhâra, commentaire à un chapitre de Hiuan-tsang,* in "Bulletin de l'École française d'Extrème Orient," vol. I, 1901, pp. 322–369. Both articles include valuable archeological maps.

dotus, Euthydemus, Demetrius and Eucratides the Greco-Bactrian kingdom valiantly defended its share of the Macedonian heritage against
native rebellions and the pressure of the nomads. At a time when the
Parthians had extended their power over almost the whole of Persia, up
here in the borderland between two worlds this epic Hellenism still
flourished with tenacious vitality. No one today can fail to be moved by
the clean profiles on those medallions which, in the absence of any
texts, are our only source for the physiology of these heroic adventurers.
Then, round about 135 B.C., came the invasion of the nomads, although fortunately on this occasion the nomads were the Yue-chi or
Indo-Scythians, that is to say they were very likely tribes of Indo-European Scythians who were capable of adopting straight away the heritage of the ancient cultures. Indeed, under the mighty Kushan dynasty
these conquerors, who were by then masters of eastern Persia and northwest India, continued to a great extent the tradition of their Greek
predecessors and, by joining the religion of Sakyamuni to Alexandrian
art, created the Greco-Buddhist civilization. But in about A.D. 425 real
barbarians swooped down on the country in the shape of the Hephthalite Huns, who were of Mongol origin. In their savage fury they subjected the Buddhist church and the Indo-Greek art by which it was
represented to frequent attacks. For more than a century they held sway
over Bactriana, only succumbing in 566 before a coalition between Sassanian, Persia and the western Turks. When the spoils were divided it
fell to the lot of the Sassanids, as represented by the greatest of their
number, Khosrau I Anushirvan. Not for long, however, for the western
Turks, taking advantage of the wars between the Byzantines and the
Sassanids, adopted Bactriana for their own. At the time of Hiuan
Tsang's visit in 630 it was called Tokharistan (T'u-ho-lo in Chinese)
and was the private fief of one of the Grand Khan's sons, Prince Tardu
Shad, who resided at Qunduz.

Accordingly Hiuan Tsang, after crossing the Oxus, left the main
caravan route from Samarkand to Balkh, the Bactrian capital, in order
to visit Tardu Shad at Qunduz. This prince was not only a son of the

Grand Khan of the Turks but also the son-in-law of the king of Turfan. The pilgrim brought him both news from his father the Grand Khan, whom he had just left, and letters from his father-in-law, the king of Turfan. This Turkish king of Bactriana was an extremely pious man. He showed great regard for Hiuan Tsang and would have accompanied him personally to India had he not been prevented by one of those harem dramas of which the history of central Asia is so full. The Turfanese princess, or *khatun* as the Turks called her, had died shortly before Hiuan Tsang's arrival. Tardu Shad had married again almost immediately. Now the new queen had been having an affair with one of the royal princes, a son of the first marriage, and this Turkish "Phaedra" poisoned the king and placed her lover on the throne. The new king, however, assured Hiuan Tsang of the same protection as Tardu Shad had done; learning that the pilgrim was thinking of proceeding directly to the Kabul Valley, the king very discreetly suggested that he should make a detour and visit Balkh: "Your disciple," he told Hiuan Tsang, "counts among his possessions the city of Fu-ho-lo (Balkh); it is known as the little royal city. It contains a multitude of religious monuments. I should like the Master of the Law to set aside some time to visit them and there offer his respects. Afterward he will take a carriage and leave for the South."

Balkh, formerly Bactra, still presented at this period the peculiar phenomenon of a basically Iranian city which was ardently Buddhist as far as religion was concerned. Its Buddhist evangelization probably dated back to the middle of the third century B.C. when the city must have received missionaries sent by the great Indian emperor Asoka. Buddhism had subsequently enjoyed the protection of the Greek dynasties and the Indo-Scythian kings, and the period of Hephthalite domination had not succeeded in destroying it. The explorations of Foucher and Hackin showed what a singular change of fortune has overtaken this region. Today, as a result of successive devastations and the abandonment of its ancient irrigation system, it is a dying land. Modern travelers say they cannot help a certain feeling of melancholy as they re-read Hiuan Tsang's description: "The plains and adjacent valleys are quite exceptionally fertile. Truly this is a privileged land." As for the "magnificent plateau" admired by Hiuan Tsang on which the city and its suburbs were built, today it bears no witness to the centuries of Buddhism except for a few ruined stupas in which the devastations of Mongols and Moslems left not one trace of sculpture.

In Hiuan Tsang's time, despite the episode of the Hephthalite Huns, the country still contained a hundred monasteries which were rich in relics of the Buddha and housed three thousand religious. All these monks were followers of the Hinayana or Little Vehicle, though this did not prevent Hiuan Tsang from getting on extremely well with them. Indeed the monasteries of Balkh not only prided themselves on their ancient stupas and their holy relics; they were no less celebrated for their learning. Hiuan Tsang admits to having benefitted greatly from his conversations with one of their scholars, Prajñakara, who at his request expounded to him certain difficult passages from the basic works of the Hinayana such as the *Abhidharma,* the *Kosa* of Katyayana and the *Vibhasha Sastra.*

After Balkh our pilgrim set out to cross the Hindu Kush or, as he says, the "Snowy Mountains." It was one of the most arduous moments of his whole journey. "The road is twice as difficult and dangerous as in the desert regions and among the glaciers. The sky is continually overcast with frozen clouds and whirling snowstorms. If occasionally one comes across a more favorable spot it is at most a few dozen feet of even terrain. It was of this country that Sung Yun once wrote: 'The ice is piled up to form soaring mountains and the snow flies over a thousand *li.*'"

Negotiating the Qara Kottal and Dandan Shikan passes, Hiuan Tsang came at last to the city of Bamian, situated in the heart of the massif or rather in the longitudinal valley separating the Hindu Kush chain from the Koh-i Baba.

Like Balkh and perhaps to an even greater extent Bamian or Fan-yen-na as the Chinese called it was an extremely important station on the route between central Asia and India. All caravans, whether of merchants or pilgrims, descending from the Hindu Kush had to pass beneath its towering cliff on their way to the upper Ghorband valley and the capital of Kapisa. The French archeologists who have worked in the area, Alfred Foucher, Mr. and Mrs. André Godard, Hackin, were all struck by the accuracy of Hiuan Tsang's description of the site. "Bamian," he wrote, "leans against the mountainside and spans the valley; the enclosure is between six and seven *li* in length. To the north it backs onto the sheer rock. The region has some winter wheat but few flowers and fruit. It lends itself to the raising of cattle and has sheep and horses in abundance. The climate is extremely cold. The manners of the people are primitive. Many furs and garments of coarse wool are worn; these too are produced locally." These proud Afghan highlanders, at that time trustees of the Buddhist Law, appealed greatly to Hiuan Tsang. Their character was tough and wild, he noted, but they were distinguished from the neighboring people by virtue of the "simplicity of their faith."

At the time of Hiuan Tsang's visit Bamian had ten or so Buddhist monasteries housing several thousand religious, all of the Hinayana school. The pilgrim visited the caves which had been dug out of the cliff on the north side of the valley and made into monastic cells. He also speaks of the two gigantic Buddha statues, respectively 175 ft. and 115 ft. high (giving their heights only as 150 and 100 ft.) which still stand in two hollows in the cliff-face. One of them in fact he thought by its gilding to be a work of bronze.

It is a fascinating exercise to try and imagine this encounter between the pilgrim from far-off China and these late products of Gandharan art, the final vestiges of Hellenism in these regions. For, as André Godard has observed, the great 175 ft. Buddha with its faultless drapery and slightly flexed left leg is simply some Hellenistic statue enlarged to a gigantic scale.

Hiuan Tsang says nothing about the frescoes of Bamian although for us these are the most interesting feature of the site. These frescoes adorn the walls of the passages carved in the rock behind the heads of the two giant Buddhas and appear to belong to two distinct periods. According to the Godards, who have carried out a methodical study of them, the frescoes in the niche behind the 175 ft. Buddha date from the third century A.D. and those behind the 115 ft. Buddha from the fifth and sixth centuries. In some of these paintings, notably those in the niche belonging to the 115 ft. Buddha, the influence of Greco-Roman art is as pronounced as in the Buddhist frescoes of the Miran district of the Gobi, south of Lop Nor Lake. The treatment of certain of the nude figures and the skill which is evident in the treatment of the draperies evoke as it were an echo of Pompeii. Did the Chinese pilgrims who cannot have helped but visit these sanctuaries in the sky suspect that what they glimpsed there was the art of the Roman Empire, the distant "Ta-t'sin" of which their geographers had a fairly precise idea? Other details, it is true, must have seemed more familiar to people who had just journeyed across central Asia; in the frescoes of the lower niche they might have detected a particular influence which they had seen already in the frescoes of Qizil, near Kucha, and which we know to have stemmed from Persia.

Several characters in the paintings in the 115 ft. niche are indeed reminiscent of the Persian horsemen we have already met in the "Cave of the Painter" at Qizil. The elegant lunar spirit who adorns the vault of the niche is a case in point. With his huge halo inscribed with a crescent moon and standing out against a blue background, he appears to us above a classical quadriga of winged white horses, shades of Pegasus unexpected in this corner of Afghanistan. His costume is in every way similar to those of the Kuchean lords. The long creamy-white or pale yellow tunic is gathered at the waist with the customary belt and afterward flares out toward the knee; it has the large Kuchean lapel on the right side, here sky-blue in color, and also the broad Kuchean border which in this case is ochre. His weapons too are like those of Qizil—

the long straight sword with the cruciform hilt and the lance with the triangular pennant.

It is the same story a little farther along with the row of donors situated, as if they were on a balcony, behind a balustrade decorated with tapestries; more "knights of Qizil" with their tight-fitting tunics opening on one side only in the large triangular lapel. And what for us is most interesting of all is that, sharing the same "balcony" as these heroes from some Persian miniature, are traditional bearded Sassanid kings, their tiaras adorned with the sun and moon, as well as Gandhararan Buddhas and Indian monks. This is probably the moment to recall that these districts to the south of the Oxus had for a time, in the middle of the sixth century, formed part of the Sassanian Empire of Khosrau I. At all events the range of donors in this "balcony" has this about it that is unique: it shows in a single fresco the transition from Sassanian art to Persian painting—a fact of great historical importance.

After leaving Bamian Hiuan Tsang, as Foucher has established, crossed the Shibar Col which lies at a height of nearly ten thousand feet and gives access to the upper valley of the Ghorband, a sub-tributary of the Kabul River. While climbing the Shibar massif he was overtaken by a snowstorm and lost his way. He was lucky enough to meet some local hunters however, who put him on the right track again. He followed the narrow winding valley of the Ghorband until this river joined the Panjshir. "At this point the two walls of hills parted at last and the beautiful plain of Kapisa spread out before him in its magnificent frame of mountains."

Kapisa (in Chinese, Kia-pi-she or Ki-pin) was that part of present-day Afghanistan lying to the north of Kabul. Hiuan Tsang did not in fact pass the site of Kabul itself because the former capital of the country, Kapisi, was situated more to the north on the middle Panjshir, corresponding to the modern Begram. Foucher, to whom we owe this identification, has confirmed every point in the Chinese pilgrim's description: "The plain of Kapisa measures between thirty-five and forty miles from north to south and about a dozen miles from east to west. It is like a smaller version of Kashmir in everything except the latter's lakes. Just as Hiuan Tsang described it, it is bordered to the north by the permanently snow-covered chain of the Hindu Kush and on the other three sides of the trapezium by the Black Mountains; mountains, that is, from which all the snow melts in summer . . . Kapisa, thanks to its geographical position, commands the principal passes of the Hindu Kush and consequently the great commercial artery between India and Bactriana; the pilgrim thus relates that it abounded in every kind of merchandise. It was no less prosperous agriculturally. Watered as it is by the Ghorband and Panjshir rivers, to say nothing of their tributaries and the numerous streams which flow down from the mountains all around, and being situated at a slightly lower altitude than Kabul with a consequently milder climate, the area is eminently suitable for the cultivation of cereals and fruit trees. From its vineyards and orchards vast quantities of almonds, apricots and fresh or dried grapes are exported to India. The region's chief disadvantage, as Hiuan Tsang also pointed out, is the frequency and violence of the north winds which sweep across it. This apart, however, there were many of heaven's blessings to account for the number of religious foundations which the Chinese traveler found worthy of mention. . . ."

Kapisa was equally important from the political point of view. In classical times Kapisi, or Capissa, as the Greco-Roman geographers called it, had been one of the capitals of the Greek state of Kabul. "It is the divinity of the city of Kapisi," writes Foucher, "which is represented on certain of the coins of Eucratides, coins which were probably struck there. It was there and not as is usually believed at Kabul that the last of the Indo-Greeks must have reigned." Subsequently Kapisi served as the summer residence of the great Indo-Scythian emperor Kanishka who governed from there the whole of eastern Persia and northwest India. In the seventh century, though he no longer headed an empire, the king of Kapisa nevertheless controlled the whole Gandhara region. In addition to his own patrimony he possessed Lampaka, Nagarahara and Gandhara itself, kingdoms whose dynasties had become extinct and which had been annexed by Kapisa. His writ consequently ran as far as the Indus. Moreover the reigning sovereign of Hiuan Tsang's time appears to have been a powerful personality. "His nature," wrote the pilgrim, "is bold and impetuous and the neighboring lands tremble before his redoubtable authority. He holds sway over a dozen kingdoms." Like the emir of Kabul in the nineteenth century, the raja of Kapisi, being master of the Asiatic trade routes, found the most powerful monarchs prepared to court his friendship. At the very period with which we are concerned the reigning raja, as we know from the *T'ang Shu,* sent as a tribute to Emperor T'ai-tsung some of those magnificent Afghan horses for which the country was already famous, a present which pleased the Son of Heaven so much that he immediately dispatched an embassy to Kapisi bearing considerable gifts in return.

To what race did the kings of Kapisa belong? Right up until the eve of the Moslem invasion these princes of the Indo-Persian borderlands all boasted that they were descended from Kanishka, the Indo-Scythian emperor who had reigned at the time of Caesar and Antoninus. In reality, however, from the second half of the fifth century A.D. when the Gandhara region had been conquered by the Hephthalite Huns, the dynasties reigning at Kapisi must have been of Turco-Mongol blood. When the pilgrim Sung Yun, Hiuan Tsang's predecessor, reached Gandhara about the year 520, he found the throne occupied by a *tegin* or Turkish prince who was a second generation descendant of the chieftain invested by the Huns. This prince was still a barbarian, hardly civilized at all: "wicked and cruel by nature, he had many people put to death." In this fundamentally Buddhist land he remained a pagan and was consequently at loggerheads with his subjects. By the time Hiuan Tsang visited the country, however, a hundred and ten years later, this Turkish element had had time to become Indianized.

The king of Kapisa who welcomed our pilgrim was an extremely devout Buddhist and indeed differed in every respect from the *tegin* of 520.

In the seventh century, then, the Kabul valley was already India, and it was in Kapisi that Hiuan Tsang met the first Jains and the first Hindu ascetics of his journey: the former were completely naked or rather "dressed in azure" for fear of denying the vow of poverty by the possession of a garment; the latter (probably Sivaite ascetics) had rubbed their bodies with ashes and wore necklaces of skulls. The majority of the population, however, was still Buddhist. Various monasteries, some of the Hinayana school, others of the Mahayana, quarreled for the honor of accommodating the pilgrim from China. So as not to disappoint his traveling companion Prajñakata, a Hinayana monk, he decided in favor of a monastery adhering to the Little Vehicle. This monastery, the site of which Alfred Foucher has identified on the banks of the Panjshir, dated from the Kushan era, and tradition had it that it was built as a residence for Kanishka's hostages. "In former times," reports Hiuan Tsang, "King Kanishka made his redoubtable authority felt in the neighboring kingdoms. He extended his realm by force of arms as far as east of the Pamirs. The subject princes living to the west of the Yellow River (in Kashgaria) sent him hostages. These he treated in a most honorable manner. The palace of which we speak was built as their summer residence." Hiuan Tsang even had occasion to supervise excavations to look for some treasure which one of the hostages had buried there, and was lucky enough to find it.

Despite the fact that he was lodged in a Hinayana monastery it was at Kapisa that Hiuan Tsang seems to have felt for the first time in complete communion of ideas with the local Buddhists. Indeed the reader will recall that in central Asia and in Bactriana the majority of monks followed the Little Vehicle. The king of Kapisa, however, like Hiuan Tsang, was a fervent Mahayanist. At his request the pilgrim took part in a chapter of the various sects which was held in Kapisi and lasted

five days. It is interesting to observe the stance which Hiuan Tsang
adopted here and which generally speaking he maintained throughout
his travels in India. Owing to his knowledge of the various schools of
theory, to his metaphysical agility and perhaps also to the fact that he
was new to the quibbling of Indian dialecticians, he tended to rise
above their verbal wrangles and find in his mystical idealism a higher
synthesis of the different doctrines. His philosophical treatise, the *Siddhi,* was to conform to this intellectual position.

After spending the summer of 630 in the "monastery of the hostages" (Sha-lo-kia) Hiuan Tsang resumed his eastward journey. He
followed the course of the lower Panjshir until it met the Kabul River
and then continued down the left bank of the latter, passing through
the province of Lampaka or Laghman as it is now called to the ancient
city of Nagarahara (now Jalalabad). It was a decisive leg of the journey. "Step by step," writes Alfred Foucher, "you come down from the
high altitudes of the Iranian plateau. Immediately the unusual warmth
of the winter, the torrid heat of the summer, the groves of palms and
orange trees, the fields of rice or sugar-cane, everything down to the
chattering of the *maina* and the antics of the monkeys tell you that you
are now on Indian soil."

Indeed Hiuan Tsang noted the contrast: "In Lan-po (Lampaka)
the terrain is suitable for the cultivation of rice and produces a great
quantity of sugar-cane. . . . The climate is fairly mild. There are (still)
occasional frosts but never snow." There was an ethnic contrast too,
after the proud Afghan warriors whom he described to us at Balkh,
Bamian and Kapisa: "The inhabitants live a life of joy and ease and are
very fond of singing. Moreover they are indolent, pusillanimous and
given to deceitfulness. In their dealing with each other they are arrogant and mistrustful and never will one give way before another. They
are small in stature and their movements are quick and impulsive. Most
of them wear garments of white cotton which they like to set off with
decorations in brilliant colors." One could hardly imagine a more picturesque diptych: on one side these nimble, restless Hindus, on the

14. Dipankara's prophesy. (*Musée Guimet*)

other side Hiuan Tsang's earlier picture of the wild gallantry, unpolished ways and straightforward chivalry of the Hindu Kush highlanders. Moreover in Hiuan Tsang's day the semi-Hindus of Lampaka were in subjection to the more purely Afghan kingdom of Kapisa.

Southeast of Lampaka lay the ancient city of Nagarahara, the site of which Alfred Foucher and his colleagues found to correspond to present-day Jalalabad, southwest of the confluence of the Kunar and Kabul rivers. The importance of the city Nagarahara during Buddhist times is shown by the number of ruins to be found there. "To the north," writes Foucher, "at the foot of the high mountains of Kafiristan (Nuristan) which come down to the opposite bank of the river, to the west along the Black Mountains (Siyah Koh) beyond which lie the Kabul highlands, and to the south along the fringe of cliffs which abruptly terminate the long slope of the White Mountains (Safed

Koh), large quantities of stupas, monasteries and more or less ruined caves testify to the magnificent golden girdle with which Buddhist piety once adorned the ancient city."

Hiuan Tsang mentions some of these ancient monuments. He refers, for example, to a great three hundred foot stupa which the Indian emperor Asoka had erected at a distance of two *li* to the southeast of Nagarahara. Indeed, one of the most venerable Buddhist legends is connected with this site. It was there that, during a previous cosmic cycle, a young man—the same who was in his last incarnation to become the Buddha Sakyamuni—had met the Buddha of that time, Dipankara. Urged by a solemn presentiment the young man had prostrated himself at Dipankara's feet, his long hair spread out before him in the mud like a most marvellous carpet; and the Buddha of that distant epoch had prophesied his worshipper's future accession to Buddhahood. Foucher found this episode illustrated in one of the Greco-Buddhist reliefs of Gandhara. Further stupas and monasteries in Lampaka contained the bone from the top of the Buddha's skull (which was known as the *ushnisha* relic), his monastic robe (the *samghati* relic) and the staff of the Blessed One "whose rings are of polished iron and whose shaft of sandalwood." In fact as a consequence of the piety of Asoka, the religious opportunism of the Indo-Greeks and the devotion of Kanishka, this whole region had become a sort of new Holy Land of Buddhism. Whereas the country around the Ganges prided itself on having provided the setting for the earthly life of Sakyamuni, the Kabul valley had acquired almost equal stature by localizing in its monasteries and stupas numerous episodes from his legendary life or his previous existences. Consequently no one in Lampaka was in any doubt but that the country had been visited of old by the Blessed One, who had arrived and departed by way of the air.

For all the details which Hiuan Tsang furnishes us with on this subject, we today know more than he appears to have known about the ancient city of Nagarahara; or rather the school of Buddhist art which

flourished in the city inspires in us sentiments which cannot have occurred to the pilgrim. The stupa decorations, reliefs and sculptures of
stucco which the French archeological expedition led by Barthoux un-
earthed on the site of Hadda (Hiuan Tsang's Hi-lo) five miles south of
Nagarahara and which can be seen in the Musée Guimet, Paris, are for
us much more than mere pious imagery. For us they constitute an unexpected, profoundly moving and almost incredible revelation of a new
art of which the Greco-Buddhist art hitherto discovered had given us
no idea.[2] Compared with the charming but sometimes slightly insipid
Apollonian Buddhas which the Gandhara region has produced in
their hundreds, the figurines from Hadda in the Musée Guimet represent an altogether more personal type of art. In the depiction of the
soldiers of Mara, the demoniac army attacking the Buddha, we are con-
fronted with a whole range of ethnic flavors. There is no doubt at all
that these are faithful portraits of the various lords and neighboring
barbarians of the Gandhara region and Hiuan Tsang's predecessors
and he himself may have known them: hooded heads of ancient Persians not unlike those of the Arbela Mosaic in the Naples Museum; life-
like portraits of Indo-European Scythians of Gallic type with long
drooping moustaches, companions doubtless of Kadphises and of Kanishka himself (bear in mind that the majority of these stuccoes date,
according to Hackin, from the second and third centuries; that is to say
precisely the Kushan period); and occasionally, though less often, we
find on some of the later pieces, which may date from as late as the fifth
century—for example in the wonderful ten-inch Mara wearing the long
cloak of the nomad herdsman and in the Chandaka of the "Great
Decease"—Mongol faces with broad, flat noses and prominent cheek-
bones, drawn no doubt from some Hephthalite Hun.

[2] We may be permitted at this point to pay homage to Alfred Goucher's gift for archeological divination which here as at Gandhara—his 1924 correspondence is the proof—located
and marked the sites of the rich harvests to come. A provisional bibliography of the Hadda
excavations is to be found in the report by M. Godard, *Exposition des récentes découvertes
et des récents travaux archéologiques en Afghanistan et en Chine*, Musée Guimet, 14 March
1924, pp. 1–36, and in J. Hackin, *Les Fouilles de la délégation archéologique française à
Hadda (Afghanistan)*, Missions Foucher-Godard-Barthoux *1923–1928*, Revue des Arts asiatiques, V.,2. See particularly the volumes by Mr. Barthoux (Van Oest).

Visitors to the museum who do not know what to expect may have the impression that they are in the presence of Gothic works. Here the head of some solemn, bearded ascetic almost evokes the "Beau Dieu" of Amiens Cathedral; other similar "barbarian" heads recall the saints of the southwest portal of Reims. There the heads of the soldiers of Mara, treated as grotesques, no longer belong to Greek art but to the caricatures of torturing demons in Western depictions of Hell and the deco-

15. Mara wearing the long cloak, from Hadda.(*Musée Guimet*)

rative heads and gargoyles of the thirteenth century. Yet other heads of
bearded demons are evocative of some "King David" figure. On certain
of the tiny stucco heads of monks we find the deep spirituality and
intense other-worldliness of other "sourires de Reims." The tall figure
carrying flowers in a fold of his robe in order to strew them in the steps
of the Buddha, he too could be an angel of Reims, direct descendant of
the spirit of Greece and Rome. And there are other "angels" too, free of
all trace of pagan sensuality, their hands held together with such artless
simplicity and such tender piety that were it not for where they were
found we should believe them to be from the West. Farther on our
attention is caught by some very curious beardless heads which in their
solid construction, intensity of expression, trueness to live and even in
their hair-styles (covered by a sort of hood) no longer have anything
classical about them but are specifically medieval, page-boys or clerks of
the Burgundian School. Or we find other figures in the same vein
which remind us of the Nuremberg School.

It is indeed a revelation. At a time when we believed Greco-Buddhist art to be (like the Roman art of the same period) virtually exhausted and reduced to a series of stereotypes, it was in the process of
undergoing a thorough renewal. Or rather, in these sheltered districts
of Afghanistan which the spirit of man had chosen for the realization
of this miracle, the Hellenistic schools of Gandhara had been eclipsed
by an art which, though emerging from their own workshops, was
entirely different; an art which was as distinct from its original models
as our own Romanesque and Gothic art was later to be from the Greco-
Roman art of the West. It was in fact an entirely analogous phenomenon. The Greco-Roman art of Kabul and the Punjab, brother to the
Romano-Syrian and Palmyrene art of the same epoch, was succeeded
by a kind of Gothic-Buddhist art which departed from fresh foundations and began on a new cycle.

It was an art, moreover, which had everything it needed for a vigorous life. It was already acclimatized to its country, as we know from
the variety of races depicted, and it was original, for we come across

nothing like it in all the Syrian, Palmyrene, Parthian and Sassanian East. Had the religious and political conditions which had given birth to it—Buddhism on the one hand and a relative independence, or at least the presence of liberal and tolerant masters, on the other—had these conditions continued to obtain and had the ancient Greco-Buddhist provinces of Kapisa, Lampaka and Gandhara not become Moslem, the curve of artistic evolution would presumably also have continued. And it might have been there that the spirit of man, having effected as it were a preliminary transition from Greco-Roman to Gothic, matured and realized the final formula that came nine centuries later in the West.

Can we imagine what it would have been like if Huns and Arabs had swooped down on Gaul on the eve of Reims and Chartres, at the very moment when the genius of our sculptors was taking wing? For that is what happened to the "Gothic" art of Kapisa and Lampaka: the Kabul valley was first invaded by Hephthalite Huns, the most iconoclastic of all the barbarians, in 475, and then after a respite which extended from the mid-sixth century to the mid-seventh, came the Arabs. Already in 652 and 664 bands of them were raiding the country and the vandalism inspired by their piety was no whit less disastrous than the vandalism of the uncultured Huns. And this ray of human genius was extinguished almost as soon as it had appeared.

The damage was already done by the time of Hiuan Tsang's visit. Lampaka and Nagarahara were still profoundly Buddhist, indeed Mahayanist. But the ravages of the Hephthalite Huns had laid waste their monasteries and works of art: "The inhabitants are full of respect for the Law of the Buddha and few among them have any faith in the teachings of the Brahmins. Yet notwithstanding the large number of monasteries one comes across very few religious. The stupas are in ruins and covered with weeds." The Arab invasion which followed twenty years later was no more than the *coup de grâce*.

Leaving the Nagarahara (Jalalabad) district Hiuan Tsang decided to follow the cliffs along the south bank of the Kabul River to the Siyah Sang valley and visit one last famous site: the cave in which the Buddha, after taming the *Naga* or dragon-king Gopala, had left the mark of his shadow.

This cave, which Foucher has identified near the present-day village of Chahar Bagh, was a dangerous place to reach. The paths were little used and were infested with bandits. Hardly a pilgrim had passed that way for the last three years. Hiuan Tsang's companions tried to make him give up the project, but their efforts were in vain: "It would be difficult," he replied, "even in the space of a hundred thousand *kalpas*, to meet as much as once with the true shadow of the Buddha. How could I, having come so far, not go to worship it? You go on ahead and have no qualms. As soon as I have spent a little time there I shall hurry to rejoin you." And taking his leave of the pusillanimous Indians he set out alone for the cave.

At the nearest monastery he found no one who was willing to act as his guide. Only an old man whom he met on the road consented to show him the way. "Hardly had they proceeded a few *li* when five brigands came upon them with swords at the ready. The Master of the Law took off his cap and showed his monk's habit. 'Master,' said one of the brigands to him, 'where do you wish to go?' 'I wish,' he replied, 'to go and worship the Buddha's shadow.' 'Master,' continued the brigand, 'have you not heard tell that there are bandits in these parts?' 'Bandits,' replied our saint, 'are men. I am now on my way to worship the Buddha and even were the roads full of wild beasts I should walk without fear. Even less then shall I fear you who are men and whose heart holds the gift of pity.' Hearing these words," adds the author of the *Life of Hiuan Tsang,* "the brigands were touched and their hearts opened to faith."

After this dramatic encounter Hiuan Tsang was able to go and make his devotions at the cave. "It is situated on the east side of a stream which runs down between two mountains. In the wall of stone out of which it is hollowed is a sort of door which opens at sunset. Casting his gaze into the cave it appeared to him dark and gloomy and he could make out nothing. 'Master,' said the old man his companion, 'walk straight in. When you have touched the eastern wall take fifty paces backward and look due east; that is where the Shadow dwells.'

"The Master of the Law entered the cave and advanced without a guide. After fifty paces he came up against the eastern wall; then, faithfully following the old man's instructions, he retreated and stood still. There, quickened by a profound faith, he performed the hundred salutations, but he saw nothing. Reproaching himself bitterly for his faults he wept and uttered loud cries and abandoned himself to grief. Some time afterward, his heart filled with sincerity, he devoutly recited the *sutras* and the *gathas,* prostrating himself after each stanza."

Then the miracle occurred: "When he had thus performed some hundred salutations he saw a glow appear on the eastern wall; it was as broad as a monk's bowl and it disappeared immediately. Seized with joy and anguish he renewed his salutations and again saw a light of the size of a basin which gleamed and then vanished like a flash of lightning. He was transported with rapture and love and swore he would not leave that place before he had seen the Divine Shadow. . . . He continued his devotions and suddenly the whole cave was flooded with light and the Shadow of the Blessed One appeared with blinding whiteness upon the wall, just as when the clouds part and allow a sudden glimpse of the wonderful image of the *Golden Mountain.* The divine face was outlined with dazzling brightness. In an ecstasy of rapture Hiuan Tsang contemplated the sublime and incomparable object of his admiration. The Buddha's body and his monastic robe were reddish-yellow in color. From his knees to his head the beauties of his person were brilliantly illuminated, but the lower part of his *lotus throne* was as if enveloped in semi-obscurity. Visible in full to the right, to the left and to the rear of the Buddha were the shades of the Bodhisattvas and of the venerable Sramanas who formed his escort.

"After witnessing this marvel he called to six men who were standing outside the door to bring fire into the cave and burn incense. When the fire was brought in the Shadow of the Buddha suddenly turned and was gone. Immediately he ordered the fire to be extinguished and in the same moment the Shadow reappeared before him. Of the six men there, five could see it but the sixth saw nothing at all. It lasted but an instant . . . Hiuan Tsang, having clearly witnessed this divine phenomenon, prostrated himself respectfully upon the ground and hymned the Buddha's praises, scattering flowers and incense; after which the heavenly light was extinguished. He then made his farewells and left the cave."

Leaving Lampaka, Hiuan Tsang continued on his way down the south bank of the Kabul River and by way of Dakka and the Khyber Pass entered the province of Gandhara.

Gandhara is one of the most celebrated regions in the history of the East. Known already by the Macedonians under the name of Gandaritis, it became one of the bastions of the Greco-Bactrian state. It was there that the Greek kings found asylum after their expulsion from Bactriana, continuing to rule there for a further century. One of their chief cities in this region seems to have been Pushkaravati (Charsadda) which was familiar to classical geographers under the name of Peucelaotis. When the Indo-Scythians came down from central Asia to take the place of the Greeks they appear to have shown the same predilection for the Gandhara region. Indeed it was at Purushapura or Peshawar that their great emperor Kanishka maintained his winter residence, his summer residence being Kapisi in the Afghan mountains. The civilization of Gandhara at this time is known to us through the many hundreds of statues, bas-reliefs and even coins which have emerged from its classical soil at Charsadda, Sahri Balol, Hoti Mardan and Shahbaz Garhi.

Such richness and fecundity can amaze us only if we have forgotten that this ancient province of Peshawar was for almost six centuries without interruption a kind of new Hellas miraculously preserved by its ring of mountains and rivers from the upheavals of the invasions. To begin with there had been two centuries of direct Greek rule under such pure Hellenes as Heliocles and Antialcidas, princes whom their coinage shows to have been as completely Western as Antiochus of Syria or the Ptolemies of Egypt. Then came almost four centuries of Greco-Roman imitation under the Indo-Scythian kings of the Kushan family—Kadphises, Kanishka, Huvishka, Vasudeva and their successors. They were the most constant Hellenophiles that the East ever saw; it was during their reign and at their court much more than under their Greco-Bactrian predecessors that the Greco-Buddhist school sprang to life. The reliquary of Kanishka himself, which was found in 1908 at Shah-ji Ki Dheri near Peshawar, bears beside the portrait of this "Clovis of India" the name of the goldsmith who made it, the Greek Agesilas. The countless Gandharan Buddhas which have found their way into our museums are further witnesses to this moving phil-Hellenism. When the Chinese pilgrims saw, as they must have done, these profiles of positively Apollonian purity beneath the waved hair, and these faultless draperies with their moulded treatment which is often so pleasing, how could they have guessed that they were looking at the first images which the hand of man had made of the apostle of their religion? How could they know that long ago, as long as six centuries probably, at a time when no one had yet dreamt of depicting the Buddha in any other way than by obscure symbols, one of these Yavana artists, as the Indians called them, living in far-off "Ta-ts'in," as it was called in China, had dared for the first time to represent the Blessed One in human form. And every other image of the Buddha had sprung from that; those venerated in the sanctuaries of Ceylon and even those of China and Japan themselves, at Lung-men and at Nara.

Buddhist pilgrims were not so knowledgeable. But Gandhara, or K'ien-to-lo as they called it, had other attractions for them. In Gandhara, barely two centuries before Hiuan Tsang's journey, had lived two of the greatest philosophers of Mahayana Buddhism, Asanga and Vasubandhu, both natives of Peshawar. Their memory was particularly precious to Hiuan Tsang's heart for it was precisely these two masters who were the chief authors of the mystical idealism which he professed.

Unfortunately the brilliant civilization of Gandhara had been almost entirely destroyed by the invading Hephthalite Huns a century before Hiuan Tsang visited Peshawar in the year 630. The Hun Mihirakula, India's "Attila," had dealt the Greco-Buddhist workshops a blow from which they had never recovered. "The royal line is extinct," wrote Hiuan Tsang sadly, "and the country has been annexed by the kingdom of Kapisa. The towns and villages are almost empty and abandoned, the inhabitants (of the country) few and far between. One corner of the royal city (Peshawar) contains about a thousand families. . . . A thousand Buddhist monasteries lie deserted and in ruins; they are overgrown with weeds and offer only a melancholy solitude. The majority of the stupas are also in ruins." A measure of the disaster which had struck the Buddhist communities of the region was the fact that the relic of relics, the Buddha's begging-bowl, which up until then had been preserved in a monastery in Peshawar, had been taken away and after many vicissitudes carried off to the infidel land of Sassanian Persia.

Hiuan Tsang visited the remains that were still standing. At Peshawar (which he gives correctly as Pu-lu-sha-pu-lo), after the pipal or Bodhi-Tree beneath which four of the former Buddhas had sat, he was shown the ruins of the giant stupa built by Emperor Kanishka. While out on a hunting expedition the Indo-Scythian ruler, still at that time a stranger to Buddhism, had been miraculously led to this spot by a white hare. There he had met a young herdsman who had repeated to him a prophesy of the Buddha concerning him: "Four hundred years after my death there shall come a king who shall win renown throughout the world under the name of Kanishka. . . ." Whereupon Kanishka had been converted and had erected a stupa upon the spot and filled it with relics. As early as 1901 Foucher suggested looking for this monument at Shah-ji Ki Dheri in the eastern suburbs of the city, and his hypothesis received full confirmation when in 1908 Kanishka's reliquary was discovered upon that very site.

Leaving Peshawar and crossing the Kabul River, which as he observes is particularly wide at this point, Hiuan Tsang paid a visit to the second city of Gandhara which he calls Pu-sho-kie-lo-fa-ti, that is to say Pushkaravati, the Peucelaotis of the Greek geographers and the Charsadda of today. There he made his devotions at a large stupa which was attributed to Emperor Asoka (according to Foucher this is the mound of Bala-Hissar) and had been erected on the site where in a former existence the Buddha had made the "gift of his eyes."

From Pushkaravati Hiuan Tsang made a two-day excursion to the northwest on the middle reaches of the Swat to visit the places where several of the principal Jatakas (birthstories or tales of the Buddha's previous lives) were set. The gaps in his account have been filled in by Alfred Foucher, who has succeeded in identifying these sites. According to the great Indianologist the two places which Hiuan Tsang went to visit are today represented by the mound of Sare Makhe Dheri, where there was apparently a stupa of Hariti, the ogress whom the Buddha transformed into a madonna of childhood, and by Periano Dheri which was the site of the stupa of Syama, the young recluse of the forests who had supported his aged and blind parents but had fallen beneath the arrows of a cruel king. A little farther to the east was the small Gandharan city which the Chinese pilgrims called Po-lu-sha and which was the setting of one of the most famous of all Buddhist legends, the legend of Visvantara.

Visvantara, or Vessantara, was a young prince with a passionately charitable nature. He had a white elephant which possessed the magic faculty of being able to cause rain. A neighboring king whose land was stricken with drought asked for the animal. Visvantara gave it; his countrymen were furious and demanded that he be punished. The charitable prince was obliged to go off into exile accompanied by his wife Madri, who had asked to share his fate, and their two children. Two Brahmins on the way asked him for the horses which drew his wagon; he gave them. A third asked for the wagon itself; he gave it. At the cost of a thousand sufferings the family finally reached the forest which has been selected for their exile. They lived in a cabin and ate roots and wild fruit. The trees were moved with compassion and themselves bowed down their branches to offer their fruit to the two sons of Visvantara and Madri. But another Brahmin arrived and asked the father to give him his two sons as servants. Despite their terror and his own despair he gave them. The god Indra, disguised as an ascetic, finally came to ask for his wife as a slave; he gave her too. In the end Indra revealed himself and restored to this hero of charity his family and his possessions.

The forest hermitage which provided the setting for this most moving and most human of the prefigurations of the Buddha was praised by every Chinese traveler, by Hiuan Tsang as well as by his predecessor

16. Amaravati Buddha,
Third Century.
(*Musée Guimet*)

Sung Yun, as one of the most charming localities in the region: "Gentle springs and exquisite fruit," wrote Sung Yun, "are to be found on this hill. Its gullies are pleasantly warm and its trees remain green throughout the bad season. Our visit took place in the first month of the year. A mild breeze fanned our faces. Birds sang in the blossoming trees and butterflies hovered over the flowered lawns. . . ." Foucher managed to locate Visvantara's hermitage, the Chinese writers' Po-lu-sha, at Shah-baz Garhi, but he could not, after the depredations of the Moslem herdsmen, find "those woods where the exiled prince wandered through verdant bowers, that enchanted flowered landscape whose charm filled the heart of Sung Yun. . . ." The Moslems, here as everywhere else they went, by deforesting the country dried up its springs and killed everything including the soil. By way of compensation Shah-baz Garhi has given us the splendid Bodhisattva statue—a young raja of majestic elegance—which is the pride of the Foucher Collection in the Louvre.

Hiuan Tsang then appears to have diverged once more from the main route from Peshawar to India for another, longer excursion toward the north, this time into the province of Uddiyana, the Chinese Wu-ch'ang-na.

In contrast to the mild climate of Peshawar this whole area of the upper Swat and Buner is already Himalayan country: "One is constantly coming across ice in spring and summer. Often snow-showers are mixed with rain, sparkling with the five colors; it is like clouds of floating blossom." [3] Hiuan Tsang's biographer describes particularly the mountain road which follows the right bank of the Indus in the Buner uplands: "The roads are extremely dangerous and the valleys

---

[3] Sung Yun, whose visit to the Uddiyana region in 520 must have taken place at a more favorable time of year, has left us a very different description: "The soil nourishes an extraordinary quantity of flowers which remain in bloom winter and summer. Religious and laymen alike gather them to make offerings to the Buddha." The landscape was similarly enchanting in the region in which the "gift of the body," made by the Buddha to a hungry tigress, was set (near Mount Mahaban in southern Buner?): "There high mountains rise steeply to vertiginous peaks which are lost in the clouds. Kalpa trees and magnificent mushrooms grow plentifully upon these mountains. The woods and streams are charming. The variegated brightness of the flowers dazzles the eye."

dark. Now they had to cross bridges of slack ropes, now cling to iron chains. Here were foot-bridges suspended in the middle of nothingness, there flying bridges flung out over precipices, elsewhere paths or ladders chiseled in the rock." Here again the interest of the region lay in its Buddhist relics. Hiuan Tsang may not at this time have explored it very thoroughly but he does at least mention a number of famous sites.

On one of these sites, identified by Foucher at Palai, stood the stupa of the monk Unicorn, whose piquant story Hiuan Tsang does not hesitate to relate: "this young anchorite, son of a *rishi* and a doe, had in his silvan innocence fallen a helpless victim to the snares of a courtesan disguised as a nun, to such a point indeed that she had been able to make him carry her on his shoulders to the palace of the king." The story was popular throughout the whole of India, appealing as much to the mischievous wit of Buddhist monks as it did in a scarcely different form to the sarcastic spirit of Hindu ascetics.

Farther north, at the source of the Swat, the traveler was shown the spot where the Buddha had tamed the dragon-king Apalala who had been devastating the country with his floods and also the mountain called Hi-lo (Mount Ham in Buner, 9,300 ft.) where he had made the "gift of his body" to five *yakshas*.

Finally there was the site, discovered by Sir Aurel Stein in the vicinity of the village of Girarai, of the "gift of the flesh," the offering made to a hawk for the ransom of a dove, as related in the *Sibi Jataka*: "Once there was a charitable king, the king of the Sibi. The god Indra, to put him to the test, took the form of a hawk pursuing a pigeon, or rather pursuing another god disguised as a pigeon, 'a pigeon whose body was as blue as the firmament and whose eyes were like red pearls.' To escape from the hawk the pigeon took refuge in the bosom of the king of the Sibi. The hawk, in the name of his own right to live, demanded his prey or at least an equal quantity of fresh meat. The king, making a sublime sacrifice, cut the flesh from his own thighs. But, by a miracle, the pigeon always weighed heavier on the scales than the ransom of flesh, so that the king was obliged to place his whole body on the balance-tray in order to save the bird. Then Indra revealed himself and the king was later reincarnated in the body of the Buddha Sakyamuni."

In Uddiyana, however, even more than in Gandhara, the invasion of the Huns had wrought dreadful havoc and the Buddhist sanctuaries lay for the most part in ruins. On the banks of the Subhavastu, as the Swat was then called, "there stood in former times one thousand four hundred Buddhist monasteries in which lived eighteen thousand religious[4]; now most of them are deserted or their inhabitants considerably reduced in number." The country had nevertheless remained at least partly Buddhist. Hiuan Tsang himself mentions that the people of Uddiyana were divided between the Mahayana and Hinduism, though he clearly had little enough sympathy for the kind of Mahayana practiced there. In fact he tells us why: "They devote themselves principally to the doctrine of *dhyana* (i.e., ecstasy). They delight in reading the texts pertaining to this doctrine but do nothing to deepen their knowledge of the meaning and spirit of those texts. . . . Their chief occupation is the study of magic formulae."

Indeed it was around this time that, in Uddiyana and the other Himalayan districts, alongside the Sivaite sects, a certain form of Mahayana Buddhism began to take a turn toward sorcery, magic, demonology and all the abnormal practices generally gathered under the heading of Tantrism. Uddiyana in fact was to play such a large part in this regrettable transformation that the very name of the country—in its Tibetan transcription of U-rgyan—was to be used before long in Tibet to refer to Tantric magic and spiritism. Such an issue of the Mahayana could only revolt a pure intellectualist metaphysician like Hiuan Tsang. We know how deep a hold the Mahayana had upon his heart. It is all the more interesting, then, that he showed much greater sympathy with his Hinayanist opponents (those of Kapisa, for example) than with the Tantric tendencies of his so-called co-religionists of the Swat and Buner.

---

[4] A hundred and ten years earlier, around 520, Sung Yun had observed that the sound of the Buddhist bells could be heard throughout the night and that it filled all the valleys.

Moreover Hiuan Tsang was now impatient to reach India proper. Leaving Uddiyana and Gandhara he crossed the Indus at Udabhanda (Und, north of Attock) and entered the Punjab region. His first port of call was the great city of Takshasila or Taxila, which he calls Ta-ch'a-she-lo.

Taxila, the ancient metropolis of the Punjab known to the Greeks in the time of Alexander the Great as the capital of the king they called "Taxiles," was later beautified by the Indian emperor Asoka who made it the chief town of his northwestern provinces. Buddhist tradition has it that he appointed his beloved son Kunala governor of the city, and Taxila, according to Hiuan Tsang, was the scene of the moving legend of this Indian "Hippolytus."

Kunala had rejected the advances of his stepmother, Asoka's new favorite, and she had sworn to have her revenge. She forged a letter in Asoka's name and took advantage of the king's being asleep to seal it, as custom required, "with the mark of his teeth." The purport of the letter was that the young man's eyes should be put out. Kunala's servants hesitated when they received the royal command, but the hero came forward and presented himself for its execution saying, "Since my father has commanded me how can I disobey?" After he had been blinded he went out to beg for alms on the highroads of India. His steps led him toward the residence of Asoka, near the royal palace. During the last watch of the night he began to sing his woes, accompanying himself on the *vina*. High up on one of the terraces the king started with surprise at the sound of his voice. He had the blind man brought to him and recognized his son. A saintly Buddhist monk restored the prince's sight and the "Phèdre" of the story was sentenced to the supreme penalty.

Shortly after Asoka's death Taxila became Hellenic once more as the capital of one of the Indo-Greek kingdoms ruled by the dynasty of Eucratides, Heliocles, and Antialcidas. The soil on which the city stood was therefore thoroughly steeped in history. Excavations by the Indian

Department of Archeology on the site of the modern Saraikala have uncovered no less than three contiguous cities: the ancient Indian city of King Taxiles on the Bhir mound, the Greek city of Eucratides and his successors at the present-day town of Sirkap, and lastly, at Sirsukh, a third city which may have been founded by the Indo-Scythian emperor Kanishka. For the Indo-Scythians of the Kushan dynasty had, here as at Kabul, faithfully continued their Greek predecessors' work of Hellenization. The Greco-Buddhist stucco figurines which Sir John Marshall dug in their hundreds from the soil of Taxila show that the artisans of this city kept up the great tradition of the workshops of Gandhara right up until the eve of the Hun invasion in the fifth century. But here too the Huns had put everything to the sack. "There are many monasteries but all extremely dilapidated"—so runs the leitmotiv which recurred whenever Hiuan Tsang took up his brush to write of the Buddhist communities of the northwest; at a time when the Moslem threat was already a reality, those communities had not yet recovered from the invasion of the Huns. The Chinese pilgrim was nevertheless able to admire one stupa at Takshasila, erected by Emperor Asoka on the spot where the Buddha had made the "gift of his head" during one of his previous lives, or rather of his heads during a thousand successive lives. Near this sanctuary could be seen the monastery which had been the home, probably in the latter half of the second century A.D., of the Buddhist philosopher Kumaralabdha (or more correctly Kumaralata), one of the principal theoreticians of the phenomenist Hinayanist school of the Sautrantika.

From the political point of view Taxila, after having been for long under the control of Kapisa, was now in the seventh century under the suzerainty of the kings of Kashmir.

At this point our pilgrim, instead of pushing on toward the Ganges basin, retraced his steps somewhat in order to visit a spot to the northeast of Taxila, on the right bank of the Indus, where one of the most famous Jatakas was located, the one in which Prince Mahasattva, the future Buddha, made the gift of his body to a famished tigress and her seven cubs. "In the beginning," writes the pious chronicler, "the land was stained with the prince's blood. Today it is still red, and plants and trees alike preserve the same color."

Hiuan Tsang was attracted by Kashmir. "Having climbed mountainous heights fraught with precipices and crossed an iron bridge he came after a journey of a thousand *li* to the kingdom of Kia-she-mi-lo." He himself describes this "paradise in the air" in extremely picturesque terms: "The country measures seven hundred leagues around and all four frontiers lie against mountains of prodigious height. It is reached by means of extremely narrow passes. For this reason none of the neighboring rulers has ever made a successful attack on it. The capital is situated to the west near a mighty river, the upper Vitasta, known to the Greeks as the Hydaspes and today called the Jhelum. The country lends itself to the cultivation of corn and produces an abundance of flowers and fruit. . . . The climate is cold and frosty; there is a great deal of snow but little wind. . . . The inhabitants are extremely good-looking though of a somewhat too devious nature. They wear woolen hats and garments of white cotton."

Strange legends were handed down in these Himalayan valleys, nurtured by the lofty atmosphere and the loneliness. "There are (up in the mountains) stupas containing relics of the great holy men. The wild animals and the monkeys of the mountains gather flowers and pay homage before them, continuing their pious offerings year in and year out as if fulfilling some appointed task." Spirits could be seen riding astride the mountain-tops: "Many things seen on this mountain are of a miraculous nature. Sometimes a wall of rock appears to be divided through, or one finds upon some high summit traces of a horse; but all these things are deceptive in appearance. They are caused by *arhats* and *sramanas* who, while a band of them was out walking, drew lines with their fingers, or galloped by on horseback and left signs of their passage. It would be difficult to recount in detail all these curious facts. . . ."

Kashmir has indeed always been a center of intense religious life. In the ninth century it was to be the home of one of the principal philosophical schools of Sivaite Hinduism. In Hiuan Tsang's time and for a short while afterward the Buddhists were still in the majority. They possessed something like a hundred monasteries numbering five thousand religious, and they proudly pointed out to visitors the three stupas erected by the Indian emperor Asoka and the memorials left by the Indo-Scythian emperor Kanishka, the "Constantine" as well as the "Clovis" of Buddhism. And everywhere throughout the country people recalled the legend of the monk Madhyantika who had made Kashmir habitable by draining the lakes and converting the dragons.

As Hiuan Tsang approached the capital, Pravarapura, now Srinagar, the king of Kashmir came out in person to meet him, accompanied by his whole court. "All along the way were sunshades and banners and the whole road lay deep in flowers and drenched in incense." The Indian monarch honored his guest by "scattering before him on the ground an immense quantity of flowers. He then bade him mount an enormous elephant and walked behind in his train." Next day, after a feast at the palace, the *raja* invited Hiuan Tsang to open a series of conferences upon difficult points of the Teaching. Learning that "his love of scholarship had brought him here from distant lands and that, wishing to study, he found himself without texts," he placed twenty scribes at his disposal to make him copies of the Buddhist gospels as well as of the later philosophical treatises (the *sutras* and the *sastras*).

Beside these bibliographical resources Hiuan Tsang also found in Kashmir a master after his own heart in the person of a venerable seventy-year-old scholar of the Mahayana. In the pages of the Chinese pilgrim's biography we glimpse something of the joy which these two great spirits experienced at meeting one another. The old man was enraptured to discover in his Chinese pupil a thinker capable of perpetuating the line of the fifth-century philosophers Asanga and Vasubandhu.

As far as Hiuan Tsang was concerned, here was full compensation for all his pains, for through this master he could absorb the tradition of the idealist school in all its original purity. And what a wonderful portrait we have of this man: "The master, a man of exemplary virtue, observed the rules of the discipline with the strictest purity. He was gifted with deep intelligence and his vast scholarship embraced all branches of knowledge. His skill and learning had a divine quality about them and his bountiful soul was filled with affection for the wise and with esteem for the learned. Hiuan Tsang questioned him freely and with an open heart and together with him devoted himself day and night to study with indefatigable zeal." As well as the idealist doctrine which corresponded to his personal inclinations, Hiuan Tsang also found in Kashmir the traditions of another Buddhist school, one which was just as well known and even more ancient, that of the integral realists or Sarvastivadins. It had been at Jalandhara, not far from the Kashmir region, that the Indo-Scythian emperor Kanishka in conjunction with two eminent patriarchs Parsva and Vasumitra had called a council of five hundred learned men who had codified the Buddhist canon according to the Sarvastivadin school. Hiuan Tsang, with his omniscience and his relatively eclectic tastes, divided his vigils in Kashmir between these two opposing systems.

In all the pilgrim stayed for two full years in Kashmir, from May 631 to April 633. They were years of study, fruitful years during which he completed his philosophical education; years of contemplation, too, before embarking upon what was properly speaking his real pilgrimage. Possessing at last the religious and metaphysical scriptures in their entirety, he came down from the high valleys of Kashmir and approached the holy land of the Ganges to find there the footsteps of the Buddha.

CHAPTER 7

On to the
Holy Land
of the Ganges

ONE OF Hiuan Tsang's first stopping-places on the way down from
Kashmir was the city of Sakala, or in Chinese Shö-kie-lo, the modern
Sialkot, just over the border of Pakistan. This ancient city was already
known in classical times; mentioned by the Alexandrian geographers
under the name of Sangala, it became the capital of one of the Indo-
Greek kingdoms, that of Demetrius, Apollodotus and Menander. If in
Hiuan Tsang's time Sakala still remembered its King "Milinda," as the
Indians called Menander, who had at one point advanced his conquests
as far as Oudh and Bihar and come close to subjugating the whole of
northern India, it was not as a conqueror. In that capacity his memory

had quite disappeared as had that of Alexander and of so many other worldly princes in this land without memory where men scorned temporal things and remembered only visions of eternity. But it so happened that the name of King Milinda was preserved in a famous text, the *Milinda-Panha* or "Questions of King Milinda," probably the earliest work of Buddhist philosophy. It is a work of capital importance for Buddhists for in it the monk Nagasena expounds to the Greek king one

17. Bodhisattva, from
Shahbaz Garhi.
(*Musée Guimet*)

of the central points of their doctrine, the purely phenomenal and illusory character of the self. The book is no less interesting for ourselves as it brings us an echo down the centuries and through successive translations, of the strange philosophical dialogues which must have taken place in the twilight of the Macedonian epic, between the last of the Hellenic adventurers and the first metaphysicians of Buddhism.

If Sakala no longer remembered that already distant time when it had been one of the capitals of the Hellenic world, it did pride itself on having been at a more recent date, approximately two centuries before Hiuan Tsang's visit, the home of the illustrious Buddhist philosopher Vasubandhu, whose conversion from Hinayana scholasticism to absolute idealism was rightly regarded as one of the greatest triumphs of the Mahayana.

Since Vasubandhu's death, it is true, this whole Punjab region had, like Gandhara, undergone the ravages of the Hephthalite Huns. During the first quarter of the sixth century the Huns had destroyed the last great united Indian empire, that of the Gupta of Magadha, and plunged India once more into chaos. Their king, the savage Mihirakula, referred to already as the "Attila" of India, set up his residence at Sakala and established a reign of terror throughout the northern provinces. "Mo-hi-lo-kiu-lo (Mihirakula) was noted for his fiery disposition and indomitable courage," Hiuan Tsang tells us. "The neighboring kings were reduced without exception to a state of trembling obedience." Buddhism he subjected to a terrible persecution, destroying monasteries and stupas everywhere and massacring their inmates. Hiuan Tsang recounts his struggle against the last Indian emperor of the Gupta dynasty, King Baladitya of Magadha. The latter, an extremely devout Buddhist, was furious at the Hun chief's persecution of his religion. He refused to pay the tribute demanded by the barbarians, and Mihirakula dispatched his hordes against him. Such was the terror which the Huns inspired that at their approach Baladitya and his officers fled into the jungle. The invaders, however, seem to have fallen into an ambush and been repulsed. Tradition even has it that Mihirakula was taken prisoner. According to other sources he was defeated by King Yasovarman of Malwa (between 530 and 545). In any event he was forced to withdraw from the Ganges region and he departed with his hordes for Kashmir, where he murdered the king and set himself up in his place. From there he established a further reign of terror over the upper Indus basin. It was thus in order to "punish" the king of Gandhara (who had no doubt refused to pay his tribute) that he invaded that country, exterminated the royal family, and destroyed every Buddhist monastery and stupa that he could find. He then returned to Kashmir taking all the wealth of the country with him as well as droves of prisoners whom he massacred on the banks of the Indus. After his death Kashmir expelled the Huns, but they continued to occupy the upper Punjab and it was only on the very eve of Hiuan Tsang's pilgrimage that they were eliminated by the kings of Thanesar of the house of Harsha. The terrible memories of which he gives such a detailed account were still fresh at the time of Hiuan Tsang's visit to Sakala.

After leaving Sakala Hiuan Tsang and his companions encountered a band of about fifty brigands while traveling through a *palasa* forest. The brigands, having stripped them of their garments, pursued them sword in hand as far as the edge of a dried-up lake. "Fortunately the bed of the lake was entirely covered with thorn bushes and creepers. The monks who were traveling with the Master of the Law discovered by peering through this dense vegetation that on the southern edge of the lake was a cave which had been hollowed out by the action of the water and was capable of sheltering several people . They signaled their discovery to the Master of the Law and he plunged with them into its depths. When the brigands had lost track of them the travelers ran as fast as they could to the neighboring village where they recounted their misadventure. A Brahmin who had been ploughing his fields and who was no doubt the headman of the village summoned the inhabitants with the conch and drum and, collecting together about fifty peasants, set out in search of the brigands to punish them. But they had already vanished into the forest and could not be found." The travelers began to commiserate with each other over the loss of their luggage. Only Hiuan Tsang preserved a smiling face, "for his soul was as a pure river which the waves may agitate but can never cloud."

In fact no sooner had they reached the next town than an aged Brahmin who felt kindly toward Buddhism gathered together the population and presented to Hiuan Tsang and his companions the equivalent of what they had lost. Moreover, to crown our pilgrim's good fortune, the Brahmin turned out to be well versed in the teachings of the Madhyamika, that school of Buddhist criticism which was so radical that it has often been taken (quite wrongly) for a sort of nihilism. Hiuan Tsang spent a month with him studying the masters of this school, Nagarjuna and Arya Deva; a fruitful month for it is not possible, in the author's opinion, fully to penetrate the Yogachara or Vijñanavada doctrine, the mystical idealism so dear to the pilgrim, without first having assimilated the dialectics of Madhyamika criticism. In the same way Fichte and Schelling can only fully be understood in terms of Kant.

The pilgrim now entered what was for him a veritable "Promised Land." Everywhere he stopped he found libraries full of essential treatises and scholars versed in all the philosophical secrets of the Great Vehicle. Sinabhukti, for example, on the left bank of the Beas, possessed so many Madhyamika and Hinayana texts that he spent fourteen months there in 633–4, and then four months of the rainy season of 634 with an eminent religious of Jalandhara (Jullundur), an important Buddhist center because the surrounding district contained no less than fifty monasteries.

Continuing his journey toward the southeast the pilgrim then came to the valley of the Jumna or Yamuna. He went straight to Mathura, the principal city of the region, which he calls Mo-t'u-lo. He was here entering tropical India. He notes: "The climate is burning hot and the soil so rich and fertile that the mango trees, of which each man tries to plant more than his neighbor, form a kind of forest." Like all the large cities of the Ganges region Mathura held as many sacred memories for Hindus as it did for Buddhists. For the former it was the homeland of their hero Krishna, the divine cowherd whose cult, so full of tenderness, was one day to replace that of Sakyamuni. For the latter Mathura was the repository of the relics of several of the Master's disciples: Sariputra and Maudgalyayana, who were among the earliest apostles; Upali, the former barber who in religion was judged superior to the sons of princes; tender-hearted Ananda, the favorite disciple; and lastly Rahula, son of the Bodhisattva's flesh who deserved to become his son in the spirit. It was also near Mathura that the delightful legend of the monkey's offering was set, as recounted in the Scriptures. This monkey had come one day to offer the Buddha a bowl of wild honey; in his joy at having his offering accepted he gamboled about so madly that he killed himself, a happy accident for as a reward for his charity he was immediately reborn in the body of a holy man.[1]

We are able to fill in the gaps in Hiuan Tsang's reminiscences with what we have learned from archeological discoveries. From the time of the Indo-Scythians onward Buddhist art had produced in Mathura a series of stupa reliefs and statues in which the Greek art of Gandhara had progressively lost ground before an invincible Indian revival, and it was in Mathura that this struggle for artistic liberation had resulted in an incomparable flowering during the fourth and fifth centuries under the great Gupta dynasty. In this city indeed Indian classicism, referred to generally as "Gupta art," gave us one of its purest masterpieces, the great fifth-century standing Buddha in the diaphanous robe beneath the vast circular halo. How delightful to imagine the silent wonder with which the philosopher pilgrim must have greeted his first sight of this statue, the serene and majestic gentleness of which remains without a doubt the most exalted expression of Mahayana idealism. It is

---

[1] One of the finds from Hadda, a small fragment of a slate relief now in the Musée Guimet, was a charming effigy of this pious simian.

surely no accident that such a work should have been contemporary with the lofty and fluent metaphysics of Asanga and Vasubandhu. Never indeed did Indian art convey more directly the idealism which inspired it than in the spare and spiritual beauty of this statue.

Leaving Mathura Hiuan Tsang proceeded up the river Jumna to visit Sthanesvara, which he calls Sa-t'a-ni-sseu-fa-lo and which is now called Thanesar. This was an extremely important fortress town by virtue of it strategic and commercial position at the center of the historic Kurukshetra region which forms a sort of slender isthmus between the

18. Fifth Century Buddha, from Mathura Museum. (*Musée Guimet*)

19. "The Legend of the Monkey," from Gandhara. (*Musée Guimet*)

Indus basin to the west and the Ganges basin to the east, and between the Himalayas to the north and the Rajputana Desert to the south. All the quarrels of history had poured through this narrow gap. Back in the time of legend it was there that the *Mahabharata* epic had placed the great clash between Kauravas and Pandavas for the hegemony of the Ganges. Hiuan Tsang's account even contains as it were an echo of the most famous episode in the epic, when the demi-god Krishna, disguised as the hero Arjuna's driver, encouraged the latter to set aside his hesitations and his humanitarian scruples and give the order to attack: "Life and death," says the hero in Hiuan Tsang's version, "are like an ocean without a shore, flowing in endless alternation; creatures of intelligence find no escape from the whirlpool in which they are caught. . . ." We can almost hear the Krishna of the poem here discovering, in his serene acquiescence in the cosmic dance, in his wisdom far above the petty considerations of humanity, in his divine indifference to all contingency; beyond joy and grief, beyond pity and hatred, a transcendent justification for the brutality of action.

The same reasons which had made Kurukshetra the battlefield of an epic had given seventh-century Thanesar a role of primary importance. The great Hun invasions, which had destroyed the united Indian empire of the Gupta, were hardly over. The Hun hordes were still encamped in the upper Indus valley. The principality of Thanesar had become a marchland against them and was hardened to its task. With the decline of the last Gupta emperors henceforth reduced to their patrimony of Bihar, the kings of Thanesar, of the dynasty of Vardhana, had become the champions of Indian independence. One of them, Prabhakara Vardhana (d. 605), had defeated the terrible Huns on a number of occasions. His eldest son Rajya Vardhana, who had reigned for no more than two years, had nevertheless had time to subdue the people of Malwa, the murderers of his brother-in-law the king of Kannauj, before being himself assassinated at the height of his conquests by a king of Bengal. But Harsha Vardhana, brother of the victim, was also to be his avenger. Acceding to the throne himself in these tragic circumstances, he spent his long reign (606–647) realizing the designs of his dynasty and establishing his hegemony over the whole Gangetic world. Once he had achieved this degree of power, however, he deprived Thanesar of its primacy and transferred his capital to Kannauj on the middle Ganges, a city which was better situated to form the center of a great empire.

Resuming his journey eastward, Hiuan Tsang came to the upper reaches of the Ganges. He observed the popular devotion which from time immemorial Hindus had accorded to the "holy Ganga," the divine river which flowed down to earth from heaven. "Near its source this river is three *li* wide; at its mouth it has a width of ten *li* or more. Its waters are bluish but frequently change color, and the breadth of its waves is immense. Great numbers of wonderful creatures live in it, which moreover are harmless to man. The water has a sweet and pleasant taste and carries with it an extremely fine-grained sand. In the Indian texts it is called the Water of Felicity. Those who bathe in it, so it is said, are cleansed of all their sins. Those who drink it or simply wash out their mouths with it are freed from every ill that threatens them. Those who drown in it are reborn among the gods. Crowds of men and women are constantly assembled upon its banks." But the cult of the sacred river, which played such a large part in Brahminical belief, was for that very reason opposed by Buddhists. Hiuan Tsang recalls how the Buddhist scholar Arya Deva once dared to stand up in the midst of the jostling throng on the Ganges banks and launch an attack on this "superstition."

We might add here what an incomparable observer of Brahminical society was our pilgrim. Here, for example, is his account of the caste system, astonishing in its scientific exactitude:

"In India the various families are divided into four classes or castes. The first is that of the Brahmins (in Chinese, Po-lo-men). They are men of spotless life. Their conduct is governed by the strictest purity. The second caste is that of the Kshatriya (Ts'a-ti-li). They are the royal race. For centuries now they have succeeded each other upon the throne. The third is that of the Vaisya (Fei-she). They are the merchants and indulge in business. The fourth is that of the Sudra (Sui-to-lo). They are the laborers. In these four families purity or impurity of caste assigns to each a separate place." And finally the lower castes, the classless and the untouchables: "Butchers, fishermen, executioners, etc., are barred from the cities. When they come and go in the villages they walk to one side, keeping to the left of the path."

In spite of Hinduism's growing influence among the masses, however, the principalities of the upper Ganges still possessed numerous Buddhist communities. Hiuan Tsang spent the spring and summer of 635 at Matipura in what is now the Bijnor district, studying certain texts of the Little Vehicle, notably those of the realist school of the

Sarvastivadins, evidence once again of the eclecticism of his mind and of the closely knit interdependence of the various schools of Buddhist philosophy.

Continuing down the Ganges Hiuan Tsang traveled through the rich country lying between the river and its two tributaries to right and

20. Buddha descending from the heavens. (*Musée Guimet*)

left, the Kalinadi and the Ramganga. This was the land of Kapitha and the ancient Kampil. He went to worship at the sacred spot where the Buddha returned to earth after his visit to the Heaven of the Thirty-Three Gods, to preach the Law of Salvation to his mother. There passed before the pilgrim's eyes those wonderful images which ten centuries later still haunted the imagination of the artists of Tibet: the Buddha, as large as the world, descending the staircase from the heavens amid a blaze of many colors. "The middle part of the staircase was of solid gold, the left part of crystal and the right of white silver. The Buddha descended by the steps in the middle at the head of the Devas. The god Brahma, holding a white fly-whisk in his hand, walked on the right on the steps of silver. Indra, shielding him with a sunshade adorned with precious stones, walked on the left on the crystal steps. A hundred thousand Devas and the multitude of the Bodhisattvas descended the steps in the Buddha's wake, scattering flowers like rain and reciting stanzas." Nearby the traveler was shown a stone which bore the imprint of the Buddha's footsteps in the form of broad lotus flowers. Let us not forget, though, that to the wonder of these miracles the true Buddhist still preferred the lessons of the Teaching. Hiuan Tsang relates a charming parable designed to bring this home to the faithful. A nun by the name of "Color of the Lotus Flower," desiring passionately to be the first to see the Buddha again upon his return from heaven, managed to get herself changed for the purpose into a "Queen of the Universe," a kind of aerial divinity with the power of being everywhere at once. But it so happened that for some time already another faithful soul, the disciple Subhuti, had been concentrating his thoughts upon the universal vanity of things. And the Buddha revealed to "Color of the Lotus Flower" that she had been forestalled, for whereas she had perceived only his material body Subhuti had previously perceived his "spiritual body" and penetrated his thought.

Hiuan Tsang then came to the great metropolis of Doab, Kanyakubja or Kannauj as it is now called, and which he calls Kie-jo-kiu-shö.

He was much taken with the beauty and wealth of this city. "Its walls are high and its ditches solidly built. Everywhere the visitor looks there are towers and pavilions. Here and there too he comes across a grove of flowering shrubs, or a pond as clear and limpid as a mirror. Quantities of the rarest goods from other lands are to be found in this country. The inhabitants live in a condition of blessed opulence." But above all, as we have seen, Kannauj was at this period the principal residence of the great emperor Harsha Vardhana and consequently the political capital of India. At Kannauj Hiuan Tsang, who referred to Harsha by his laudatory cognomen Siladitya—"Sun of Virtue"—began to become imbued with the Indian monarch's fame and excellence.

Indeed Harsha united in his person all the qualities of the warrior and the statesman. During the course of his long reign (606–647) he gave the Gangetic world a unity and peace such as it had not known since the collapse of the Gupta dynasty.

From the moment of his accession a sacred cause had summoned him to arms. He had, as we have seen, to avenge his elder brother Rajya Vardhana who had been treacherously massacred by a prince of Gauda or Gaur (Bengal) by the name of Sasanka. We know very little of the details of this campaign for all the eulogies of Harsha's chronicler, the poet Bana, afford us few definite facts. His enthusiasm for the struggle must have been all the greater for the fact that he was a fervent adept of Buddhism whereas his enemy, Sasanka, not only openly persecuted the Buddhist church but went as far as to lay impious hands upon the Bodhi-Tree at Gaya. Harsha was to be victorious everywhere. Hiuan Tsang tells us that after avenging the murder of his brother "he marched from west to east, chastising the insubordinate kings. For the space of six years the elephants were never without their saddles nor did the men unstrap their breast-plates." Doubtless Harsha found allies in the persons of the last Guptas of Magadha, now become his dependents and protégées. At any rate we find that shortly afterward he had extended his possessions as far as the Gulf of Bengal and even farther to the east, for the king of Kamarupa (Assam) spontaneously accepted his suzerainty. We must assume that Harsha also had his vengeance on the people of Malwa who a few years earlier had killed his brother-in-law, the previous king of Kannauj, and taken prisoner his sister Rajyasri, for Malwa too was annexed to Harsha's empire. He even reduced to vassalage the wealthy kingdom of Valabhi which lay to the southwest of Malwa and included Gujarat and the Kathiawar Peninsula. If we are to believe Bana, his chronicler, he also, in pursuing the last of the Hun hordes in the northern Punjab, repeated the exploits of his father Prabhakara and of his ancestors, for we find him leading his armies "as far as the inaccessible land of snow-clad mountains, Tokharistan." Only the Deccan had escaped his conquering hand, the king of Maharashtra, the Chalukya monarch Pulakesin II, having repulsed all his attacks in that direction with the result that his empire remained bounded to the south by the Vindhya Mountains.

Now this conqueror, this peacemaker, this last emperor of independent India was a most pious Buddhist. Like Asoka before him he was a veritable saint upon the throne. His wars once over, Hiuan Tsang tells us, his only concern was for the material and moral well-being of his people. His ideal as sovereign was to impregnate the laws and customs of the country with the gentleness and charity of Buddhism. It was a worthy effort, coming as it did on the eve of the great tidal wave of Sivaism and its wake of violence. "His rule," says Hiuan Tsang, "was just and humane. He forgot his food and drink in his eagerness to accomplish good works." Like Asoka he attempted to forbid the killing of animals; and like him he erected thousands of stupas and monasteries. "In the towns and villages, at cross-roads and other meetings of the ways he built houses of relief in which were stored food, drink and medicaments to be given as alms to travelers and to the poor and indigent."

No monarch took his kingly task as seriously as he. "When the kings of the small neighboring kingdoms or when their ministers or chief officers performed good works and sought to attain virtue," writes Hiuan Tsang, "he took them by the hand and seated them upon his throne, calling them his good friends." Except during the rainy season he spent the whole time traveling from province to province of his empire, personally inspecting everything and putting right things that were wrong.

Like Asoka and also Kanishka before him, Harsha took an active part in the life of the Buddhist church. Each year he called a council of monks drawn from the whole of India, discussing points of doctrine with them, sustaining their faith, and heaping alms upon the deserving religious. He invited the most scholarly and the most saintly among them to sit on his throne and himself received instruction from their lips.

Furthermore, and this is another feature which he had in common with his saintly predecessor Asoka, we find this monk-like ruler endowed with a spirit of tolerance that does great honor to Indian Buddhism. He made himself personally responsible for supplying the daily wants not only of a thousand Buddhist monks but also of five hundred Brahmins. And every five years he called an "assembly of distribution" to which he invited the poor of every confession and the clergy of every cult for a general distribution of alms.

During his stay at Kannauj Hiuan Tsang did not in fact meet Harsha, who was no doubt absent from the city. The pilgrim nevertheless spent three months of 636 there in the Bhadravihara monastery, rereading the commentaries on the Three Baskets (Tripitaka) which constitute the epitome of the Buddhist scriptures.

Once on the road again the pilgrim crossed the Ganges and entered the province of Oudh, the ancient realm of Ayodhya (A-yu-t'o, in Chinese). The capital, also called Ayodhya and corresponding to the ancient city of Saketa, was still deeply imbued with the fame of the two great scholars of the Mahayana, the brothers Asanga and Vasubandhu, founders of the idealist school to which Hiuan Tsang was so attached. With the deepest respect he visited the ancient monastery, situated in a grove of mangoes five or six *li* to the southwest of the city, where two centuries earlier the two brothers had conceived and propounded their system. They had come to Oudh from the Gandhara region, and at first they had not by any means followed the same line of development. While Asanga, the elder of the two, had immediately embraced the then new doctrine of absolute idealism the younger brother, Vasubandhu, had remained loyal to the old disciplines of the Hinayana, notably of the school of the Vaibhashika, whose realism bordered on a kind of atomism. Vasubandhu even edited the summary of Vaibhashika philosophy, the enormous *Abhidharma Kosa Sastra* which on any reckoning remains one of the most impressive monuments of Buddhist philosophy. But the hour of grace was to strike for him too. According to the *Life of Vasubandhu,* written around 560 by Paramatha, this conversion was brought about by Asanga himself.

The great idealist had arranged to meet his brother at Ayodhya, at the monastery in the mango grove. As night fell he led him out into a terrace overlooking the river and then withdrew. It was a clear autumn night with the moon shining on the waters. A voice began to speak, an unknown voice reading a Mahayana treatise. No doubt it told of the liberation of the spirit and of its flight on the wings of idealism. This fluent and luminous theory held that the world of forms must wane away, just as, that night, the appearances of earth and water floated in the lunar mists above the Gogra. Above all vain materiality, beyond all concrete things, the Indian night was filled with dream; for things were no more than that, the dream of a dream. The ideality of the universe took the place of the material cosmos, and seen from this new aspect everything became intelligible, accessible, possible. . . . The ecstatic Vasubandhu finally understood the full beauty of the Mahayana. He resolved to cut out the tongue that had hitherto spoken in opposition to the Great Doctrine. Asanga, hiding in the shadows, leapt out in time to prevent him from doing so. The two brothers, now inseparably united, were to fight side by side for the triumph of the teachings of idealism.

Another legend set at Ayodhya relates how the two brothers, together with their disciple Buddhasimha, had one day taken an oath that the first of them to die should come back and instruct the others. Sure enough, as Asanga was meditating one night following Vasubandhu's funeral, the transfigured body of the deceased appeared to him and revealed the wonders of the paradise of Maitreya. The Bodhisattva Maitreya, the Buddha-to-be, played a large part in the molding of the idealist school. Hiuan Tsang himself relates how one night Asanga was carried off to the heaven of the blessed gods where Maitreya dictated to him the texts of his doctrine. As a result many Chinese and Japanese believers still regard the school of Asanga and Vasubandhu as being placed under the direct protection of the Buddhist messiah.

Leaving Oudh, Hiuan Tsang rejoined the Ganges and there embarked with about twenty companions, intending to sail down the river to Prayaga, the modern Allahabad. At this point occurred one of the most dramatic episodes in his biography and one which very nearly marked the end of his journey.

After sailing down the Ganges for a dozen miles or so the pilgrim's boat came to a spot where both banks of the river were shaded by a forest of *asoka* trees whose foliage was particularly dense. Concealed in these trees were a dozen pirate vessels. Pulling hard on their oars the pirates swept out towards the pilgrim and his companions and cut them off. Several of the passengers were so panic-stricken that they flung themselves into the river. Hiuan Tsang's boat was surrounded by the pirates and the pilgrim was taken to the bank. All the passengers were pillaged and stripped of their garments. To crown their plight, the pirates turned out to be worshippers of the Sivaite goddess Durga, a ferocious divinity who required her votaries to perform human sacrifices. Consequently every autumn they selected a victim, preferably a well-built, handsome man, immolated him and offered his flesh and blood to the goddess. "When they had examined the Master of the Law, and their cruel eyes had observed his noble stature and distinguished face, they looked at one another with joy. 'We were about,' they said, 'to let the time of the sacrifice demanded by our goddess pass for want of a victim who should be worthy of her, but here is a monk of fine bearing and pleasing countenance—let us kill him to obtain happiness.' 'Were this vile and contemptible body,' replied Hiuan Tsang, 'able worthily to answer to the intention of your sacrifice, I would truly not begrudge it to you, but since I have come from a far-off land to pay my respects to the Holy Places and to obtain the sacred books and acquire knowledge of the Law, and since this vow is not yet accomplished, I fear, men of generous heart, that in depriving me of my life you will bring upon yourselves the greatest misfortune.' All the passengers from the boat together beseeched the pirates and some of them even offered to die in Hiuan Tsang's place, but this he obstinately refused to allow. Whereupon the chief of the pirates sent men to fetch water from among the flowering *asoka* trees and ordered them to build an earthen altar with mud from the river. He then instructed two of his henchmen to draw their swords and to drag Hiuan Tsang up onto the top of the altar and sacrifice him immediately. The Master of the Law, however, permitted no trace of fear or emotion to appear upon his face. The pirates were surprised by this and almost touched. Meanwhile, Hiuan Tsang, seeing there was no escaping from his fate, begged the pirates to grant him a few moment's respite and not subject him to such violent haste: 'Allow me,' he asked them, 'to enter Nirvana with a calm and joyful soul.' "

The Master of the Law then meditated lovingly upon the Bodhisattva Maitreya and turned all his thoughts to the Heaven of the Blessed Ones, praying ardently that he might be reborn there in order to offer his respects and pay homage to the Bodhisattva; that he might hear the most excellent Law expounded and reach perfect enlightenment (Buddha-hood); that he might then redescend and be born again on earth to teach and convert these men and bring them to perform the acts of higher virtue, to abandon their infamous beliefs; and finally that he might spread far and wide all the benefits of the Law and bring peace and happiness to all creatures. He then proceeded to worship the Buddhas of the ten countries of the world, sat down in a posture of contemplation and eagerly bent his thoughts upon the Bodhisattva Maitreya, allowing no other ideas to intrude.

"All of a sudden, in the depths of his enraptured soul, he felt himself raised up to Mount Sumeru, and after having passed through one, two and then three heavens he saw the true Maitreya seated upon a glittering throne in the palace of the Blessed Ones, surrounded by a multitude of gods. And in that moment body and soul were overcome with joy and he knew not that he sat near the altar of sacrifice, and was unaware of the pirates thirsting for his blood. His companions, however, had given themselves up to crying and weeping when suddenly a furious wind sprang up all around them, uprooting trees, raising the sand in whirling gusts, beating up the waves of the river and swamping all the boats. The pirates were terror-struck and turned to Hiuan Tsang's companions saying, 'Where does this monk come from and what is his name?'

" 'He is a religious of high renown come from China in search of the Law,' they replied. 'If you kill him, my lords, you will bring endless punishment upon yourselves. Can you not see already, in the anger of the winds and waves, the terrible signs of the vengeance of the spirits of heaven? Make haste and repent!' "

The terrified brigands threw themselves down at Hiuan Tsang's feet. But the Master of the Law, in his ecstasy, had observed nothing of what was going on around him. When one of the brigands respectfully touched the edge of his robe he opened his eyes and asked softly whether his hour had come. On learning of the change in his situation he greeted the news of his salvation with the same serenity as he had earlier greeted the announcement of his death, and he invited the bandits to alter their lives for once and all. They promised to do so and as a mark of repentance threw their weapons into the Ganges. "Soon the fury of the winds and waves was calmed. The pirates, beside themselves with joy, bowed down before the Master of the Law and bade him farewell."

Following this dramatic episode Hiuan Tsang came to the confluence of the Ganges and the Jumna where stood the city of Prayaga,
called Po-lo-ye-k'ie by him and known today as Allahabad. Prayaga
had been one of the capitals of the Gupta emperors during the fourth
and fifth centuries and it was still a very large city. In spite of its stupa
built by Asoka, however, and in spite of the memory of the Mahayana
philosopher Arya Deva who had preached there in the third century,
the Buddhists were in a minority in the city. The two monasteries
which they possessed there (moreover of the Hinayana school) could
not compete with the hundreds of Hindu temples which, as Hiuan
Tsang tells us, were frequented by prodigious numbers of the faithful.
Furthermore the city would have been famous were it only for its
"plain of alms." Such was the name of the level plateau to the east of
Prayaga to which the princes and lords of the land had from time
immemorial come to perform the pious office of distributing alms to
religious and to the poor and orphaned.

Hiuan Tsang observed at Prayaga as he had higher up the river the
cult of which the Ganges formed the object on the part of the Hindu
masses. Vast numbers of people tried to meet their death in its sacred
waters, hoping by this means to be reborn in the heaven of the gods.
Even herds of deer and tribes of monkeys gathered on its banks, bath-
ing at great length in the water; and occasionally, so Hiuan Tsang as-
serts, these animals would refuse to leave the river, fasting there piously
until their decease. The pilgrim quotes by way of example the story of
the monkey who sat in a tree near the bank and allowed itself to die of
hunger during the reign of Harsha, the event inspiring a fresh access of
zeal in those who were given to the practice of austerities. Long poles
had been fixed in the river at this point, each one fitted with a peg or
ledge near the top by which the devout could hold on. At sunrise one
day Hiuan Tsang saw one of them performing a strange exercise out in
the middle of the river: the Hindu, supporting himself on the pole by
one hand and one foot and holding the other arm and leg out horizon-
tally with his body suspended in mid-air, followed with burning gaze

the course of the sun through the sky. He came down from his column only when the sun had disappeared in the west, resuming at dawn the next day. The object of these painful austerities was to release the soul from transmigration, and they were pursued daily without interruption for decades at a time.

Hiuan Tsang goes on to point out, again speaking of Prayaga, the demoralizing effect of certain of the sectarian devotional practices of Hinduism. His account here reads like one of the more disturbing pages of Kipling. "There is in the city a temple of the gods which is dazzling in its splendor and is the scene of many miracles. Whoever donates a single coin there acquires greater merit than one who gives a thousand elsewhere. Moreover, whoever commits suicide in the temple attains the paradise of the gods. Before the main hall of the temple stands a great tree whose branches and dense foliage cast a deep shade. In the tree lives a man-eating demon, whence the quantities of human bones to be seen on the ground to right and left. A man has only to enter this temple to sacrifice his life thereby. He is drawn both by the magic of error and the seductions of the spirit. From the depths of antiquity right down to our own times this senseless custom has not ceased for an instant."

During Hiuan Tsang's visit there occurred a further example of the danger of the strange mental contagion of the temple of the dead. A Brahmin of the highest intellectuality had resolved to put an end to this murderous superstition. As soon as he stepped inside the temple, however, the suicidal obsession took hold of him. "He climbed up into the tree and leaning down toward his friends cried, 'I shall die. I said before their teaching was a lie; I acknowledge that it is true. The *rishi* and the musicians of heaven, hovering in the air, are at this moment calling me toward them. In this blessed spot I must now cast down this worthless body.' " And so he did.

We must never forget such scenes as this nor lose sight of all the weird and dangerous superstitions that seethed against the background of Hinduism if we would appreciate at its true value the moral contribution made by the religion of the Buddha. Human nature is full of such contradictions. The entirely theological religion and fervent ontology of the Brahmins could not prevent the development of the most cruel and immoral practices; the history and iconography of several of the Sivaite sects are sufficient proof of this. Buddhism, on the other hand, which theoretically speaking has been described as "nihilist," preserved at least in its official forms a simplicity of manners, a moral stability and a smiling moderation which recall Socratic Greece when set against the medieval manifestations of Hinduism. Hiuan Tsang, faced with Hinduism's excesses, reacted like a European.

Leaving Prayaga in a southwesterly direction and passing through a forested zone full of wild animals including elephants, the pilgrim came to another former Gupta capital on the lower Jumna, Kausambi, (Kiao-shang-mi in Chinese) the present-day Kosam. There too were traces of the Buddha's passage as well as a stupa erected by Asoka, the two-storied pavilion in which Vasubandhu had written one of his works and the mango grove where Asanga had lived. But the city possessed only about ten Buddhist monasteries which moreover were partly in ruins or deserted and included only three hundred religious, all Hinayanist. On the other hand Kausambi contained almost fifty Brahmin temples frequented by the mass of the people. Thus at the very period which appears to us to mark the apogee of Buddhist thought in India, to the eyes of an alert observer the Hindu reconquest was becoming daily more threatening.

CHAPTER 8

The Holy Places of Buddhism

AFTER KAUSAMBI Hiuan Tsang's journey took a different direction. Instead of continuing down the Ganges to Benares he turned due north along the trails leading to northern Oudh and Nepal. The pilgrim, in fact, wished to put off no longer his visit to the birthplace of the Buddha Sakyamuni.

The first place Hiuan Tsang came to was Sravasti, called She-lo-fa-si-ti in Chinese and corresponding to the present-day town of Sahet-Mahet on the right bank of the Rapti. In the Buddha's day it had been the capital of the old kingdom of Kosala (Oudh) and its king Prasenajit. By the seventh century, however, the site was already virtually abandoned and the former capital consisted of little more than ruins.[1]

---

[1] For the condition of the site today see Ph. Vogel, "Excavations at Sahet-Mahet," *Archaeological Survey of India,* notably the Report for 1907–8, p. 81.

Yet how steeped in memories was this dead city! There was situated the Jetavana Grove, given to the young church by the wealthy merchant Anathapindika; the limpid ponds, luxuriant vegetation and innumerable flowers which still inspired, many centuries later, the admiration of the first Chinese pilgrims. Asoka had marked the site with two engraved pillars bearing the Wheel of the Law and the Bull, and by Hiuan Tsang's time these were all that was left standing; the monastery itself was in ruins. It was at Sravasti too that the Buddha had performed what is known as the "Great Miracle," the traditional account of which the sacred iconographers have ever since vied with each other in celebrating. King Prasenajit had organized a tournament of miracles between Him and three opposing ascetics, an event which turned into the apotheosis of the Blessed One. He ascended into the air and reached the realm of light and immediately his body began to shine with many-colored lights. Whorls of flame sprang from his shoulders and at his feet rained a stream of fresh water. Soon afterward he was seen to be seated on a lotus created by the *naga* kings with Brahma on his right and Indra on his left; then, by a miracle of his omnipotence, he caused further lotuses to appear in uncountable numbers filling the sky, each of them containing a magic Buddha like himself.

Hiuan Tsang saw the tower that marked the site of the convent of nuns founded by Prajapati, the Buddha's aunt and adoptive mother—Prajapati who with the support of Ananda had after repeated refusals finally obtained the Buddha's consent to the entry of women into the Order.

A little farther on was the stupa of Angulimala, which referred to one of those conversions of evil-doers which were such frequent occurences in the life of the Blessed One. Angulimala was a fanatical bandit, probably connected with some homicidal sect, like the Thugs of more recent history, who used to murder people and sever their fingers to make a "holy garland." His dreadful trophy was complete but for two fingers and he was about to kill his own mother to obtain them when the Buddha, seized with compassion, substituted himself. "The bandit rushed upon the Blessed One, brandishing his sword. The Blessed One slowly retreated backwards and Angulimala, pursuing him, was unable to catch him up." In spite of the extreme blackness of his soul the Buddha consented to convert him, and the former head-hunter finished his days in the habit of a devout and faithful monk.

Near the former Jetavana Grove Hiuan Tsang saw the stupa "of the healing of the monk." This stupa preserved the memory of one of the most tenderly humane episodes in the life of the Buddha. There was a sick monk who, having given himself up to despair, was living in solitude apart from the rest of the community. The Blessed One, finding him in this state of seclusion, asked him the reason for it. The monk replied, "I am of so slothful a disposition that I lack even the will to appeal to the doctors. I am very ill and have no one to look after me." The Buddha was moved with pity and said to him, "My friend, I shall be your doctor." Whereupon he touched the poor man with his hand and the sickness disappeared. The Buddha then carried him out of his room, remade his bed, stood him up, dressed him in fresh clothes and left him with an injunction that he be zealous and strong.

Farther on was a small stupa recalling the charming story of Maudgalyayana and Sariputra, two of Sakyamuni's earliest and most famous disciples. One day when the Buddha was preaching to the crowds by Lake Anavatapta he noticed that Sariputra was absent and asked Maudgalyayana to go and look for him. Maudgalyayana had received supernatural powers from the Blessed One and in a matter of seconds transported himself by air to Sravasti. He found the saint in his monastery, where he was busily darning his monastic robe. He tried in vain to bring him away with him. Unable to do so, he returned through the air to the gathering by the lake. What was his surprise when, arriving there, the first person he saw beside the Buddha was Sariputra. A story, says Hiuan Tsang, which shows us how in Buddhism the supernatural powers accorded to the saints, however great those powers may have been, came a long way after spirituality.

21. Sravasti miracle. (*Musée Guimet*)

Sravasti in fact possessed innumerable holy places, each of which was marked with a commemorative stupa. One of these stupas indicated the spot where the Brahmins who had murdered a courtesan accused the Buddha of the crime, and there was a hole where Devadatta, the Judas Iscariot of Buddhism, had been cast down to hell; another hole showed where the earth had swallowed up a girl who had slandered the Buddha's virtue. There too was the spot where the Buddha had first saved his homeland. Virudhaka, the king of Kosala, having a grievance against the Sakya people which demanded vengeance, marched against them at the head of a vast army. The Buddha stationed himself on their route, sitting on a dead tree-trunk. When the king saw him he stepped down from his chariot, saluted him and asked him why he had chosen to pursue his meditation while seated upon a withered log instead of in the plentiful shade of the nearby trees. "My clan," replied the Buddha, "was my branches and my leaves. Now that you are going to strike it down I shall be like a tree that is stripped of its foliage." The king was touched by the Buddha's lesson and on this occasion turned around and went home. Later, it is true, he renewed his attempt and laid waste the land of Sakya, taking away with him five hundred girls and, when they refused to be his, cutting off their hands and feet and throwing them into a pit. As they were about to die they appealed to the Buddha. He appeared to them, preached to them the Excellent Law, received their last breaths and caused them to be reborn in the heaven of the gods. Hiuan Tsang made his devotions at the stupa which bore witness to their martyrdom.

He also worshipped at the "stupa of the healed eyes" which was situated at a distance of four or five *li* from the Jetavana Grove. The tradition was that five hundred Awahdi brigands whom the king of Kosala had taken prisoner here had their eyes torn out and were left in this state in the midst of a dense forest. Thus tormented, their thoughts turned toward the Buddha. Their crimes were numberless but their expiation had been terrible and the Master's mercy was infinite. He took pity on them. A refreshing breeze began to blow upon Sravasti from the snowfields of the Himalayas and the tortured criminals recovered their sight.

Continuing in a northeasterly direction the Chinese pilgrim came at last to "Kie-pi-lo-fa-su-tu" or Kapilavastu, the city of the Buddha's birth. We know what trouble the archeologists had to discover this famous place on the unpromising and indeed wretched site of Tilaura

22. The sleeping women, from Gandhara. (*Musée Guimet*)

Kot in the heart of the Nepal Terai.[2] The region was already abandoned in the seventh century. "There are ten deserted towns lying covered with wild plants. The capital is in such a state of ruin that it is
impossible to determine its original extent. The walls of the royal palace
can still be made out, however; they were built of brick and their foun-

[2] The definitive identification of the site of Kapilavastu was made possible by the discovery
at Rummindei near the Nepali village of Paderia, two miles north of Bhagvanpur, of an
engraved pillar erected by Asoka. Rummindei is the modern name of Lumbini, the garden
just outside Kapilavastu in which the Buddha was born. See Purma Chandra Mukerji, "Antiquities in the Terai, Nepal. The Region of Kapilavastu," *Archaeological Survey of India,
1901; The Journal of the Royal Asiatic Society, 1914*, pp. 391, 751; Jarl Carpentier, "Note
on the Pandaria or Rummindei Inscription," *Indian Antiquary*, January 1914, p. 17.

dations are still whole and solid." Near what used to be the palace was a monastery inhabited by thirty or so Hinayanist monks. What was this against the thousands of monasteries whose ruins could be seen everywhere in the surrounding jungle? "The country has been deserted and uninhabited for centuries and one comes across only a few inhabitants in villages here and there. They have neither princes nor supreme chief, each community being led by its own local chieftain." And yet as Hiuan Tsang himself observed the country was fertile and well irrigated with an invariably moderate temperature and very regular seasons. What then was the curse that lay upon this other "Holy Land," that had made sterile such abundance and turned this blessed soil into a desert?

Hiuan Tsang evokes with melancholy the sacred memories that hovered among these ruins. Near the royal palace, once the palace of King Suddhodana, the Buddha's father, he was shown the site of the room in the gynaeceum to which Queen Maya, visited by a solemn presentiment, had withdrawn in order to spend in prayer and meditation the hours preceding the conception. Hiuan Tsang was also able to see a representation of this famous scene, in which no doubt the Bodhisattva was depicted, as in the reliefs of Bharhut and Amaravati, as a young elephant descending from the Heaven of the Blessed Gods into the bosom of the chosen queen. And all around were further sites where the various episodes of the Childhood and Youth had taken place. A stupa to the northeast of Queen Maya's room marked the spot where the aged saint Asita had foretold to the parents of the divine child the greatness for which he was destined. A stupa near the southern gate of the former city of Kapilavastu commemorated the place where the Bodhisattva, as a young *raja* of marriageable age, had vanquished the other claimants in a contest of arms. Elsewhere the pilgrim was shown the spot where the young prince, while out in his chariot for a gallop across country, had had his first meeting with Old Age, Sickness and Death, that symbolic encounter which was to determine his vocation. Due southeast of Kapilavastu was the path he had cut through the undergrowth when, leaving the sleeping harem in order to adopt the monastic life, he had stolen out of the city on his faithful horse Kanthaka, whose guardian spirits had held his hoofs in their hands so as not to alert the gate watch.

The country around Kapilavastu was no less rich in memories. At a distance of four *li* to the south of the city was a stupa which Asoka had erected to mark the site of a moving scene. It took place many years after the Great Renunciation. The Buddha had attained Enlightenment

23. The departure, from Amaravati (the Buddha is not shown). (*Musée Guimet*)

and founded his religion. Back in his native city his father was now an old man and sent message after message that he wished to see him again before he died. The Buddha yielded to this desire. As he was approaching Kapilavastu King Suddhodana came out to meet him, and it was this meeting between father and son which Asoka's stupa commemorated.

Another monument indicated the site of the first meditation, as recounted by the poet of the *Buddhacharita*. The Bodhisattva was still only a youth. He had gone out into the country to help with the work in the fields. "At the sight of the young grass being torn up and shredded by the ploughshare, all covered as it was with the eggs and young of insects that had been killed, he was deeply affected with grief, as if it had been his own family and friends that were thus massacred. And at the sight of the workmen with their faces shrivelled with the dust and burnt with sun and wind, he was filled with deep compassion." He sat down under a pink apple tree and began to meditate. The time was midday. He was still deep in meditation when the sun went down. But the shade of the pink apple tree had not moved and continued to cover the divine youth.

The most sacred place of all in this region lay to the northeast of Kapilavastu. This was the Lumbini Gardens, the actual birthplace of the Bodhisattva. There Queen Maya, in the posture popularized by Buddhist iconography—standing and holding with her right hand onto the branch of an *asoka* tree—had given birth to the hero of charity. The divine child had emerged from her right side where he was received into the arms of Indra and Brahma, the supreme god of Vedism and the supreme god of Brahminism having both hurried to greet him. Two spirits or *naga* kings, appearing in mid-air visible from the waist upwards, had created two springs, one of warm and one of cold water, in order that Brahma and Indra might give the child the ritual bath. The child had taken possession of the world by taking seven steps in the direction of each of the four points of the compass. Celestial music had been heard and perfumed breezes had wafted over the land. There in the middle of the garden King Asoka erected the engraved pillar which still stands today and which enabled archeologists to locate the Lumbini Gardens at what is now Rummindei.[3]

Proceeding in an easterly direction deeper into the Nepal Terai, an area of wild forests which are even today infested with tigers and herds of elephants, Hiuan Tsang came to the stupa of Ramagrama, a venerable monument in which a former king of the country had enshrined some relics of the Buddha. Abandoned and even completely forgotten by men, lost in the middle of the jungle, this stupa was for centuries maintained by wild elephants. The monk who rediscovered it was able to witness this miracle: "The elephants gathered flowers and came and laid them before the reliquary; they tore up the grass and weeds all around and watered the soil with their trunks." A little farther on was another stupa erected by King Asoka in the clearing at the edge of a forest where the Bodhisattva, after leaving his father's house, divested himself of his princely garments, his jewels and his royal turban and bade farewell to his tearful squire and to his horse which, equally moved, licked his feet.

The saintly King Asoka had called this stupa the stupa of Chandaka, which was the name of the squire. Another stupa to the east of this monument marked the spot where the Bodhisattva had exchanged his luxurious clothes for the rags of a poor hunter and where he had cut off his hair and thrown it into the air, from which it had been recovered by the gods.

Later in life, as we have seen, after he had achieved Enlightenment, the Buddha was to return to the country of his birth in answer to the entreaties of his father. Hiuan Tsang was shown the place where he came down out of the sky, for he had traveled through the air. "Eight Vajrapani were his escort and the four Celestial Kings went before him. Indra stood on his left hand and Brahma on his right, together with the multitude of the gods. The Buddha towered in their midst like the

[3] There are some excellent photographs of the countryside around Rummindei in Perceval Landon, *Nepal*, London, 1928, vol. I, pp. 1–10.

moon shining amid the stars. Shaking the three worlds by his divine power and effacing the seven planets by his dazzling brightness, he came through the air to the kingdom of his birth. When King Suddhodana and the ministers accompanying him had completed their acts of homage, the entire procession entered Kapilavastu. . . ."

The holy places connected with the Buddha's death were situated in the same region as had seen his childhood. Leaving the province of Kapilavastu Hiuan Tsang came to Kusinagara, which he calls Kiu-she-na-kie-lo and which has been identified as corresponding to the present Kasia, on the right bank of the middle Gandak.[4] He saw the landscape amid which the Blessed One had entered Nirvana, and evoked that page from the Pali scriptures whose message, reaching down the centuries and through the vanity of things, still has the power to move us:

In a grove of *sala* trees on the banks of the Hiranyavati River the Buddha had a couch prepared for him between two twin trees which immediately became covered with blossom. Gently consoling his disciple Ananda, who was in despair, he said, "Do not weep, Ananda, do not despair. From all that man loves he must one day part. How could that which is born a prey to instability not pass away? Perhaps you are thinking: 'Now we have no master.' Think not so, Ananda! The doctrine I have preached to you, that is your master." He said again, "Truly, my disciples, all things created are subject to decay. Struggle without respite." They were his last words. "His spirit," says the Buddhist catechism, "plunged into the depths of mystical absorption, and when he had reached that point where all thought and all conception are extinguished and where the awareness of individuality ceases, he entered the supreme Nirvana. Before the gate of Kusinagara which

---

[4] The reader will find archeological maps of this famous site as well as photographs of the countryside around Kusinagara and of its ruined monasteries in the articles by Ph. Vogel, Hirananda Sastri, *et al.*, in "Excavations at Kasia," *Archaeological Survey of India*, 1904–5, pp. 42–58; 1906–7, pp. 44–67; 1911–12, p. 134; 1924–5, plate IV; etc.

faces toward the east the noblemen of Malla cremated the body of the Buddha with royal honors."

Hiuan Tsang visited the site of the Nirvana at the beginning of A.D. 637, approximately eleven hundred and twenty years after the Buddha's death. A number of stupas marked the successive phases of this great drama. One stood on the site of the house of Cunda the blacksmith with whom the Blessed One had taken his last meal. Farther on was the site of the *sala* grove in which he had fallen asleep; there was also the place where the gods had worshipped his corpse for seven days with celestial singing and showers of blossoms; the place where the Blessed One's body had been placed in its coffin; the place where it had been burned on a pyre of precious woods; the place where the "War of the Relics" had almost broken out over the distribution of his remains; and lastly the place where the relics had been apportioned. Like the Vajrapani who fainted with grief at the Blessed One's death, the pilgrim must have pronounced the threnody which he gives as follows: "To cross the vast ocean of life and death, who shall serve us for our skiff and oars? When we walk through the shadows of a long night, who shall henceforth be our guide and torch-bearer?"

And since in Indian Buddhism our brothers the animals can never be left out of any of the great scenes of our salvation, close by these stupas erected in memory of the historical Buddha stood a monument commemorating the "Charitable Deer," the Bodhisattva in one of his former lives, who had died during a fire while saving the jungle folk.

"There stood on this site in former times a great forest. One day a fire broke out in a wild plain which lay at the middle of the forest. The birds and the four-footed beasts were driven to the very last extremity. Before them flowed a rapid torrent which brought them to a halt. Forced on by the violence of the fire they plunged into the water and lost their lives. The deer was moved to pity and placing himself athwart the torrent which tore at his skin and snapped his bones he did his utmost to save them from drowning. The last to arrive was a lame hare and the deer, forgetting his exhaustion and agony, somehow found the force to see him safely to the other bank. But his strength was drained and he sank into the water and died. The gods gathered up his bones and raised a stupa to his memory."

The "Francolin Miracle," which tradition also set in the same place, likewise had a forest fire for its theme. "There was a huge and dense forest filled with birds and four-footed beasts, the former living in nests and the latter in holes in the ground. One day a terrible wind sprang up and violent flames whirled and flew through the air. At that moment a francolin, moved to pity, went to dip itself in a stream of pure water and then flew up and began to sprinkle the forest with its wings." The god Indra, noticing the little bird, jeered at its efforts: "How can you be so stupid as thus to tire out your wings? The fire is already consuming the trees of the forests and the grass of the plains. How could such a paltry creature as you ever put it out?" Then the francolin made the god ashamed of his indolence, whereupon the god, taking some water in the palm of his hand, threw it upon the fire and extinguished it immediately. "The flames fell, the smoke blew away, and all the birds and four-footed beasts were saved." This miracle too was commemorated by its stupa.

Leaving the sacred site of the Nirvana the pilgrim made his way through the vast forests lying between the Gandak and the Gogra and Gumti rivers and arrived in Benares.

Benares or Varanasi (Hiuan Tsang's Po-lo-na-ssu) was by then already the holy city of Hinduism. Hiuan Tsang's description of it has a curiously up-to-date ring. After some remarks about the luxuriant vegetation of the region he goes on to mention the density of population, the accumulated wealth of this metropolis of the Gangetic world, the city's ancient culture and above all the multitude of Brahminical temples. "These temples stand several stories high and are richly adorned with sculptural decoration, the wooden parts being brightly painted in many colors. They are set in thickly wooded parks and surrounded by pools of clear water." He also noticed the profusion of ascetic sects within Brahminism and Jainism. "Most of them worship Siva. Some cut off all their hair; others gather their hair up in a knot at the top of their heads. There are some (these are the Jains) who go naked. Yet others rub their bodies with ashes or indulge in cruel mortifications to obtain release from transmigration. . . ."

24. Fifth Century Buddha, from the Sarnath Museum. (*Musée Guimet*)

25. The deer park, where Buddha preached his first sermon. (*Roger-Viollet*)

Hiuan Tsang particularly noticed in one of these Brahminical temples at Benares a colossal statue of Siva "full of grandeur and majesty; at the sight of it one is filled with a fearful respect as if one were in the very presence of the god. . . ." These lines, coming from the brush of a Buddhist writer, are most interesting. Might they not serve as a definition of the Gupta sculpture of the early Middle Ages in which the Indian aesthetic finally realized its ideal? And does not Hiuan Tsang's description of this Siva of Benares, which we shall never know, immediately evoke that of the cave-chapel on Elephanta, the three-in-one "Mahesamurti Siva" which is probably the finest figuration of the pantheistic deity ever to have been formed by the hand of man?

In Sarnath just outside Benares Hiuan Tsang was able to admire another magnificent statue, this time a Buddhist one. I refer to the

26. Buddha's first sermon, Hadda. (*Musée Guimet*)

Buddha of the Sarnath Museum, dating from the fifth century A.D. and depicting the Buddha seated in the posture of preaching or, to use the hallowed expression, "Turning the Wheel of the Law"—a work whose solemnity, simplicity and gentleness make it, in my opinion, the purest realization of the Gupta ideal.[5]

For Benares, despite the numerical superiority of the Hindus, had

[5] For further documentation on Buddhist Sarnath—monastery plans, photographs of the ruins, statuary, etc.—the reader is referred to the articles by Sir John Marshall and Sten Konov, "Excavations at Sarnath," *Archaeological Survey of India, Report for 1904–5*, pp. 59–104; *1906–7*, pp. 68–101; *1907–8*, pp. 43–80; *1914–15*, pp. 97–131; etc.

not forgotten its memories of the Buddha. This same Sarnath quarter on the outskirts of the city contained the Deer Park, scene of the Blessed One's first sermon or, as the scriptures put it, the "Setting in Motion of the Wheel of the Law." There, in a state of proud asceticism, lived the first five disciples of the Buddha, who deserted him, scandalized, when on the eve of the Enlightenment he gave up the exhausting mortifications which he had been practicing in vain. And then, after the Enlightenment, back the Buddha came to Benares and presented himself before them. "Calm breathed from his whole person and a divine light shone out from him. His hair gleamed like jade and his body was as pure gold. He came forward with tranquil step and all creatures were moved by his majesty." The five ascetics had sworn to give him a scornful reception but an invincible force prostrated them at his feet. And then it was that he delivered for them the Benares Sermon, one of the most beautiful ever to have emerged from purely human lips.

The Master told them, "There are two extremes, oh monks, which you must always avoid. The life of pleasure is base, ignoble, contrary to the spirit, unworthy and vain. And the life of mortification is sad and unworthy and vain. From these two extremes, oh monks, the Perfect One has kept away, and he has discovered the way which passes through the middle and which leads to peace, to knowledge, to Enlightenment, to Nirvana. . . . This, oh monks, is the sacred truth about pain: birth, old age, sickness, death and separation from what is loved are pain. This is the origin of pain: it is the thirst for pleasure, the thirst for existence, the thirst for what is impermanent. And this is the truth about the suppression of pain: it is the quenching of the thirst by the abolition of desire."

Hiuan Tsang lingered long in the Deer Park, his heart overflowing with these great memories. He saw the engraved pillar erected there by Emperor Asoka with its bell-shaped capitol surrounded by a charmingly naturalistic frieze of animals and crowned by four addorsed lions, the earliest masterpiece of Indian art. Not far off was the stupa marking the spot where Maitreya, the Buddha-to-be, received the Blessed One's

27. "The Story of the Elephant," from Gandhara. (*Musée Guimet*)

announcement of his Messianic role. To the east of the Deer Park could still be seen the pond where the Buddha used to bathe during his sojourns in Benares, the pool in which he used to wash his clothes and that in which he would clean out his monastic vessels. These holy places were all devoutly looked after, for the Deer Park also contained a vast monastery whose galleries Hiuan Tsang praised as being ideal for meditation and which housed fifteen hundred Hinayanist monks.

Benares was also the traditional setting of several of the Buddha's former lives, notably of some of the Jatakas on animal subjects, so movingly informed with the universal tenderness of Buddhism. One of the best known Jatakas, that of the elephant with the six tusks, had taken place in the forest near the sacred pools, as if the Blessed One had been pleased to revisit in his last human incarnation the scene of the most touching of his animal lives, for in a previous existence the Bo-dhisattva had been a king of the elephants, a white elephant armed with six magnificent tusks "like water-lily roots." "One day, out walking with his two wives, he knocked against a tree that was in flower.

Chance willed that the pollen and petals fell on one of the queens while the other received only twigs and dead leaves." The latter queen, consumed with envy and determined to have her revenge, contrived to die and be reborn in the body of a queen of Benares. She then sent out a hunter to kill the elephant and get hold of his tusks. The hunter, who in his treachery adopted the disguise of an inoffensive monk, came upon the divine animal—"like a walking mountain"—some little way apart from the herd by a lotus-covered pool, and fired a poisoned arrow at him. The elephant was in such pain that he was on the point of killing his enemy, but he restrained himself and even prevented his herd from trampling the hunter to death. Hearing of the mission with which the latter had been charged he tore out his own tusks with his bleeding trunk and, quivering with pain, offered them to his executioner. He died on the instant and was reborn in the body of the Buddha-to-be. And the queen? When she received the tusks and learned of the sacrifice made by one she had so greatly loved in another life, she was seized with such remorse that her heart broke with it. . . .

This countryside around Benares was saturated with tender and wonderful legends. Hiuan Tsang was taken to a clearing in the middle of a forest which had provided the setting for the Jataka of the king of the deer, another prefiguration of the Buddha. He commanded a herd of five hundred deer. The king of Benares sent out beaters who surrounded the whole herd. The king of the deer went to him and secured the release of the captives on condition that they send one deer a year to the butcher-shops of Benares. It so happened that the lot fell to a hind who was pregnant. Before going to her death she sought out the king of the deer and "prostrating herself before him on the knees of her front legs she said, 'Wait only until I have dropped my young and then I shall give myself up without regret.'" The king of the deer was filled with compassion and offered himself to the king of Benares in her place. Touched by such generosity the latter renounced his cruel tribute, and the story, as related in the *Sutralamkara,* ends with some stanzas of quite Franciscan tenderness: "All these forests and all these woods, all these springs and pools I give to the deer folk and forbid anyone to do them harm."

Farther on was a stupa commemorating the story of the kind hare, as told in the scriptures by the Buddha himself: "And in another life I was a hare and dwelt in a mountain forest. I ate grass and leaves and fruit and harmed no one. A monkey, a jackal and myself lived together. I would instruct them in their duties and teach them what was good and what was evil." One day an aged Brahmin, or rather Indra disguised as a Brahmin, approached the three friends. " 'My children,' he asked them, 'are you happy in this quiet retreat?' 'The greensward is thick that we tread beneath our feet,' they replied, 'and the forest we walk through is a dense one. And although we are of different species we enjoy one another's company. We are happy and at peace.' 'When I learned,' resumed the old man, 'of the bond of friendship which united you I forgot the weight of my years and came expressly from far away to make your acquaintance. But just now my hunger is urgent. What can you give me to eat?' " The three friends immediately set out hunting. The jackal caught a fresh carp in the stream and the monkey culled fruits and flowers of the most unusual kinds. "Only the hare came back empty-handed and began dancing about this way and that." When the old man expressed surprise the animal replied, "A noble gift, a gift such as has never before been given, such a gift I give you today. Gather wood and light a fire! " The story-teller continues, "When the wood began to blaze I leapt in the air and threw myself into the middle of the fire. As plunging into cool water allays the torments of heat so did that blazing fire allay all my torments. Skin, flesh, bones, heart, my whole body and my every limb gave I to the Brahmin! "

Having worshipped at all these sites, whether historical or legendary, Hiuan Tsang left the Benares area and went a little way northward to the lower reaches of the Gandak where he visited the city of Vaisali (Fei-shö-li), the present-day Besarh. The city had once been famous for its groves of banana and mango trees and had been one of the Buddha's favorite places of residence. By Hiuan Tsang's day it was a dead city.

The pilgrim spent a long time strolling in the Mango Grove in the southern part of the city which had once been given to the Order by Amrapali, the dancing-girl saint. He was shown the "Monkey Pool" which had been dug for the Buddha by his friends the monkeys; a stupa nearby recalled how the monkeys had carried off the Blessed One's begging-bowl and brought it back to him filled with wild honey. The city was full of tender memories; of melancholy ones, too, for Hiuan Tsang was shown the hillock from which the Buddha, on the way to the place where he was to die, had turned for another look at these familiar horizons, a last lingering contemplation of his favorite city and his favorite monastery. But for a theologian like Hiuan Tsang the city of Vaisali was interesting for yet another reason: it was there that a hundred years after the Buddha's death the second council of the Buddhist church had been held.

Of all the provinces of India, however, the most important for our pilgrim, as much for its sacred memories as from the point of view of his Buddhist studies, was the ancient kingdom of Magadha (the Mo-kie-t'o of Chinese writers) in southern Bihar. This truly imperial land had twice brought political unity to India, once under the Maurya dynasty and again under the Gupta dynasty. Hiuan Tsang, describing the southern Bihar countryside with his usual geographer's accuracy, gives us a number of details which still hold good today: "The towns have few inhabitants but the villages are densely populated. The soil is rich and fertile and seed grows abundantly in it. A most unusual type of rice is harvested there, very large-grained and of exquisite flavor. The land is low-lying and damp and the villages are built on slightly higher ground. From the first months of summer until the second month of autumn the plains are flooded and can be crossed by boat."

Hiuan Tsang writes first of the historic capital of Magadha, Pataliputra (Po-t'o-li-tsu in Chinese) the site of which is now occupied by Bankipore and Kumhrar in the suburbs of Patna, between the Ganges and the old bed of the Son. The city had once been famous. There the first Maurya emperor, "Sandrocottus," had received ambassadors from Greece. From there his grandson Asoka had governed the whole of India. And it was at Pataliputra that Asoka had called his celebrated council, reckoned as the third, where it was decided to evangelize the world; it was from there that those missionaries set out who as we know from inscriptions were to carry the faith to the courts of the Greek princes, the Seleucids of Syria, the Ptolemies of Egypt and the Antigonids of Macedonia. The city had at that time rivaled Alexandria and Antioch, and indeed the excavations carried out there earlier in this century revealed traces of a hypostyle hall reminiscent of the colonnades of Persepolis. After a period of obscurity Pataliputra had once more, in the first century A.D. at the beginning of the Gupta period, become for a time the capital of India, before sinking back finally into obscurity. By the time of Hiuan Tsang's visit its decline appears to have been complete. Nothing, at any rate, could be seen of its ancient palaces except the foundations, and of the hundreds of monasteries it had once possessed only two or three at most were still standing.

These Hiuan Tsang visited. He saw a stupa erected by Asoka, one of the eighty-four thousand monuments of this kind with which the saintly emperor had covered the whole of India. On the bank of the Ganges he worshipped the Buddha's farewell stone on which the imprint of his holy feet were still visible. The Buddha, knowing that his time was near, had left this ancient land of Magadha where he had fought, suffered and triumphed and had taken once more the road toward the north, the road to the Decease. "Standing on a large square stone on the south bank of the river he turned in deep emotion to Ananda and said, 'This is the last time that I shall look upon the Diamond Throne and the royal city.'" How infinitely precious is this emotion on the part of the Master of Renunciation, this involuntary sadness at the approach of death, and how doubly disturbing on the part of the apostle of Nirvana this confession of an earthly attachment that suddenly makes the Sage look so human. . . .

The land to which the aged Buddha addressed this final farewell had indeed been the principal theater of that great mystical drama that was his life. This, for the Buddhist, was the true Holy Land.

Hiuan Tsang's own emotion is evident in every line as he describes to us the road from Pataliputra to Bodh Gaya. For Bodh Gaya was the very heart of Buddhism, the sacred site of the Buddha's Enlightenment. The pilgrim saw the river Nairanjana, now called the Lilajan or Phalgu, "with its clear waters and lovely steps, adorned with trees and shrubs and surrounded by meadows and villages"—that temperate landscape which the Buddha, looking for a hermitage, had selected for its gentleness.[6] Hiuan Tsang came to the divine Bo or Bodhi Tree beneath which the miracle of the Enlightenment had occurred, and he evoked that sacred scene as it had been handed down by the scriptures, with every detail immutably fixed:

". . . The Bodhisattva, renouncing his fruitless mortification and all the practices of Hindu asceticism, had just restored to his mind its indispensable physical support by taking the milk and rice prepared for him by a devout girl named Sujata from the nearby village. He had refreshed his weary limbs in the clear waters of the Nairanjana. Then he had set out for Bodh Gaya where stood the sacred fig tree which was to witness the central scene of the Buddhist gospel.

"The Bodhisattva (here the texts are particularly precise) sat down at the foot of the tree on a handful of freshly cut grass with which he had covered the seat that had miraculously appeared there—the Diamond Throne, hub of the Buddhist world. Then began the "sublime meditation" from which the salvation of all creatures was to result. In vain did Mara, the Buddhist devil, assail the meditating sage with all the hosts of hell: darts, boulders and jets of burning flame turned to garlands of flowers and a halo of light about the Blessed One. In vain did the daughters of Mara resort to every means of seduction: the Bodhisattva transformed them into old crones. Against all these attempts he called the Earth to witness the excellence of his strength, and the

6 The reader will find a photograph of the village of Urel, formerly Uruvela and the site of the Buddha's hermitage, in the article by Th. Bloch, "Notes on Bodh Gaya," *Archaeological Survey of India, Report for 1908-9*, p. 143.

Earth, emerging from the waist upward between the gaping furrows, paid him solemn homage.

"The Bodhisattva, having triumphed over temptation, still sitting motionless at the foot of the tree, bent his thoughts upon the universality of suffering and upon the means of abolishing it. His gaze took in the whole universe. He saw the endless cycle of rebirth unfolding to infinity, from the infernal world and the world of the animals right up to the gods themselves, through all eternity. And every birth, every life, every death was suffering.

"Then the Bodhisattva, his mind thus in contemplation and completely pure, during the last watch of the night, just as dawn was breaking, at the hour of the beating of the drum, achieved Enlightenment. Tracing back the chain of causality, he discovered that the cause of universal suffering was the thirst for existence, and that the thirst for existence was based upon our false conceptions of mind, the self and the material world. Thus to abolish the thirst for existence by doing away with its intellectual causes was to abolish suffering. . . . Such was the inner Enlightenment, the revelation of perfect wisdom by which the Bodhisattva had finally become a Supreme Buddha."

After the Enlightenment the Buddha stayed for a further four weeks by the Bodhi Tree. In the fifth week the country was ravaged by a terrible storm. But a divine serpent called Mucilinda came and coiled himself up beneath the Buddha's body, lifting him above the flood, and by forming a hood with his seven heads he sheltered the Blessed One's head from the violence of the storm. Then, at the instigation of the gods Brahma and Indra who had come to entreat him to this purpose, the Buddha departed to evangelize the world or, as the texts say, to "set in motion the Wheel of the Law."

All these sacred scenes were recalled at length by Hiuan Tsang. First the Bodhi Tree received his adorning worship. Meticulously he described everything about it: "The trunk of the Tree is yellowish white and its leaves, which are green and shiny, fall neither in summer nor in winter. Only at the anniversary of the Nirvana do they come away, to be born again as beautiful the next day. On that day kings and lords gather beneath its branches, sprinkle milk upon the ground, light lamps, scatter flowers, and withdraw after they have gathered up the leaves."

Since Asoka's time, as we know from a relief at Sanchi which shows the emperor visiting Gaya, the Bodhi Tree had been protected by a brick wall. "The main gate of the enclosure lies to the east, facing the river Nairanjana. The southern gate is situated near a large pool covered with lotus flowers. To the west all access is blocked by a wall of steep mountains. The north gate communicates with a large monastery inside which the visitor finds sacred monuments at every step, whether viharas or stupas, which kings, ministers and wealthy citizens have erected for love of the saints and in order to preserve and honor their memory. At the center of this monastery is the Diamond Throne, so-called because it is firm, solid, indestructible, and capable of withstanding all the shocks of the world. Every Bodhisattva who would overcome the demons and attain Buddhahood must sit upon this throne. The place where Sakymuni attained Buddhahood is known also as the Seat of Understanding. When the rest of the world trembles to its very foundations, this place alone remains unshaken."

Near the Bodhi Tree stood a statue of the Bodhisattva Avalokitesvara. There was an ancient prophecy to the effect that when this statue disappeared into the earth the religion of the Buddha would disappear from India. By this time it had already sunk in up to the chest, and Hiuan Tsang himself predicted that it would need only another hundred and fifty or two hundred years for the prophecy to be fulfilled. And strangely enough between the eighth and ninth centuries Buddhism was indeed virtually eliminated from India except for Magadha and Bengal.

What makes the figure of Hiuan Tsang so vivid and so true—it is difficult to read his biography without loving the man—is the fact that in this formidable metaphysician the most tender piety went hand in hand with a deeply speculative bent. Take the scene which occurred at the end of his pilgrimage to the Bodhi Tree: "After contemplating it with burning faith he prostrated himself upon the ground with sighs and groans and abandoned himself to grief: 'Alas!' he cried, 'when the Buddha attained perfect understanding I know not in what conditions I was dragging out my miserable existence. And now that I am here in this place in the latter age of the statue I cannot contemplate the depth and enormity of my faults without a blush coming to my face!' At these words a flood of tears began to stream down his cheeks. Crowds of religious returning from their summer retreat began to arrive in their thousands at that moment from all directions. All who saw the Master of the Law in this posture of grief were unable to restrain themselves from sighing and weeping."

One by one Hiuan Tsang made his devotions at all the sacred sites of Bodh Gaya. He saw the pool created by Indra in which the Buddha washed his clothes; another pool where had dwelt the serpent-king Mucilinda who sheltered the Blessed One at his meditations by forming a canopy with his seven heads; the hermitage where, before the Enlightenment, the Bodhisattva had given himself up to such austerities that the gods themselves had feared for his life; he was shown the spot in the Nairanjana where the Blessed One had bathed before going to the Tree of Wisdom, the place where the gods came successively to offer him begging-bowls made of the most precious metals all of which he refused in favor of the stone bowl of the very poorest mendicants; and finally at Uruvela he saw the clearing in which the hermitage of the Kasyapa brothers had stood, those most famous of Brahminical ascetics whose pride the Buddha tamed to such a point that they became the pillars of his church.

Here too was the scene of more of the animal Jatakas. In a forest on the banks of the Nairanjana, near a pool, stood a stupa commemorating the touching adventure of the "perfumed elephant." This young elephant supported and fed his blind mother by gathering lotus roots for her. When he was captured and taken off to the royal stables he refused all food until the king, moved by his filial piety, had set him free again.

Near Gaya, after traveling through a region of forests and jungles, Hiuan Tsang made the ascent of the Cock's Foot Mountain, a wild, deserted mountain where tradition had it that Maha Kasyapa, Sakyamuni's great disciple, had been waiting for several centuries in ecstatic immobility for the advent of Maitreya, the Buddha-to-be. "Its faces are sheer and its cave deep. Swift torrents wash the foot of the mountain and its valleys are wrapped in vast forests. Three peaks thrust boldly up into the sky, their imposing mass reaching to the clouds." When the patriarch Kasyapa reached a great age he wished to retire from the world. "He went to the mountain and ascended by the winding paths of the north face. Reaching the southwestern chain he found his way barred by a wall of rock. He smote it with his stick and it split in two. Proceeding up this path which he had opened up through the mountain he came to the center of the three peaks. Through the force of his desire the three peaks drew themselves together and hid him from the sight of men. . . ." Farther along on the same mountain slept five hundred *arhats* or Buddhist saints; they too were waiting for a mysterious awakening.

To the northeast of Bodh Gaya lay Nalanda, a veritable monastic city consisting of some ten monasteries linked together by an enclosure of brick walls and comprising, apart from the monks' dwellings, a number of halls for meetings and for prayer. Hiuan Tsang describes with great delight the appearance of this *samgharama* with its regularly laid-out towers, its forest of pavilions and harmikas and all its temples "seeming to soar above the mists in the sky." From their cells the monks "might witness the birth of the winds and the clouds." His description has taken on even greater interest for us since excavations carried out by the Indian Archaeological Department have allowed us to reconstruct the topography of this complex of monasteries and to place all its stupas, verandas, cells and courtyards.[7] "An azure pool winds around the monasteries, adorned with the full-blown cups of the blue lotus; the dazzling red flowers of the lovely kanaka hang here and there, and outside groves of mango trees offer the inhabitants their dense and protective shade."

The space between the monasteries was divided into eight courts. Each of the houses for religious in these various courts comprised four stories. "The monasteries of India," writes Hiuan Tsang's biographer, "today number in their thousands, but there is not one to equal these whether in majesty, in richness or in the height of the buildings. There are ten thousand religious here at all times, both internal and external, and all follow the teaching of the Great Vehicle. Members of the eighteen schools are all assembled here and all manner of works are studied, from popular books, the Vedas and other accounts of that kind, to medicine, the occult sciences and arithmetic. Within the monastery a hundred lectures were delivered each day and the disciples gave zealous attention to the teachings of their masters without ever a moment being wasted.

"The lives of all these virtuous men were naturally governed by habits of the most solemn and strictest kind. Thus in the seven hundred years of this monastery's existence no man had ever contravened the rules of the discipline. The king showers it with the signs of his respect and veneration and has assigned the revenue from a hundred cities to pay for the maintenance of the religious. Regularly each day two hundred families send them several hundred bushels of rice as well as butter and milk. The students therefore ask nothing of anyone and

---

[7] See *Archaeological Survey of India, Report for 1922–3*, p. 104, and particularly plates XIX and XX for some fascinating photographs of the uncovered walls. See also *ibid., Report for 1923–4*, plate XXIX, and *1924–5*, plate XXVIII. Thanks to this series of methodical excavations and the accompanying articles the plans of the various monasteries described by Hiuan Tsang can be drawn virtually in their entirety. It is one of the achievements which does the greatest credit to Sir John Marshall and his colleagues in the Archeological Department.

have no difficulty in securing the four necessary things. The progress they have made in their studies and their brilliant achievements are the result of the king's liberality."

At Nalanda Hiuan Tsang received a fraternal welcome. Two hundred monks and a thousand laymen came out in procession to meet him carrying banners, torches and parasols and scattering incense and flowers. On arrival at Nalanda they were joined by all the rest of the religious. "When the Master of the Law had finished greeting them all they set a special chair on the president's dais and entreated him to be seated. The multitude of monks and believers sat down also. Thereupon the vice-president was instructed to strike the gong and pronounce the invitation to the Master of the Law to reside in the monastery and enjoy common use of all the implements and effects of the religious there assembled." Hiuan Tsang was then solemnly ushered into the presence of the man who was in effect the superior of this enormous monastery, the aged and saintly Silabhadra, surnamed the Treasure of the Good Law.[8]

"Hiuan Tsang, following his guides, passed in to greet him. Once in his presence he performed all the duties of a disciple and exhausted every token of respect. In accordance with their hallowed rules and customs he walked on his knees and elbows, drummed with his feet and beat his forehead upon the ground. Silabhadra, when he had questioned him and heaped praises upon him, had chairs brought in and begged the Master of the Law and the monks to be seated. He then inquired as to the Master of the Law's intentions. 'I have come from China,' replied the latter, 'in order to study under your direction the philosophy of Idealism.' "

Hearing these words Silabhadra was unable to contain his tears, and he recounted to Hiuan Tsang the extraordinary premonition he had had of his arrival. Some time before, while suffering from a cruel

---

[8] Hiuan Tsang's biographer writes that in 637, the date of the pilgrim's arrival at Nalanda, Silabhadra was a hundred and six years old, which would mean that he was born around 531. It should be pointed out, however, that Hiuan Tsang himself says merely that his master was very old without mentioning a figure.

disease, he had formed a wish to die. One night three deities had appeared to him in a dream. Beautifully formed and with faces that were full of dignity, they had been dressed in ceremonial robes as light as they were brilliant. The first was the color of gold, the second of lapis lazuli and the third of white silver. They were the Bodhisattvas Mañjusri, Avalokitesvara and Maitreya. They had appeared to him and commanded him to live in order to spread far and wide the Holy Law and the teachings of Idealism and to await, to that end, the arrival of a certain religious from China to whom he was to impart his knowledge. "Since my coming tallies with your dream," replied Hiuan Tsang, "I beseech you to instruct and enlighten me, and complete my happiness by allowing me to entertain on your account the sentiments of a devoted and submissive disciple!"

The Chinese pilgrim had finally found the omniscient master, the incomparable metaphysician who was to make known to him the ultimate secrets of the idealist systems. For in the person of Silabhadra Hiuan Tsang encountered the pure tradition of the Mahayana as handed down from master to pupil by a line of metaphysicians of genius. The founders of Mahayana idealism, Asanga and Vasubandhu, whose works date according to Sylvain Lévi and Junjiro Takakusu from the fifth century A.D.,[9] had had the logician Dignaga as their disciple; Dignaga had trained Dharmapala, head of the Nalanda school, who had died around 560, and Dharmapala had in turn trained Silabhadra. Silabhadra was thus in a position to make available to the Sino-Japanese world the entire heritage of Buddhist idealism, and the *Siddhi,* Hiuan Tsang's great philosophical treatise of which we shall have occasion to speak later, is none other than the *Summa* of this doctrine, the fruit of seven centuries of Indian thought.

Hiuan Tsang stayed with Silabhadra at Nalanda all through the rainy season of 637. He lodged at first in a two-story pavilion in the middle of a monastery built by Baladitya, the king of Magadha, and subsequently in a house that stood near the philosopher Dharmapala's

---

[9] Between approximately 420 and 500, by J. Takakusu's reckoning.

former residence. "Each month the king of Magadha sent him three measures of oil and daily the necessary quantity of butter, milk and other provisions. By order of the king a monk and a Brahmin accompanied him on a daily outing by carriage, on horseback or in a palanquin."

Hiuan Tsang interrupted his philosophical studies for a moment to pay a visit to Rajagriha (Rajgir), the ancient capital of Magadha, which lay to the north of Nalanda.[10] This city, we recall, had been the metropolis of the country in the time of the Buddha, who had often begged there during the reign of the pious king Bimbisara, his protector and friend. Now, long since abandoned in favor of Pataliputra, it was virtually a dead city, living only on its great memories of the Buddha.

Hiuan Tsang gives us a gloomy description of this historic city, the ruins of which were already disappearing beneath the luxuriant vegetation of tropical India. "Apparently sheer hills rise up on all four sides. Access from the west is by a narrow path; to the north stands a broad gate. Within (the old city) is another smaller city whose foundations extend over thirty *li*. Everywhere are groves of kanaka trees which bloom without interruption all the year round."

He was shown the place where Devadatta, the Buddhist Judas, and his accomplice Prince Ajatasatru, unworthy son of King Bimbisara, had set loose the infuriated elephant in the Buddha's path; subdued by the power of his gentleness, it had pulled up short before him and worshipped him. Hiuan Tsang visited the Vulture's Peak which lay to the northeast of Rajagriha and was one of the most picturesque spots in the whole region. "This mountain," notes his biographer, "possesses cool springs, extraordinary rock formations and trees covered with the richest foliage. In days of old when the Buddha was in this world he fre-

---

[10] In actual fact the Buddhist Rajagriha was not at Rajgir itself but slightly to the south, on the site of Kusagarapura, as Hiuan Tsang very correctly points out. I refer the reader to the excellent map and fine photographs published by Sir John Marshall in his article "Rajagriha and Its Remains," *Archaeological Survey of India; Report for 1905–6*, pp. 86–106.

quently made this mountain his dwelling-place and it was there that he taught his disciples the *Lotus of the Good Law,* the *Sutra of Transcendent Wisdom* and numerous other sutras." Also in the neighborhood of Rajagriha was the Bamboo Grove, one of the most celebrated monastic parks in the Buddhist scriptures. The holy man Kalanta or rather King Bimbisara himself had presented it to the Buddha, and it had become one of the latter's favorite places of residence. It was the very type of the monasteries described in the texts: "Not too far from the city nor too close to it, easy of access, not too busy by day, silent by night, apart from the press and tumult of men, places of retreat and sojourn suitable for meditation in solitude."

He was also shown the place near Rajagriha where King Bimbisara and all the people of the city had come out to meet the Blessed One, a scene that became so vivid to us when those reliefs at Sanchi and Bharhut were discovered.

Another of the sights of Rajagriha was the Tower of the Relics in which Ajatasatru, by then king of Magadha, had placed his share of the holy remains after the Master's cremation. Later Emperor Asoka had removed a part of its precious contents as part of his design to erect reliquary stupas in the four corners of India, but had left the rest in the

28. The sharing of the relics, from Gandhara. (*Musée Guimet*)

holy tower which, Hiuan Tsang assures us, still shone with an extra-ordinary luster.

A further monument in the vicinity evoked memories of a quite different sort. This was the stupa erected to a wild goose; a wild goose, though, who was none other than one of the incarnations of the Bodhi-sattva. Again we notice the close comradeship which Buddhism estab-lished between ourselves and our animal brothers. The legend, as Hiuan Tsang relates it, is a quite delightful one. Once upon a time, in a monastery in Rajagriha, the good monk who was charged with the stewardship of the monastery, having been unable to secure the neces-sary provisions, was in a state of great perplexity. As a flock of wild geese flew overhead he cried out with a laugh: "Today the monks' al-lowance is completely non-existent. Noble creatures, this is a circum-stance of which you must take note!" Hardly had these words left his lips than the leader of the flock came tumbling out of the clouds as if his wings had been cut and fell at the monk's feet. All the other monks came running at once: the bird was a Bodhisattva who had given his life for them. A tower was erected to contain the body and furnished with an inscription telling the story.

Rajagriha was of additional interest to the theologian because it had been the seat of the first Buddhist council. Immediately following the death of the Blessed One, so the tradition goes, his disciples had gathered there to establish the texts which were to form the collection known as the Three Baskets. The council opened with a scene in which the whole essence of early Buddhism is reflected. Kasyapa, who pre-sided, refused a seat on the council to Ananda, who was the Buddha's cousin and had been his favorite disciple but had been guilty of grave distraction. "Your faults, Ananda, are by no means effaced. Sully not the purity of this august assembly with your presence!" Ananda with-drew, covered in confusion. "During the night he strove with all the strength of his spirit to break the ties that bound him to the world and attain arhatship. Then he came back and knocked at the door. 'Are your ties all broken? Kasyapa asked him. 'They are all broken,'

Ananda replied. 'If that is so,' resumed Kasyapa, 'there is no need to open the door for you. Enter where you will . . .' Ananda then entered through a crack in the door, greeted the monk and kissed his feet. Kasyapa took him by the hand and said, 'I wanted to see you efface all your faults and obtain the fruit of the Bodhi. That, I must now tell you, is why I sent you away from the assembly. Do not resent this.' 'If my heart bore any resentment,' replied Ananda, 'how could I say that I have broken all my ties?' He bowed again to Kasyapa, expressing his gratitude, and took his seat on the council. Then, at the invitation of Kasyapa himself, he mounted the dais and recited the discourses of the Buddha. The entire assembly received them from his lips and wrote them down upon palm leaves."

After paying homage to these great memories Hiuan Tsang returned to the monastery at Nalanda. For the next year and more—fifteen months, according to the pilgrim's biographer—the saintly old Silabhadra expounded to him the texts of the idealist and mystical philosophy of the Yogachara school; he had already studied these in Kashmir but he was keen to go through them a second time in order to resolve all difficulties and dispel his doubts. His *Siddhi* treatise was to be the fruit of this instruction. He also studied the texts of Brahminical philosophy and perfected his knowledge of Sanskrit. His biographer even inserts at this point an extremely accurate summary of Sanskrit grammar.

Eventually, however, Hiuan Tsang had to tear himself away from this interlude of peace and scholarship at Nalanda, take up his stick again, and resume his pilgrimage along the arteries of India. On the way to Bengal he stopped for several days at the monastery of Kapota, which occupied a charming situation. "Two or three *li* from the monastery stands a solitary mountain the sides of which are formed into terraces and the top of which is adorned with rich vegetation, pools of clear water and scented flowers. This place being noted for its beauty spots, a large number of sacred temples have been erected there in which miracles and wonders of the most extraordinary kind frequently occur.

In a monastery occupying the center of the plateau stood a sandalwood statue of Avalokitesvara; the divine power of this statue arouses the very deepest respect."

The statue was the occasion of one of the most popular acts of devotion in the entire region. It was protected by a balustrade from which the faithful would pitch flowers at the Bodhisattva. Those who succeeded in lodging their garlands on the statue's hands considered their prayer granted. Hiuan Tsang's three wishes are indicative of the philosopher's purity of heart: "Firstly, after completing my studies in India I wish to return to my homeland. As a presage of the fulfillment of this wish I desire that these flowers shall lodge upon your venerable hands. Secondly, I wish one day to be born again in the heaven of the Blessed Gods and to serve Maitreya. If this wish is to be fulfilled I desire that these flowers shall lodge upon your two venerable arms. Thirdly, I Hiuan Tsang have doubts about myself and know not whether I am among the number of those gifted with Buddhahood. If I possess this nature and if, by practicing virtue, I too may become a Buddha, grant that these flowers lodge around your venerable neck." So saying he threw his garlands at the statue and was overjoyed to see them land where he had wished.

The summer of 638 Hiuan Tsang spent in the kingdom of Irana in West Bengal. Tradition had it that this was where the Buddha had converted a man-eating *yaksha* who subsequently became a saint. In Hiuan Tsang's day it possessed a dozen monasteries housing some four thousand religious, all of whom adhered to the Little Vehicle and, within the Little Vehicle, to the realist system of the Sarvastivadins. This was the doctrine which stood in greatest opposition to the idealist system professed by Hiuan Tsang. Nevertheless he placed himself under the local scholars in order to study their texts, and the time he devoted to receiving their teaching shows the extent to which his dogmatic preferences were tempered by liberalism.

The Chinese traveler then plunged into the very heart of present-day Bengal, a tropical region bordered to the south by a zone of dense, dark forests where roamed hundreds of herds of wild elephants noted for their size and strength as well as rhinoceroses and other wild animals of every sort. Hiuan Tsang remarked that the kings of Bengal possessed vast numbers of war elephants and that their hunters combed the forests all the year round to keep their stables stocked.

Crossing the Ganges, Hiuan Tsang pushed on into East Bengal (Pundravardhana and Karnasuvarna) and then turned down toward Samatata in the Ganges Delta, "a low-lying, damp region, abundantly fertile, growing prodigious quantities of flowers and fruit and inhabited by a small, black-skinned people whose character is harsh and cruel." Finally he reached the Bay of Bengal and the port of Tamralipti, the present-day Tamluk, intending to embark there for Ceylon.

CHAPTER 9

A Journey Around the Deccan at the Time of Ajanta

TAMRALIPTI, as we shall see from the memoirs of Yi Tsing, was the great emporium of India for the East Indies and Indochina trade. Hiuan Tsang evidently questioned closely the Bengali and Malay seamen calling in at the port for he was able to give a very precise account of the lands for which they embarked: "Sailing in a northeasterly direction up the coast one comes to the kingdom of Sri Ksetra," which is indeed the name of a former capital of Burma. "Farther to the east is the kingdom of Dvaravati"—and this certainly is the name of a former Mon kingdom in what is now Thailand, as discovered by Coedès and his pupils earlier in this century. "Farther to the east still is the kingdom of Isanapura," Isanapura having indeed been, before the foundation of Angkor, one of the capitals of Cambodia, possibly corresponding to the ruins of Sambor Prei Kuk excavated by Victor Golowbew. "Yet farther to the east is the kingdom of Maha Champa," the "great kingdom" of Champa, then at the height of its splendor, occupying as our traveler quite rightly states, the whole of the southern and even central seaboard of present-day Vietnam.

Of all the realms to which ships sailed from Tamralipti, however, the one which interested Hiuan Tsang most was Ceylon, the holy isle, headquarters of the Hinayana, and notably of the realist school of the Sarvastivadins, a knowledge of which was indispensable to any complete picture of Indian Buddhism.

Hiuan Tsang's biographer depicts him, as he waited here by the Bay of Bengal, dreaming of the relics in the ancient sanctuaries of that island in the south. In the warm tropical nights he allowed his thoughts to wander far out over the ocean's vastness, and he believed he could already see, shining like a star above the watery horizon, the Tooth of the Buddha. "Two hundred leagues to the south in Ceylon, every night when the sky is clear and cloudless, the precious diamond at the top of the Stupa of the Tooth projects its dazzling light; it can be seen from far off, and its shimmering form is like that of a planet suspended in the sky."

Some monks from the south, however, who were passing through Tamralipti, dissuaded Hiuan Tsang from taking ship. They pointed out to him that to get from Bengal to Ceylon there was absolutely no need to expose himself to the hazards of a long voyage; much better, they said, to proceed by land to the southeastern tip of the Carnatic from whence it was a mere three days by sea to the island.

Adopting this course, Hiuan Tsang set out to travel the whole length of the Deccan from north to south, following the eastern coast. He passed thus through Odradesa, corresponding to the present-day state of Orissa, and Kalinga or the Coast of the Circars, where he remarked upon the burning climate, tropical fertility and luxuriant vegetation. A notable feature of these forests was a breed of very black wild elephants which were particularly highly prized by the Indian rajas. The natives Hiuan Tsang describes as being dark-skinned, tall, of a blunt and savage character and possessing the most ferocious customs, and indeed even today the bulk of the population consists of aboriginal Munda and Telugu tribes who have been only superficially Indianized.

Despite the presence of a number of pockets of Buddhism the region was by and large deeply attached to the various different sects of Hinduism. Hiuan Tsang mentions the large number of Hindu temples in Orissa and Kalinga, all frequented by crowds of natives. The Vishnuite or Sivaite sanctuaries of Bhuvanesvar, Konarak and Puri certainly bear him out on this score with their forests of curved and bulging towers thrusting vigorously up into the sky. Although the majority of these Orissa temples were built between the ninth and twelfth centuries the temple of Muktesvara at Bhuvanesvar does appear to have existed in Hiuan Tsang's time. Can the pilgrim have had any idea that this blooming growth emerging from the tropical soil would one day smother the seed of Indian Buddhism?

Continuing his journey southwest Hiuan Tsang then visited Maha-Kosala, a region of forests and plains situated in the heart of the Deccan and inhabited by primitive tribes of Gonds, aboriginals "of a black skin, lofty in stature, harsh and violent in their customs and by nature bold and impetuous." This was the wild country where Rudyard Kipling was to set his *Jungle Books*. What was to become Mowgli's homeland, however, had in the second and third centuries A.D. witnessed the finest years of two of the greatest metaphysicians of Buddhism, Nagarjuna and Arya Deva, the former a native of a neighboring district (Berar) and the latter Sinhalese by birth. These two men had between them founded the subtle and influential critical philosophy of the Madhyamika. But then such contrasts were by no means unusual for this multifarious and yet homogeneous land of India, where brute barbarism and genius existed side by side.

Traveling through the vast forests irrigated by the Godavari river system the pilgrim came to the former kingdom of Andhra, corresponding more or less to the portion of Andhra Pradesh state lying between the Godavari and Krishna rivers. Only a few years before his visit the region had been conquered by a Chalukya clan from the Maratha region who had set up their capital at Vengipura. Correctly speaking it is this Chalukya state of Vengipura that Hiuan Tsang refers to as the kingdom of Andhra. The southeastern part of the former Andhra, together with Bezvada and Amaravati, cities situated on opposite banks of the lower Krishna, constituted in the seventh century the separate kingdom of Dhanakataka. Up-river from Amaravati on the same south bank of the Krishna were two other sites which have become famous in the history of archaeology, Goli and Nagarjunikonda. Jouveau-Dubreuil, the historian of southern India, has established that in Hiuan Tsang's time a Chola, i.e. Tamil clan had settled in this essentially Telugu area between the Krishna and the Pennar, so this is where we should place the Chola kingdom mentioned by the pilgrim.

Although Sanskrit culture was current everywhere among the upper classes of society, Hiuan Tsang was here entering the domain of the Telugu language, and he points out how this differed from the Indo-Aryan dialects. Andhra, however, had nonetheless played a role of considerable importance in the history of Buddhism. During the first few centuries A.D. when northern India was, both artistically and politically, under foreign domination by the Greeks and by the Scythians, Andhra had preserved intact not only its independence but also the Indian aesthetic tradition. Between the second and fourth centuries A.D. Amaravati, Goli and Nagarjunikonda had become covered with stupas whose sculptural decoration provided the link between the "primitive" Buddhist art of Sanchi and the output of the Gupta workshops of the fourth to the seventh centuries.

We are familiar with the work of this great school of sculpture from the pieces preserved in the Madras Museum and the British Museum, and since 1928 from the admirable collection of reliefs originating from this same region of Amaravati and dating from the second, third, fourth and fifth centuries on exhibition at the Musée Guimet, Paris. We have only to glance at these fine marbles with their scenes from Buddhist mythology lovingly chiseled by the old masters of Andhra to understand the eminent position occupied by this school in the formation of the Indian aesthetic. Buddhist works they certainly are, by virtue of the gentleness of their inspiration, but in their delicately pagan workmanship we also feel something of the perpetual youthfulness of the Hindu character. What freshness there is here, what spring-like verve, what feeling for the play of living forms! Such naive *joie de vivre,* and such voluptuousness, too, in the scene depicting the Bodhisattva's life of pleasure in the gynaeceum, faithfully modeled on the texts of the *Lalita Vistara* itself. "Musings of a mystical pagan" which show us how far the Buddhist doctrine of renunciation was able to adapt itself in practice to a mentality that was very like that of ancient Greece, and not the Greece of the tragedians and philosophers either but the Greece of the *Anthology.* Greco-Roman art, moreover, had itself not been entirely without influence upon the art of Amaravati, as might have been supposed from the commercial relations we know to have existed in Pliny's time between the "Andarae" and the classical world, and as was proved by the imperial coins and the Buddha with an emperor's face found in the region by Jouveau-Dubreuil.

Andhra had also done much for Buddhist culture in the field of doctrine. The illustrious philosopher Dignaga had compiled part of his treatises on logic and the critique of knowledge at Amaravati in the latter half of the fifth century, and eminent teachers professing the doctrines of the Great Vehicle were still to be found there in Hiuan Tsang's time. He spent the rainy season of 639 with them in Amaravati and Bezvada.

Leaving Amaravati and traveling southwest through Nagarjuni-konda and the Kurnul forest, then turning south and continuing by way of the Pennar basin, Hiuan Tsang came to the Carnatic, a tropical region with a hot, humid climate. This ancient Tamil region was the Dravidian land *par excellence,* "Dravida" the pilgrim calls it. It belonged at that time to the Pallava dynasty whose capital was Kancheepuram and whose principal port was Mahabalipuram or "Seven Pagodas," both cities situated on the north bank of the lower Palar.

The Pallava dynasty was one of the most glorious in Indian history. At this period, having taken over the hegemony of the eastern Deccan from the kings of Andhra, the dynasty was having to hold its own against another Deccanese house, that of the Chalukya of the Maratha region, who had just robbed it of the area lying between the lower reaches of the Krishna and Godavari rivers. Despite this loss the Pallava were yet to wreak terrible vengeance upon their Maratha rivals. In 642 the Pallava king Narasimhavarman (clearly a Vishnuite name) who reigned from 625 to 645 and was thus on the throne at the time of Hiuan Tsang's passage through his kingdom, conquered and killed the powerful king of Maharashtra, Pulakesin II.

At the same time the Pallava dynasty numbered among those that made the greatest contribution to Indian culture. They had created very early their own architectural style from which all the styles of the South were to spring, and Mahabalipuram was already, at the time of Hiuan Tsang's visit, beginning to fill up with the magnificent works which have made it one of the capital cities of Indian art. Victor Golowbew's fine work has made us familiar with this complex which is perhaps unique in India—the monolithic temples covering the entire area, foreshadowing their Cham and Indonesian replicas, the rocks carved into animal statuary of a magnificently bold and powerful naturalism, the entire cliffs worked as "frescoes" of stone in vast tableaux which in their composition, movement and lyricism surpassed anything produced in India up until that time.

Some of these masterpieces Hiuan Tsang probably saw, for among the Mahabalipuram sculptures two at least, those of the Yamapuri and Valadalandha caves with their splendid reliefs depicting the incarnations of Vishnu, date from the seventh century. The pilgrim may even have seen the beginning of work on the cliff of the "Descent of the Ganges" with its throng of gods, spirits, ascetics and animals adoring and worshipping the life-giving waters. And very likely this glorification, this deification of the forces of nature, whether good or evil (or rather all good because the expression of Life itself, and in any case here relatively humanized because the inspiration of the work was largely Vishnuite)—very likely this tremendous unfurling of vital lyricism did nothing but shock our apostle of Buddhist renunciation. Indeed it is not without interest for us to note that the idealist speculations of a Silabhadra or a Hiuan Tsang were contemporary with the outburst of naturalism that occurred at Mahabalipuram; such was the torrent of creative forces of lasting value whether in the spheres of aesthetics or metaphysics which swept irresistibly through the seventh-century India.

Hiuan Tsang appears to have spent quite some time in the Pallava country during 640. It was with particular emotion that he visited the city of Kancheepuram, for this had been the home of Dharmapala, one of the greatest metaphysicians of the Mahayana, who had died c. 560. Dharmapala, as we have seen, was the master of Silabhadra, the saintly old man who became the dean of the monastic university of Nalanda and who taught Hiuan Tsang. The pilgrim relates how Dharmapala had once refused the hand of a princess of Kancheepuram in order to embrace the religious life, a decision to which the literature of the Mahayana was to owe a number of its most celebrated works.

However, Hiuan Tsang's real reason for coming so far south had been his hope of being able to embark there for Ceylon, but here a grave disappointment awaited him. The holy isle, following a series of palace revolutions, lay in the grip of civil war and famine. Far from being able to make a peaceful retreat there as he had desired, he found Sinhalese monks arriving in Kancheepuram who had been obliged to flee for their lives, and who appear to have advised him against making the trip.

So, giving up his plans for visiting the island, Hiuan Tsang continued his journey around the Deccan. He calls the next country he passed through Malakottai, that is to say the Tamil region of Tanjore and Madura, which had been formerly and was again in the future to constitute the powerful empire of the Chola. It was a hot and humid region of tropical vegetation rich in precious essences, made wealthy by the pearl-fishing industry and by the spice trade with the East Indies. The Chola Empire, however, was not to enter the full phase of its development until very much later, during the tenth century. The people spoke Tamil and were very dark-skinned. The area had once been evangelized by Buddhism but had reverted almost immediately to the Hindu cults, particularly to Sivaism, although there were also a number of pockets of Jainism.

Having descended the Deccan by the Bay of Bengal coast, Hiuan Tsang now turned northward again to follow the coast of the Arabian Sea, passing through Konkan and the Maratha country, a region which at that time constituted the empire of the Chalukya.

The Chalukya, a vigorous warrior clan of Rajput origin who played a role of the first importance in the history of the period, had organized the Maratha people at the end of the sixth century. At the time of Hiuan Tsang's visit they dominated the whole of the northwestern Deccan. The pilgrim gives us an extraordinarily precise account of their empire. He notes the climate, which is relatively mild and temperate owing to the proximity of the sea and the height of the Ghats, and also the war-like character of the Maratha people, on which point his observations possessed an eternal validity; from Pulakesin II the Chalukya, conqueror of Emperor Harsha, to Sivaji the "Mountain Rat," who led the Marathas against the Mogul emperor in the seventeenth century: "The inhabitants are tall in stature and though their customs are plain and straightforward their character is proud and impulsive. They value (above all else) honor and duty and think nothing of death. Whoever does them a good service may count on their gratitude, but the man who has given them cause for offense will never escape their vengeance. If they are insulted they will immediately risk their lives to wipe out the affront. But should anyone in distress come in quest of their help they will scorn their own safety to provide it. When they have a score to settle they never fail to give their enemy prior warning. Then each man prepares his weapons and goes out to fight with his lance at the ready. In battle they pursue those that flee but never kill those that give themselves up. If one of their own generals has suffered defeat he is not punished physically in any way but is simply dressed in women's clothes, when in many cases, to escape dishonor, he kills himself." One of the most powerful warrior races of India, in short, and also one of the most chivalrous. Hiuan Tsang's brief tableau already contains a hint of the epic Rajput era of the Middle Ages and that of the Marathas in the eighteenth century.

The king of Maharashtra at that time was Pulakesin II who, as we have seen, had victoriously repulsed all the attacks of the northern Indian emperor Harsha. He was then at the height of his fame and in the final period of his reign, which had begun in 608 and was to end in 642. Hiuan Tsang, notwithstanding his admiration for Harsha, his co-religionist and later his protector and friend, did full justice to the merits of the Maratha sovereign. Hwui-li writes: "His vision is both wide and deep and the influence of his humanity and good works extends far and wide. His subjects serve him with a devotion that is absolute. . . . His preference runs to war-like pursuits and with him martial glory takes pride of place. In his realm, therefore, infantry and cavalry are fitted out with the very greatest care and the military regulations strictly observed." Hiuan Tsang himself writes: "The state is responsible for the maintenance of a corps of intrepid champions several hundred strong. When preparing to go into battle they drink a sufficient quantity of wine to intoxicate themselves, and then one of these men by himself, with a lance in his fist, is capable of defying ten thousand of the enemy. If, while he is in this condition, he should kill a man who happens to be in his way, the law takes no action against him. Each time the army goes into battle these bold fellows form the vanguard, marching to the sound of the drum." Furthermore the king of Maharashtra maintained a stable of several hundred of the most ferocious war-elephants. These too would be primed with strong drink just before the battle, and then, infuriated by the alcohol, they would be unleashed on the enemy in a massive charge that crushed everything in its path.

With a military organization like this King Pulakesin II was the most feared prince of the entire Indian peninsula. Harsha, the other potentate of India, emperor of the Gangetic world, could do nothing against him. "Today," writes Hiuan Tsang, "Emperor Harsha's armies are victorious from east to west. He holds distant peoples in subjection and causes neighboring nations to tremble with fear. The men of this kingdom alone have never submitted to him. Though he has several times led against them all the troops of the Five Indias he has never been able to overcome their resistance."

Hiuan Tsang may possibly have spent the rainy season of 641 at Nasik, Pulakesin's capital. At any rate, after describing the political state of the country, the Chinese pilgrim remarks upon the intellectual aptitude of the Maratha race as if with personal knowledge of what he is talking about, telling us that "the inhabitants are ardently given to study." The Chalukya dynasty professed the Hindu faith, being particularly attached to the Sivaite sects, but the two religions still co-existed peacefully and Hiuan Tsang speaks of there having been some two hundred Buddhist monasteries in Konkan and Maharashtra at the same time as several hundred Brahminical temples.

The progress of Indian archeology has made it possible for us to give names to some of these temples mentioned so briefly by Hiuan Tsang. And what magic those names hold for us! The capital of Maharashtra was Vatapi (modern Badami) where the majority of the temples, including the Malegitti Sivalaya, dated precisely from Hiuan Tsang's era (c. 625). The earliest masterpieces of Ellora farther to the north, such as the Cave of the Avatars, the Ravana ka Khai, the

29. From the Ajanta frescoes. (*Roger-Viollet*)

Dhumar Lena and the Ramesvara, also go back to the seventh century. No doubt the ideal represented here was singularly foreign to Hiuan Tsang's way of thinking, even more so than what he had seen recently at Mahabalipuram. Indeed nothing could be more opposed to the transcendent idealism of the Mahayana than these Sivaite beliefs, a tumultuous flood that carried with it every kind of monstrosity and every kind of cruelty as well as every nuance of the sweetness of Being; a desperate,

30. From the Ajanta frescoes. (*Roger-Viollet*)

superhuman, almost inhuman effort to attain the supreme mysticity by
means of a total and joyous acceptance of the whole of life.

And yet, to the unbiased eye, was it after all such a leap from the
Buddhist art of the Gupta workshops to the Hindu works of the
Maratha region? The triumphant Sivas of the caves of Ellora or Elephanta are basically, are they not, very similar to the Bodhisattvas we
know from the paintings of Ajanta and the sculptures of Borobudur?

The bodies are as harmonious, as pure and as smooth as those of the earlier works, only here they are free of any idea of renunciation; they have emerged from their disenchanted meditations and have plunged into the very heart of things, into the alternately mystical and sensual intoxication of life.

The traveler to the Maratha country might also find there a number of masterpieces of Buddhist art. Near Kalyan, one of the chief towns of the region, could be seen several monuments of the earliest Sunga and Andhar schools such as the vihara (monastery) at Bhaja and the chaitya (shrine) at Bedsa, which went back to the second century B.C., or the great chaitya at Karli, dating probably from the beginning of the Christian era. But above all in the heart of King Pulakesin's realm there were the famous catacombs of Ajanta with their underground monasteries and their immortal frescoes. Strangely enough Hiuan Tsang makes no mention of these sanctuaries. And yet it was in his time, during the first half of the seventh century, that the finest frescoes at Ajanta, those of Caves I and II, were executed. But what does his silence matter? The important thing in our opinion is the profound harmony which exists between the impassioned idealism to which his work bears witness and the supernatural apparitions which illuminate the walls of Ajanta. The vision which the Bodhisattva Mañjusri was shortly afterward to grant the pilgrim is surely comparable to that which visitors to Ajanta experience before the "Bodhisattva of the Blue Lotus"—who may in fact be Mañjusri himself—that slightly stooping figure with the crown of solid gold, a figure of such ardent mysticity that it has been compared to Leonardo's drawing of Christ of the "Last Supper." Indeed it is while looking at Victor Golowbew's excellent reproductions[1] of these tender and wonderful images, the fruit of Indian Buddhism's declining years in this sequestered spot in the heart of the Maratha country, that we come closest to evoking the ideals of Hiuan Tsang's contemporaries, the object of their burning faith and the substance of their dream.

[1] V. Golowbew, *Ajanta: les peintures de la première grotte*, 1926.

Leaving Maharashtra and crossing the Narmada Hiuan Tsang stopped for a few days at Broach, the Barygaza of Greek geographers, which as he observes was an important commercial port. Indeed Barygaza is described by Greek and Byzantine writers as having been the principal depot for traffic between the Indian world and the province of Egypt.

Nor did Hiuan Tsang miss visiting Malwa farther to the north, one of the most civilized and cultured countries in the whole of India and one which occupied an honored place in the history of Sanskrit literature. Hiuan Tsang rightly compares it with Magadha in this respect. Malwa was above all the erstwhile home of Kalidasa, possibly the greatest of Sanskrit poets, author of *The Recognition of Shakuntala* and so many immortal dramas. His fame must still at this time have been at its height for he had lived in the fifth century, only a century and a half before.

To the west Malwa bordered on the kingdom of Valabhi in the Kathiawar Peninsula. Valabhi and the contiguous region of Saurashtra (Surat) depended for their livelihood upon maritime trade with the Persian Gulf and the eastern Mediterranean. Hwui-li writes: "Large quantities of precious merchandise from foreign lands are to be found in the country. There are more than a hundred families whose fortune exceeds a million ounces of silver." From the beginning of the sixth century until the last quarter of the eighth this rich land belonged to the energetic Maitraka dynasty, remembered for their beautiful coinage. Between 633 and 640 the king of Valabhi had had to acknowledge the suzerainty of Emperor Harsha, and at the time of Hiuan Tsang's visit the reigning monarch Dhruvasena openly involved himself in Harsha's political system by becoming his son-in-law. Although the Valabhi dynasty had been Hindu up until then Dhruvasena, on the example of Harsha, had adopted the Buddhist faith. "Each year," records Hiuan Tsang, "he holds a great seven-day assembly at which he distributes to the multitude of religious the most exquisite dishes, the Three Garments, medicines, the Seven Precious Things and jewels of the greatest value. He respects the virtuous and honors the wise. The religious of distant lands are particularly favored with his homage and respect."

During his stay in this maritime region Hiuan Tsang was able to gather a certain amount of information about Persia, and although he himself never traveled there his notes on the country are of great interest when we consider that they were written on the very eve of the collapse of the Sassanid Empire. He particularly mentions the importance of irrigation for the means of life on that high and partly desert plateau, and anyone who has traveled between Teheran and Isphahan and Shiraz, following the underground canals which are punctuated at intervals by the series of ancient royal wells, will be struck by the rightness of his observation. Moreover does not the *Avesta,* the sacred book of ancient Persia, place the upkeep of the irrigation canals among the number of good works? Hiuan Tsang also mentions the high quality of Persian textiles: "They are skilled in weaving figured silk and other fabrics as well as various kinds of carpet." And such indeed remained, from Sassanian times up until the present century, the principal industry of Persia.

Furthermore, although pilgrims from China never crossed the frontiers of the Persian Empire they can hardly have helped observing during the course of their travels across central Asia such rich Persian materials as those of which the von Le Coq expedition found some remains, and which so clearly dated from the Sassanian period. Had the fancy taken them to penetrate to the heart of Persia itself they would have discovered the source of the decorative themes that were current in the Kuchean region. They might even have found, on the robe of the equestrian Khosrau II at Taq-e Bostan near Kirmanshah, that heraldic bird which occurred so often on the brocades of Kucha and Turfan.

On the subject of commerce Hiuan Tsang also mentions, as every subsequent traveler was to mention, the excellence of Persian horses and camels. He alludes to the beauty of the Persian silver coinage, examples of which he clearly saw himself, and no numismatist who has ever handled those marvelous coins minted by Khosrau and Shapur will fail to echo his enthusiasm. Marriages between siblings, as encouraged by Zoroastrianism, naturally provoked him to some sharp criticism. He was equally shocked by the Zoroastrian custom of exposing corpses to the vultures on the "towers of silence": "When a man dies his body is dumped on the refuse-heap." The *T'ang Shu* likewise observes: "Whenever anyone dies they are abandoned in the mountains," adding that "the vultures of Persia are so enormous as to be capable of devouring sheep."

Although the state religion was Zoroastrianism the Sassanian Empire was fairly tolerant of Buddhism, at least in the Afghan borderlands, as it was also of Nestorianism in the Mesopotamian region. Hiuan Tsang remarks that there were two or three Buddhist monasteries in Persia numbering several hundred religious of the Hinayana school of the Sarvastivadins. This assertion was confirmed by discoveries made in Afghanistan earlier in this century. On the Bamian frescoes of the third to the fifth centuries uncovered by André Godard and his wife we find, against a background of Buddhist inspiration, features which are purely Sassanian. And in the astonishing spectacle of a bearded and be-crowned Sassanid monarch, a veritable Shapur or Khosrau indeed, rubbing shoulders in these frescoes with Buddhist monks and a Gandharan Buddha, there is surely occasion to speak of a kind of nascent Sassano-Buddhist school, following in the wake of the Greco-Buddhist schools of the past. Indeed a little distance away at Dokhtar-e Noshirwan, Hackin was to find other frescoes which were purely Sassanian, royal frescoes by the hand of some Indian Buddhist artist—irrefutable proof of the good relations existing between the Zoroastrian empire and the Indian communities of these Afghan marchlands which had lately become attached to the Sassanian realm. Moreover this same Indian influence was to be found as far as the west of Sassanian Persia on Khosrau's hunting-elephants at Taq-e Bostan.

From the political point of view Persia was the scene of profound upheavals at the time of Hiuan Tsang's pilgrimage.

While in the Far East the T'ang dynasty was extending its power as far as the T'ien Shan and the Pamirs, recreating the great Chinese Empire of the Han emperors, in Persia the Sassanid dynasty under Khosrau II (590–628) had for a time almost succeeded in recreating the mighty Achaemenid Empire of former days. Between 611 and 616 the Persian armies had conquered Syria, Egypt and Asia Minor, and in 626 they had even laid siege to Constantinople. In the following year, however, a counterattack by the Byzantine emperor Heraclius in the Caucasus and Assyria had broken Khosrau's power. The exhausted empire had then been assaulted on its southwestern flank by the invading Arabs. An initial victory at Qadisiya in 636 had given the Arabs the plains of Mesopotamia, including the Persian capital Ctesiphon which they had occupied the year after. A second victory at Nehawend in 642 brought them the Iranian plateau itself from Zagros to Khorassan. The last of the Sassanids, Yazdegerd III, fled to Merv on the frontiers of Transoxiania, vainly imploring the assistance of the Chinese. He was to die in 652 without getting the help he had hoped for; Persia was too far off for the T'ang armies to carry their banner thither, though the T'ang court did at least offer hospitality to the exiled Sassanids. Such was the dismal end of a dynasty which for four centuries had trimmed the fortunes of Rome and restored for a time the glory of Darius and Artaxerxes.

What a momentous historical force was Islam, whose shattering intervention was to change the whole basis of Middle Eastern culture. We can be glad that on the very eve of the great upheaval there was a witness of the caliber of Hiuan Tsang to give us an account of this doomed civilization.

CHAPTER 10

Nalanda, the Monastic City

Hiuan tsang pushed on west as far as the middle reaches of the Indus. Then, after visiting Sindh and Multan, he returned to Magadha for a further stay at Nalanda, which was to prove as fruitful as the first. His tour of the Holy Places now completed, he could devote the rest of his time to seeking instruction from the masters of Indian philosophy. He found out that a learned monk of the Sarvastivadin school named Prajnabhadra was living in another monastery about twenty-five miles from Nalanda, and he spent two months with him. An even more famous Buddhist hermit by the name of Jayasena was also living near Nalanda, on Mount Yashtivana Giri. He was one of the most remarkable philosophers of the Mahayana. Although he had also studied under Silabhadra, Jayasena had been trained principally by Sthiramati, the leader of another branch of the idealist school which had remained closer to the critical philosophy of the Madhyamika. As he appears to us through the notes of Hiuan Tsang and his biographer, he was a philosopher of a truly eclectic breadth of knowledge, a kind of encyclopedist for whom the *Vedas,* Indian science and even the teachings of Hinduism itself held no secrets. His hermitage, which was thronged with several hundred pupils, was one of those "schools of wisdom" such as have always existed in India. Hiuan Tsang spent many months with him, studying the idealist texts.

It was here, according to the account of Hiuan Tsang's disciple, that a curious "revelation" took place. The Master of the Law was transported in a dream back to the monastery of Nalanda. "The cells were empty and deserted and the foul and noisome courts full of buffaloes that had been tied up there. Neither monks nor novices were anywhere to be seen. . . . The Master of the Law entered, and there he saw on the fourth story of one of the courts a figure who was of the color of gold and whose grave and solemn face shone with a bright light." The Bodhisattva Mañjusri, for it was he, indicated the horizon, where the pilgrim saw an immense fire devouring whole towns and villages. In a loud voice he prophesied the forthcoming death of Emperor Harsha, lord of northern India, and the wars and revolutions into which the country would be plunged by this catastrophe.

Not long afterward Hiuan Tsang was favored with another supernatural vision. He had returned to Gaya on a pilgrimage to the Bodhi Tree to celebrate the feast of the Relics of the Buddha, and one night he saw the stupa in which they were exhibited ablaze with light, while from the top there issued an immense flame which reached as high as the sky. "Heaven and earth were lit as if by the broad light of day. The stars and the moon could no longer be seen, and the precinct of the monastery was filled with a mild and perfumed breeze. After a few moments this brilliant light began gradually to diminish, leaving heaven and earth in darkness once more as the stars recovered their former brightness."

It was in this atmosphere of mysticism that the pilgrim continued his metaphysical researches, and at this elevated level the debates of the schools sometimes seemed to him to be rather unreal. The thinkers of the Mahayana were, as we know, divided between two systems: on the one hand there was the school, at once idealist and mystical (Vijñana-vara and Yogachara), to which Silabhadra adhered and which went back to the two great fifth-century metaphysicians Asanga and Vasu-bandhu; and on the other hand there was the school founded by Nagarjuna and known as the Madhyamika or Middle Path school which, despite its modest name, practiced a critical philosophy of a very much more radical kind. Though it is undoubtedly true that the two systems had their origin in the same principles—the preliminary critique of the data of pure reason and the data of experience with, to counter-balance speculative negations, an affective mysticism of the most consoling efficacy—Nagarjuna and his pupils, confining them-selves to this position, arrived at a kind of Buddhist Kantianism; whereas the disciples of Asanga and Vasubandhu succeeded, under the cloak of absolute idealism, in adapting the old master's prolegomena and achieving an almost complete rehabilitation of metaphysics.

Hiuan Tsang, as we know from his biographer, was unable to keep out of these discussions; he was even obliged to take sides. It appears, however, as though his ambition at this stage in his career was to recon-cile these two great systems within a more comprehensive Mahayana eclecticism. Such at any rate was the attitude he took against a saintly monk by the name of Simharasmi who professed the teachings of Nagarjuna and opposed the idealism of the Yogachara. In particular Simharasmi rejected the notion of *bhutatathata,* or "absolute nature," of which we shall have occasion to speak later and which was a kind of crown which the idealists placed upon the critical philosophy of the Madhyamika. "The Master of the Law," writes his biographer, "had studied the treatises of Nagarjuna and moreover possessed an excellent knowledge of the Yogachara. He felt that the holy men who had com-posed these various works had each followed his own particular ideas without however being in any way opposed to the others. He held that if it was not possible to harmonize them perfectly that did not give one any right to consider them as being mutually contradictory. The fault must lie with the commentators. These divergencies of opinion are without importance as regards faith." Hiuan Tsang composed then and there a treatise "On the Concord of Principles" (*Hwui-tsung-lun*) which was greeted with approval by the Nalanda masters.

The Master of the Law reserved his polemical shafts for the Buddhists of the Little Vehicle or Lesser Path, as the men of the Mahayana termed those rather backward pietists who refused to crown Buddhism with a philosophy but limited their entire effort to the study of monastic discipline. Nor did these latter spare their attacks against the adherents of the Great Vehicle. The Hinayana monks of Orissa, in an address to Emperor Harsha, accused the monks of Nalanda point-blank of being nihilists who believed in *sunyata* or "universal emptiness" and were Buddhist in no more than name. As we shall see, the efforts of idealist metaphysicians of Hiuan Tsang's school consisted precisely in absolving the Mahayana of this charge and in gradually correcting the negative content of the Madhyamika by means of metaphysical and mystical data of a sort that were capable of satisfying mind and heart.

Hiuan Tsang was particularly engaged at Nalanda in combatting the various Brahminical schools.

At that time the two principal Hindu philosophical systems opposed to Buddhism were the Vaiseshika and the Samkhya. The Vaiseshika was a realist system, utterly direct and immediate in its realism, based upon the acceptance as such of the data of experience and awareness; an atomic philosophy, in short, with an overlay of monadology. The Samkhya was a metaphysical poem of a very much more powerful kind, and based on very much more elaborate data; but it too implied a dualism of mind and nature. Such doctrines stood in total opposition to the acosmic idealism of Yogachara Buddhism, which refuted the objective existence of matter no less vigorously than it refuted the substantial existence of the self. Hiuan Tsang consequently battled against them without mercy, as he did against the Jainist system.

As far as the Jains were concerned the picture was the same: nothing could be more opposed to the phenomenist and monist idealism of Hiuan Tsang than their atheistical monadology. But what exasperated the pilgrim most was the kind of caricature of Buddhism which, to his mind, Jainism represented. Indeed, ever since the Buddha's time Buddhism and Jainism had been two warring brothers. "These sectaries," writes Hiuan Tsang, "practice severe austerities. Day and night they manifest the most ardent zeal without taking so much as a moment's repose. The law expounded by their founder (Mahavira) was in large part ransacked from the books of the Buddha, which he took as his guide for the establishment of his rules and precepts. In their religious exercises and observances they follow the rule of Buddhist monks virtually in its entirety. Only they retain some hair upon the head and furthermore go naked. If they should happen to wear clothes these are distinguished by being uniformly white in color. The statue of their master resembles and is a kind of usurpation of that of the Buddha."

We find recalled in Hiuan Tsang's biography a discussion in which the pilgrim sought to destroy *en bloc* all the enemy doctrines, both Hindu and Jain, by comparing them one with another. By means of his dialectical virtuosity he demonstrated in particular the divergencies between the Samkhya and the Vaiseshika, the two great Brahminical philosophic systems then in force. He then proceeded to mock the extravagant asceticism of the various sects who reduced religion to a matter of certain peculiarities of dress and practice. "Some ascetics rub their bodies with ash under the impression that they are thereby performing a work of great merit. Their skin is a livid white all over, like a cat that has been sleeping in the hearth. The Jains believe they distinguish themselves by leaving their bodies entirely unclothed, and they make a virtue of plucking out their hair. Their skin is full of cracks and their feet are chapped and calloused; in appearance they resemble those rotten trees that stand near rivers." The peculiarities of Hindu asceticism proper came in for all the mockery of which Chinese positivism was capable: "Some wear a feather from a peacock's tail, others cover their bodies with pads made of plaited grass, and there are others again who pluck out their hair and cut their moustaches, or who wear bushy side-whiskers and tie their hair up on top of their heads." Lastly the follies and excesses of Sivaism were passed under review: "Others there are who thread themselves strings of the bones of skulls which they place upon their heads or hang around their necks; they live in holes in the rock like the yakshas who haunt tombs. Some go to the length of wearing garments soiled with dung and eating filth and putrid meat. They are as foul and disgusting as swine wallowing in a sewer. And yet you Hindus regard such things as acts of virtue! Are they not rather the height of madness and stupidity?"

The speech is particularly interesting because it reveals in its full light the attitude of Buddhist wisdom, so moderate, humorous and humane as occasionally to evoke the turn of mind of a Socrates or Plutarch when faced with the follies of Brahminical yogism. Had not the Buddha himself in the Sermon of Benares accorded the same censure to mortification as to voluptuousness? Indeed one has only to think of all the excesses and all the monstrosities of unbalanced asceticism and sensuality to which the disappearance of Buddhism was to give free reign in India in order to understand how much the Indian mind lost by that disappearance. But this speech attributed to Hiuan Tsang reveals something else as well. For all his unqualified adherence to the religion of Sakyamuni the pilgrim nevertheless retained the habits of thought inculcated by a Chinese education—an innate positivism, sound good sense, and the religion of social decorum—and there can be no doubt that it was this ancient Confucian foundation that was revolted by the excesses of Hindu mysticism.

There is a further passage in the *Life of Hiuan Tsang* which is even more revealing of the extent to which the Master of the Law retained, in this capital of Indian Buddhism, his Confucian citizenship.

The monks of Nalanda believed him to be so much one of themselves that they tried to dissuade him from returning to China: "India," they told him, "is where the Buddha was born, and though he has now left this earth, here the traces of his sacred presence remain. To visit them one by one, worship before them and sing his praises will crown your life with happiness. Why did you come here only to forsake us so abruptly? Furthermore China is a barbarian land, treating religious and the faith with scorn. For that reason the Buddha did not desire to be born there. The minds of the inhabitants are narrow and deeply tainted with falsehood, which is why the (Indian) saints and sages have never been there. . . ."

Hiuan Tsang's reply, as rendered by his biographer's brush, is an outburst of national pride. First of all he quite rightly protests in the name of Buddhist charity: "The Buddha laid down his teaching that it should spread to all lands. What man would partake of it alone and abandon all those whom it has not yet reached?" Then comes a protestation of imperial pride which represents the *ego sum civis sinicus* of this subject of T'ai-tsung and the great T'ang dynasty: "In our realm the magistrates are stern and the laws respectfully observed. The prince is distinguished by the highest virtue and his subjects by their loyalty; fathers by their ready affection and sons by their ready obedience." This is pure Confucian doctrine, the state religion of filial piety. It is followed by a passage in praise of Confucian traditionalism, humanitarianism and humanism: "(In our land) humanity and justice are respected and the highest honor is accorded to the aged and wise. Nor is that all, for science holds no mysteries for them. Their perspicacity equals that of the Spirits; they take the heavens as their model and know how to calculate the movements of the Five Brightnesses. They have invented all manner of instruments, divided up the seasons of the year, and discovered the hidden properties of the six tones and of music. Hence their ability to drive out or tame wild animals, reach and bring down the demons and the Spirits, calm the opposing influences of the Yin and Yang and win peace and happiness for all creatures."

Doubtless this apostrophe, which was composed some time afterward by an official panegyrist, was designed to include everything calculated to satisfy Chinese pride. It is a splendid piece of oratory nonetheless. How forcefully it contrasts the organization, mental precision and scientific outlook of the Chinese with the political ineptitude and pragmatic indifference of the people of India.

Returning then to the question of religion, Hiuan Tsang points out the immense progress accomplished by Chinese Buddhism: "Ever since the Law bequeathed by the Buddha made its entry into China all men respect the Mahayana and their lights are as pure as clear water; their virtue spreads about them like a perfumed cloud; lovingly they go about doing good and have no other wish than to attain by means of meritorious deeds the six steps of perfection. Folding their arms in postures of profound meditation they aspire to reach the Three Bodies of Buddhahood. If of old the Blessed One came down to earth it was for no other reason than himself to spread the beneficial influences of the Law. I have had the good fortune to hear his wonderful words and to see with my own eyes his golden face. How can you say that this country is to be scorned because it was never visited by the Buddha?"

The writer has Hiuan Tsang end his speech with a kind of Platonic allegory: "Why does the sun traverse the world? To dispel the shadows. Precisely for that very reason do I wish to return to my own country."

CHAPTER II

Harsha, the Poet King

The victories won by Hiuan Tsang in his philosophical and religious controversies had attracted the attention of a number of Indian potentates. It is a well-known fact that Indians, from the haughtiest *raja* to the humblest outcast, have always been passionately fond of the subtleties of doctrine and religious speculation. The king of Kamarupa (i.e., Assam) asked him to come and spend a few weeks at his court before returning to China.

This Bhaskara Kumara, king of Assam, was a most cultured ruler. Although he professed Hinduism himself, he would have been deeply disappointed had a Buddhist scholar of the caliber of Hiuan Tsang departed before he had had a chance to converse with him. Indeed a few years later, after meeting the Chinese ambassador Li Yi-piao, he was to push his philosophical inquisitiveness so far as to ask the latter for a Sanskrit translation of the Taoist canon. There could be no better illustration of the religious syncretism of the period and the philosophical openness of the Indian mind before the triumph of Hinduism and the invasion of Islam.

Hiuan Tsang's notes on Assam are remarkably accurate. It is a land of lakes and rivers, abundantly watered by the Brahmaputra which swallows up the monsoon winds in its broad valley; physically and ethnographically it belongs not so much to India as to neighboring Indochina. "The terrain is low-lying and humid. The towns are surrounded by rivers, lakes and ponds. The bread tree and the coconut palm flourish admirably. The people are small, dark-skinned, and of a wild and violent disposition. They worship spirits and believe not in the Law of the Buddha. Consequently there has never been built in this kingdom, from its origin until today, a single monastery for religious. The few true believers encountered by chance confine themselves to thinking upon the Buddha in the privacy of their own hearts. There are some hundred Brahminical temples in the country. The present king is descended from the god Vishnu; he is of the caste of the Brahmins and his name is Bhaskara Varma, 'Breast-plate of the Sun.' He is passionately given to study. Gifted men from distant lands are attracted by his fame and love to journey up and down his lands. Although he does not believe in the Law of the Buddha he treats religious with great respect."

Farther to the east, as Hiuan Tsang goes on to say, the country consists of no more than a succession of mountains and hills with no towns of any note. There it bordered on the regions inhabited by the aborigines of southwest China, the Man and Lolo. The pilgrim learned from some natives that the Chinese province of Ssu-ch'uan was only two months' journey away. He may have thought of returning home that way, but this mountainous tract of country, deeply scored from north to south by the valleys of the upper Salween and the tributaries of the Yangtze, would have been far too difficult to cross. Moreover the region was ridden with malaria and on its southeast versant ravaged by herds of wild elephants. Hiuan Tsang consequently did not follow up the temptation to gain his nearby homeland by this dangerous route, but answered instead the summons he had received from Emperor Harsha to visit him on the Ganges.

Harsha, surnamed Siladitya or "Sun of Virtue," ruled as we have seen over practically the whole of northern India from the Brahmaputra to Gujarat and the Vindhya Mountains. He had transferred his capital from Thanesar to Kannauj and either by force of arms or by the simple prestige of his authority he had succeeded in making the most ancient dynasties acknowledge his suzerainty, dynasties like that of Assam, the last of the Guptas, the Maukharis of Magadha, and the Maitrakas of Valabhi. At the same time Harsha was one of the finest scholars of his century. His name occupies an honored place in Sanskrit literature. He had attracted to his court a pleiad of writers such as the poet Mayura and the romance-writer Bana. To the latter we owe that epic and romantic history of his master, the *Harshacharita,* which unfortunately remains incomplete. Harsha was himself a poet and several Sanskrit dramas are commonly attributed to him, notably the *Priyadarsika,* the *Ratnavali* and the *Nagananda.*

Above all Harsha was the last of the great Buddhist sovereigns to reign in India. In spite of the material prosperity and blossoming of intellect to which Hiuan Tsang testifies, Buddhism was undeniably on the decline in India in favor of a still peaceful but nonetheless persistent Brahminical recovery. The Bengali emperors of the Gupta dynasty who had ruled over almost the whole of India during the fourth and fifth centuries had already tended toward Hinduism; for all their toleration of an even sympathy toward Buddhism the majority of them had adhered for preference to the Vishnuite sects. Then it had been simply a question of personal tendencies which the philosophical syncretism and religious eclecticism of the time had still been able to neutralize. But the period of brutal persecution was about to begin.

As early as the first quarter of the sixth century the Hun chieftain Mihirakula had directed a terrible persecution against the followers of

Sakyamuni in the northwest, and the monasteries of the Punjab still bore the marks of his fury. Even more recently, in the early years of the seventh century, a king of Gaur or Karnasuvarna in Bengal by the name of Sasanka, an aggressive Sivaite, had gone so far as to lay sacrilegious hands on the Bodhi Tree at Gaya, daring to remove the statue of the Buddha from this forever venerable site and replace it with one of Siva. The king of Magadha, Purnavarman, had had great difficulty in repairing the damage occasioned by this impious assault.[1] In the face of such symptoms, heralding as they did only too clearly the mighty storm beneath which Buddhism was to succumb a century and a half later, the protection of a conqueror like Harsha was of inestimable value to Sakyamuni's church.

Harsha of course never broke with official Brahminism nor even with the Hindu sects, any more than did any other Indian ruler of his day. Hiuan Tsang depicts him showering the Brahmins with gifts, and in his own works he declared himself a worshipper of Siva; moreover his confidant and friend, the romance-writer Bana, was a Brahmin by caste and a Hindu by belief. But the monarch's personal preference clearly lay with Buddhism and, within Buddhism, the school of the Mahayana. And even within the Mahayana his sympathies appear to have run to Yogachara idealism as taught in the monasteries of Nalanda and as professed by Hiuan Tsang. It is not surprising then, that he and the latter got on so well together. Indeed in the few weeks that they were to spend together a close friendship was to form between the Indian *maharaja* and the pilgrim from China.

Harsha, already somewhat impatient with the dilatoriness of his

---

[1] Th. Bloch is of the opinion that Sasanka's assault against the Bodhi Tree does not necessarily imply any suggestion of persecution, just as Purnavarman did not have to be a Buddhist to carry out his work of restoration. The Gaya pilgrimage represented an important source of income for the king of the region and it is possible that the Bengali prince, being hostile to Purnavarman, simply wished to harm him by stemming the flood of pilgrims, and that Purnavarman's only object in restoring the Tree was a financial one. See Th. Bloch, "Notes on Bodh Gaya" in *Archaeological Survey of India, Report for 1908–9*, pp. 140–1. However it should not be forgotten that, according to Hiuan Tsang's (contemporary) account, Sasanka had attempted to replace the statue of the Buddha by one of Siva. This would certainly seem to indicate a war of religions.

vassal, ordered the king of Assam to accompany Hiuan Tsang on his visit. The king of Assam's procession, consisting of twenty thousand elephants and thirty thousand boats, sailed up the Ganges as far as "Kajughira" (Kankjol?), the site of Harsha's camp. Night had just fallen as they reached this rendezvous, but Harsha had no desire to wait until next day to pay his respects to the Master of the Law. "Messengers came to tell Hiuan Tsang and his companion, the king of Assam, that thousands of torches had been sighted in the middle of the river and the sound of drums could be heard. The king of Assam immediately called for torches and went out to meet him (Harsha) with his principal officers." It was indeed the Indian emperor who was approaching for, as Hiuan Tsang tells us, whenever he moved about he had a hundred drummers go before him with metal drums and sound the beat at each step. This privilege was reserved to Harsha alone and none of the vassal kings had the right to do the same.

As soon as Harsha arrived he bowed low before the Master of the Law and respectfully kissed his feet. He then scattered flowers before him and, gazing at him with a sort of ecstasy, proceeded to address him in terms of unbounded praise. When asked why he had not come sooner in reply to the emperor's invitation Hiuan Tsang answered with the lofty freedom of the sage that he had been unable to do so, having been occupied at the time in studying a treatise on Yogachara philosophy. In reply to another of Harsha's questions the chronicler attributes to Hiuan Tsang this vibrant eulogy of the Chinese emperor T'ai-tsung: "At the time of his coming heaven and earth were in a state of the most violent agitation; the people had no master, corpses were heaped up in the fields and the rivers and canals were awash with blood; by night strange stars threw down their baleful light; by day deadly vapors gathered and hung in the air; the banks of the Three Rivers were laid waste by the voracious onslaughts of the wild boar and the Four Seas (the Celestial Empire) were infested with venomous snakes. Then the imperial prince (Li Shih-min, the future T'ai-tsung) obeyed the commands of Heaven. Filled with noble ardor he deployed his invincible forces;

wielding now axe and now lance he delivered the provinces from tur-
moil and restored peace to the world. . . ."

Harsha eagerly studied the treatises which Hiuan Tsang had recently written in refutation of the opponents of the Mahayana, both
Hinayana and Hindu. The emperor's sister, who was probably the
former queen of Kannauj, Rajyasri, robbed of her husband by Sasanka's treachery, was equally devoted to the Mahayana. This princess
shared power with Harsha, sitting behind him on the occasion of the
second audience granted to Hiuan Tsang, and she also enthusiastically
congratulated the Master of the Law on his assaults against the Little
Vehicle. Harsha then decided to hold an enormous philosophical joust-
ing match at which Hiuan Tsang might "dispel the blindness" of the
"heretics" of the Hinayana and "shatter the overweening pride" of the
Brahmins and adherents of the Hindu sects.

This assembly was convened at Kannauj itself, Harsha's capital.
Harsha and Hiuan Tsang traveled up the Ganges "amidst a great forest
of blossoming trees" at the very beginning of 643.

The procession was headed by the two kings, with their four army
corps forming an impressive escort. Some traveled in boats and others,
mounted on elephants, marched up the bank. The column advanced to
the sound of drums, conches, flutes and guitars. The whole country and
all the vassal kingdoms hurried to keep this rendezvous with their
suzerain. "There came eighteen kings from central India, three thousand religious versed in the Great and Little Vehicles, two thousand
Brahmins and Jains and some thousand religious from the monastery
of Nalanda. All these sages, who were as renowned for their vast
knowledge as for the wealth and facility of their eloquence, had re-
sponded with eagerness to the invitation to this assembly. Each was
accompanied by a large retinue. Some came riding upon elephants and
others were borne in palanquins; banners and standards surrounded
each group. Gradually the throng grew more and more numerous as
the clouds gathered and unfolded in the sky, filling the space of several
leagues. The king had had two enormous thatched buildings erected in

advance at the place of assembly; these were to house the statue of the Buddha and to receive the multitude of attending religious." Harsha's traveling tent was set up at a distance of five *li* to the west of this point.

On the first day Harsha had a gold statue of the Buddha borne ceremoniously across the plain on a costly dais on the back of a large elephant. He himself walked on the right of the statue, carrying a white fly-whisk and dressed as the god Indra, while the king of Assam, bearing a parasol of costly material, walked on the left dressed as Brahma. "Both wore divine crowns upon their heads from which hung garlands of flowers and ribbons laden with precious stones. Two further large elephants, also decorated, followed behind the Buddha bearing baskets of rare flowers which were scattered at every step." A hundred elephants ridden by musicians beating drums went before and after the statue.

The Master of the Law occupied a place in the front rank of the royal procession. "He and the palace officials," writes his biographer, "were each invited to mount a large elephant and ride in line behind the king. Then came three hundred large elephants assigned to the *rajas,* ministers and religious of the other kingdoms; these had to line the sides of the route and sing praises as they marched. Preparations for the procession began at dawn. The king (Harsha) led the way in person from his traveling tent to the place of assembly. Arriving at the gate of the enclosure he ordered everyone to dismount and carry the statue of the Buddha into the palace that had been built for it and place it upon a precious throne." Hiuan Tsang himself recounts: "At each step Harsha scattered fine pearls, all manner of precious stones and flowers of gold and silver in honor of the Buddhist Trinity. He mounted the altar which was made of precious materials and bathed the statue with perfumed water. The king then took it upon his own shoulders and bore it to the top of the tower." After paying homage to the statue, together with Hiuan Tsang, Harsha commanded the eighteen *rajas* to bring in the most learned and illustrious of the religious, to the number of a thousand, five hundred of the Brahmins and "heretical" scholars most renowned for their works, and two hundred ministers and high officials of the different kingdoms. The religious and laity who could not be admitted he ordered to form up in separate troops outside the gate of the enclosure. He then ordered food to be served to everybody, both without and within. He presented valuable gifts to Hiuan Tsang and the other religious: a gold bowl for the service of the Buddha, a gold cup, seven gold pots and three thousand garments of fine cotton.

"When this distribution was completed Harsha had a costly seat set up on one side and begged Hiuan Tsang to sit down and preside over the solemn conference, to speak in praise of the Mahayana and to expound the subject for discussion." A monk from Nalanda made Hiuan Tsang's propositions known to the multitude. Harsha had them written down and hung a copy at the gate of the enclosure where it might be seen by all present. He himself added at the bottom that "if anyone found in it a single erroneous word and showed himself capable of refuting it, he would offer his own head to be cut off in token of his gratitude." It need hardly be added that no one came forward to refute a text which was guaranteed on the emperor's head.

Hiuan Tsang was thus able to argue the case for the Mahayana without meeting any serious opposition. However, the emperor's intervention was not greeted without a certain impatience by the opponents of the Great Vehicle, and we learn from Hiuan Tsang's own biography that on the fifth day of the assembly "the heretics of the Little Vehicle, finding that the Master of the Law had overthrown the principles of their doctrine, were seized with hatred against him and hatched a plot against his life." How sad that a sectarian quarrel should lead the disciples of universal charity to such a pass. Had the pilgrim from China covered those thousands of miles in order to deepen his belief in the very country of the Buddha, and faced so many dangers and shown such faith, only to find himself in peril of his life at the hands of his co-religionists? Emperor Harsha was forced to issue a threatening proclamation: "If in this multitude there is a single man who shall attack or wound the Master of the Law I shall have him beheaded, and I shall cut out the tongue of anyone who shall be guilty of any insult or calumny regarding him. Those on the other hand who, placing their trust in my justice, wish to make a point in the approved manner, shall be entirely at liberty to do so." "From then on," Hwui-li naively adds, "the partisans of error stole away and disappeared, and there followed eighteen days during which no one dared open his mouth in dispute."

According to the biographer Hiuang Tsang's sermons to the assembly at Kannauj were followed by the conversion *en masse* of the adherents of the Hinayana. "They left the paths of error and entered the right way; abandoning the narrow views of the Little Vehicle they came to embrace the sublime principles of the Great."

It is a sad reflection to note the gulf that always separates pure ideas and the realities of human feeling. No sooner was the Buddha dead than the kings of India had forgotten the lessons of peace and gentleness that had been constantly on his lips and had practically joined battle over the distribution of his relics. And here was one of the greatest metaphysicians of medieval Buddhism expounding to Buddhists the doctrines of their faith and courting death at their hands for the sake of arguments as Byzantine as that of "Three Pure Foods."

Threats uttered against Hiuan Tsang had both alarmed and shocked Emperor Harsha. We know how much importance the Indian monarch attached to the friendship of China from the embassies which he exchanged regularly with the T'ang court. In 644–5 he was to receive two of T'ai-tsung's envoys, Li Yi-paio and Wang Hiuan-ts'ö, who took advantage of their visit to go and raise a commemorative inscription at the Bodhi Temple at Gaya. Hiuan Tsang was in no way an official ambassador, having even left China against the will of the court, but his assassination could have done nothing but harm to the excellent relationship which existed between Kannauj and Ch'ang-an. Not that such considerations even necessarily entered the picture, for Harsha had obviously formed a deep personal attachment for the pilgrim, besides admiring his superior understanding. "He gave the Master of the Law ten thousand gold pieces, thirty thousand silver pieces, and one hundred garments of fine cotton. He ordered one of his officers to caparison a large elephant with a rich adornment of costly materials and invited the Master of the Law to ride upon it. Finally he ordered the highest dignitaries of the land to form his escort and thus to make a tour of the assembled multitude and announce publicly that he had expounded the principles of truth and firmly established them without being vanquished by a single contrary voice." This was the traditional form of the Indian triumph, "accorded to whoever has carried the day." Hiuan Tsang's efforts to escape the honor were in vain. The king's wish was an order. "Holding the Master of the Law by his monk's robe, he cried out to the multitude, 'The Chinese Master has brilliantly laid down the doctrine of the Mahayana and overthrown all the errors of the sectarians. For the last eighteen days no one has dared dispute his teaching. Such a triumph must be made known to all and sundry!'" Everyone present heaped praises upon Hiuan Tsang, burned incense before him and scattered flowers before respectfully withdrawing.

Such is the version given by Hwui-li in his *Life* of his master. Hiuan Tsang himself, however, in his own account gives us some rather disturbing details on the subject of this assembly. We read there that an arsonist set fire to the sanctuary which Harsha had prepared and that the emperor himself very nearly fell victim to an assassination attempt.

Harsha, as we have seen, had built a tower at Kannauj to house the statue of the Buddha. "On the final day of the assembly this tower caught fire and the two-storied pavilion that rose above the gate of the monastery was engulfed by the flames." Hiuan Tsang puts the following melancholy observations into his hero's mouth: "I have drained the coffers of my kingdom in alms. After the example of the kings of old I have built this monastery and have sought to distinguish myself in worthy deeds. But my feeble virtue has found no encouragement. In the face of such calamities and such gloomy auguries, what need have I to live any longer?" The members of his entourage were similarly struck with anguish: "We had hoped that the holy monument which you had just completed would have lasted through the generations of the future.

Who would have thought that on the first day it would be reduced to ashes? The Brahmins furthermore are rejoicing from the bottom of their hearts, congratulating one another. . . ." It proved possible to put the fire out, however, which Hiuan Tsang took to be a miracle of the Buddha. And Harsha in any case appears to have made a rapid recovery: "In what has just taken place we recognize the truth of the Buddha's words. The Brahmins obstinately maintain that everything is eternal. But the Buddha has taught us the instability of all things. As for me, I have completed my alms and fulfilled the vow of my heart." But the Brahmins, for it was indeed they who had provoked the disaster, were to take their brazenness even further. Harsha, still very upset after the calamity, had climbed to the top of the great stupa, followed by the vassal kings. "At the top he gazed about him in every direction and then began to descend the stairs. Suddenly a stranger came running up to him, brandishing a dagger. The king, hard pressed, took several steps backward up the staircase. Then, reaching down, he managed to seize the man and hand him over to his officers." It had all taken place so quickly that the members of the royal retinue had not had time to come to their master's help.

His face showing not the slightest sign of anger, Harsha questioned the assassin, who confessed to having received money from the Brahmins. The plot had indeed been hatched by members of this sacerdotal class who were jealous of the favor which the king was bestowing on the Buddhist religious. Having set fire to the tower they had hoped that the king would meet his end in the ensuing disorder. When this had failed they had hired an assassin to stab him.

The conspiracy was put down with some severity. "The king punished the leaders but pardoned their followers. Five hundred Brahmins were banished beyond the frontiers of India."

There is surely something strangely symbolic about this scene. Harsha, the poet-king, was truly an anachronistic figure. Notwithstanding his personal inclinations, which seemed to revive the days of Asoka, the Brahminical reaction was becoming daily more threatening.

The triumph of Hinduism was at hand. The hour was drawing near when the monks of Ajanta would be driven from their cells and their places taken by Sivaite or Vishnuite sectarians. Another century and a half and it would all be over. . . .

Harsha invited Hiuan Tsang to another great assembly which took place on the great plain of Prayag (Allahabad) at the junction of the Ganges and Jumna where, following an ancient tradition, the Indian monarch made a general distribution of alms. "For thirty years," he says, not without a certain melancholy, in the *Life of Hiuan Tsang,* "I have reigned over India. I was disturbed to see myself making no (suffi-cient) progress in virtue. Deeply grieved at the impotence of my efforts in the direction of the good, I assembled vast quantities of wealth at Prayag and every five years I have distributed it. . . ." As it was now time for the "Distribution of Deliverance" for the year 643, Hiuan Tsang was able to be present at this so specifically Indian ceremony and to leave us a highly colorful description of it.

"To the west of the confluence of the Ganges and the Jumna," writes his biographer, "there stretches a vast plain as even and smooth as a mirror and measuring between fourteen and fifteen *li* in circum-ference. From ancient times the *rajas* of the land have come there to distribute alms. Tradition has it that it is a worthier deed to give one coin in this place than a hundred elsewhere. The king (Harsha) had a space measuring a thousand feet square surrounded with rush fences and in the middle he erected several dozen thatched halls to contain vast quantities of costly objects, gold, silver, fine pearls, red glass, prec-ious stones, etc. He further had erected several hundred sheds to house the silks and cottons. A little way beyond the fence he built an immense dining-hall. In front of the buildings containing all manner of riches he had a further hundred sheds erected, arranged in straight lines like the booths of our Ch'ang-an market. Each of these was long enough to shelter a thousand persons."

When Harsha arrived at the Plain of Alms-Giving followed by

Hiuan Tsang and the eighteen vassal *rajas* he found a crowd of five hundred thousand people assembled there by his officers. He set up his tent on the north bank of the Ganges. One of the vassals from southern India placed his to the west of the meeting of the two rivers. The king of Assam pitched his camp in a grove of flowering trees on the south bank of the Jumna. "Next morning the army corps of Harsha and of the king of Assam came in vessels and that of the southern prince riding upon elephants, all advancing in an imposing array and meeting at the Plain of Alms-Giving. The *rajas* of the eighteen vassal kingdoms joined them there, each one taking his appointed place.

"On the first day the statue of the Buddha was installed in one of the thatched temples and precious things and garments of the greatest value were distributed. Exquisite dishes were served and flowers scattered to the accompaniment of harmonious music, and in the evening all withdrew severally to their tents.

"On the second day the statue of the sun-god (the Brahminical god, Aditya, identical with Vishnu) was set in place and precious things and garments distributed, though only half the quantity of the first day.

"On the third day the statue of the god Isvara (i.e., Siva) was set in place and the same alms distributed as for Aditya.

"On the fourth day alms were distributed to some ten thousand religious sitting in rows and forming some hundred separate lines. Each man received a hundred gold pieces, a cotton garment, and various drinks and foodstuffs as well as perfumes and flowers.

"On the fifth occasion distributions were made to the Brahmins, lasting twenty days.

"On the sixth occasion alms were distributed for ten days to the 'heretics.'

"Then for a further ten days alms were distributed to Jain mendicants who had come from distant lands.

"Finally alms were given to the poor, the orphans and those without family, lasting for a month. At the end of that time all the wealth accumulated in the royal coffers over a period of five years was entirely spent. Nothing remained to the king but the horses, elephants and weapons of war necessary to maintaining order in his realm."

This Indian fairy-tale of the Festival of Alms-Giving—the "Festival of Salvation" as the Buddhists called it—ended with a curious scene. Harsha, the poet-king, was seized with a kind of fever of charity. Like the Visvantara of Buddhist legend, a prefiguration of the Buddha Sakyamuni who had given in alms his goods and family, the emperor of Kannauj resolved to strip himself utterly: "The clothes he was wearing, his necklaces, his earrings, his bracelets, the garland of his diadem, the pearls that adorned his throat and the carbuncle that blazed at the crest of his hair, all this Harsha gave in alms, keeping nothing back. . . .

"When the whole amount of his wealth was exhausted he asked his sister to bring him a worn and common robe and, dressing himself in this, went to worship before the Buddhas of the ten countries." Then, clasping his hands together, he abandoned himself to transports of joy: "Before," he cried, "while amassing all this wealth, I lived in constant fear of never finding a storeroom solid enough to keep it in. But now that I have spread it in alms upon the field of happiness I regard it as forever preserved! Oh that I may thus in the future lives again amass immense wealth in order to distribute it in alms among men and by this means acquire the ten divine faculties in all their fullness!"

It was no doubt in a similar access of bliss that Harsha wrote the poem with which his *Suprabhatastotra* opens:

"I salute the Buddha! I salute the Law! I salute the Order! Him who is praised by the multitude of the gods and by the Siddhas, by the Gandharvas, by the Yakshas, in heaven and upon earth, and by the principal ascetics, with many and varied praises I too salute, arrogating to myself this power, Him the Noble One, the Enlightened One. But do not the bees fly in the sky that is traversed by Garuda?"

This Buddhist litany continues in iridescent images like a stanza from the *Lalita Vistara*. The Buddha is declared to be "He in whom all tendency to evil is annihilated, in whom there is no fault, who is of the color of molten gold, whose eyes are as long as the full-blown lotus, whose garments gleam and who has the brightness of a brilliant sphere, He who is conqueror of the power of Mara, destroyer of the ways of evil, doer of good in the Three Worlds, He who unravels us from the entanglements of the lianas (of temptation) and in whose gift are the fruits of bliss."

This spate of mystical exaltation once over, however, there was the coming down to earth. Hiuan Tsang's biographer tells us himself that the eighteen vassal kings "gathered afresh precious things and large sums from among the peoples of their realms, redeemed the rich necklace, the carbuncle and the royal garments given in alms by King Harsha, brought them back and gave them to him once more." The same cycle was repeated several times. Possibly it is this extreme religious romanticism which provides us with a clue to the ephemeral and transitory nature of Harsha's empire. At any rate we are struck by the contrast between the poet-king, the lyrical, passionate Indian, and his Chinese contemporary, the robust T'ai-tsung, a man thoroughly imbued with Confucian prudence and positivist wisdom.

It is easy to imagine how deeply Harsha desired to keep a man like Hiuan Tsang beside him. Indeed he was so insistent that the pilgrim, in order to get away, was obliged to "speak with him in words which revealed the bitterness in his heart." "China," he cried, "lies at an immense distance away from India and it was long before she heard tell of the Law of the Buddha. Although she now possesses some brief knowledge of it she is unable to embrace it in its entirety. Therefore have I come to seek instruction in foreign lands. If I now desire to return thither, it is because the sages of my homeland sigh for my coming and draw me thither with their every prayer." And he reminded the pious monarch of the words of the scripture: "Whoever hides the Law from the sight of men shall be struck with blindness in all his lives." Harsha yielded. He offered Hiuan Tsang the company of his official envoys should he wish to return by way of the Indian Ocean and the China Seas. But the pilgrim had made up his mind to travel back via central

Asia, where he had made a number of invaluable friendships. In particular he had not forgotten his promise to the king of Turfan that he would pass through his country on his way home; this was in the nature of a debt of honor, bearing in mind all that the king of Turfan had done to facilitate the pilgrim's journey through the Tokharian and Turkish kingdoms.

So Harsha allowed Hiuan Tsang to depart, not without lavishing gifts upon him and placing him in the safe-keeping of an escort which was to take him as far as the borders of India. This escort was to be extremely useful to the pilgrim during the crossing of the brigand-infested sub-Himalayan zone. Harsha had furthermore given Hiuan Tsang one of his finest elephants to ride, and finally had dispatched couriers bearing letters patent "written on pieces of white cotton and sealed with red wax" instructing the princes of the realms which lay on the pilgrim's route to make him welcome. As for the books and statues which Hiuan Tsang was taking back with him, they had been entrusted to a northern Indian *raja* who had agreed to have them transported by easy stages on horseback or in army wagons. The king of Assam for his part had given Hiuan Tsang a garment of fine down to protect him against damp and rain in the mountains. "The two kings, each with a large retinue, accompanied the Master of the Law for several tens of *li* through the Prayag countryside. When the time came to say farewell they both shed tears and were shaken by deep sighs."

Three days after the pilgrim's departure Harsha and the king of Assam gave him a fresh and touching surprise. Wishing to see him once more they galloped out with several hundred cavalry and caught up with him, escorting him for several further leagues before the final separation. We feel through the notes we have of Hiuan Tsang's life the emotion with which he took his leave of the two kings, this time forever.

This was in April 643. Four years later Harsha was gone and his place usurped by a man who was to commit such acts of vandalism that

Wang Hiuan-ts'ö's Sino-Nepalese army had to come and take him prisoner. Henceforth all was chaos in northern India. The Rajput feudality took possession of the thrones of Malwa and the Ganges but was unable to recreate the united empire of which Harsha had been the last defender. And with the Rajputs came the triumphant reaction of the non-Aryan element, the revenge of Sivaism and Tantrism. Then, sweeping down from the Khyber Pass in squadrons of iconoclastic Mamelukes, came the Moslem avalanche.

Harsha's death marked the end of what was definitely the finest, most glorious period in Indian history. That last prince of the Thanesar dynasty, a man who knew no successor, was indeed the last of the Arya, men of our own race in a world become foreign once more.

Passing through Kausambi (Kosam) on the Jumna, Hiuan Tsang came to the Bilsar (Etah) region to the northwest of Kannauj, where he spent two months of the rainy season of 643. He then crossed the Punjab by way of Jalandhara and Taxila, retracing the route he had traveled in the opposite direction ten years before. The passes of the upper Punjab were infested with brigands, about whom Hiuan Tsang had been warned. His saintly soul, however, found the necessary words to disarm their hostility. He sent one of his monks ahead as a scout, with instructions to say to the brigands, "We are religious who have come from afar to obtain instruction in the Law. What we carry with us are sacred books, relics and statues. Men of generous heart, we ask your help and protection." The Master of the Law followed at a distance with his disciples and traveling companions. His appeal to the brigands' hearts was heard and accepted, and though he frequently ran into bands of them they did not so much as lay a hand on him.

Hiuan Tsang crossed the Indus at the beginning of 644. The crossing was fraught with mishaps: "The books and statues and the travelers were embarked upon a large boat and the Master of the Law crossed the river on the back of an elephant. He had instructed one of his men to keep an eye on the books and the seeds of rare Indian flowers on the boat. But as they arrived in mid-stream the boat was violently shaken by an eddy and almost swamped. The guardian of the books was filled with terror and fell into the water. He was pulled out by his companions but he lost fifty manuscripts and the flower seeds and it was only with great difficulty that they were able to save the rest."

It was probably one of the most vexing things which happened to Hiuan Tsang on his whole journey. By great good fortune the king of Kapisa, whose realm he had just entered and who had come as far as Udabhanda (Und) on the Indus to meet him, sent all the way to Uddiyana to have fresh copies made of the books which had been lost. The king of Kashmir, learning that the pilgrim's return journey was not going to include his kingdom, also came to the Udabhanda region to say his farewells.

Hiuan Tsang then left for Nagarahara and Lampaka, escorted by the king of Kapisa who is here clearly depicted as being the suzerain of all these little Gandharan principalities. The inhabitants came out in procession to await the caravan with flags and banners. At Nagarahara (Jalalabad) the local king distributed alms in his honor. There Hiuan Tsang was put up at a monastery of the Great Vehicle, probably close to one of the stupas excavated by André Godard and his wife and Barthoux. The king of Kapisa, who had accompanied him all the way from India, also gave him a particularly friendly reception in his own realm at his capital, Kapisi; here too there was a distribution of alms in the pilgrim's honor.

Religion did not entirely account for the interest which the little princes of the Gandharan region showed in the great Chinese; it was partly political as well. As proof of this we need look no further than the official documents of the T'ang chancery. These kings of Kashmir and Kapisa were anxious to obtain the help of the Chinese court against the threat of their barbarian neighbors, the hordes of central Asia. How could they know that a much greater peril lay in wait for them down in Arabia? The Turco-Mongol invasions attacked no more than their material existence, and in any case at that time the Turkish hordes always ended up being converted to the Law of the Buddha. Islam, on the other hand, was to alter the very soul of the country and expunge from this soil, so saturated in history, every last memory of its Greco-Buddhist civilization.

CHAPTER 12

From the Pamirs
to Tun-huang

Taking his leave of the king of Kapisa, Hiuan Tsang followed the caravan trail over the Hindu Kush and the Pamirs toward Kashgar.

The king of Kapisa had made careful arrangements for this part of the journey, sending one of his officers with a hundred men to accompany the Master of the Law through the mountains and carry his fodder, provisions and other supplies. The crossing, which must have begun in July 644, was nonetheless a difficult one. After a seven-day march they reached the top of a great mountain which presented a vista of dangerous summits and terrifying peaks soaring up on all sides and taking the strangest and most varied forms. Now the eye picked out a plateau, now a slender pinnacle; at each step the view was different. It would be hard to relate all the perils and hardships to which they were exposed while negotiating these mountains. From this point on it was impossible to travel on horseback and the Master of the Law led the way leaning upon a stick.

"After a further seven days they came to a mountain pass and at the bottom of this pass lay a village of a hundred families who raised sheep the size of donkeys. He slept in this village on the first day and left in the middle of the night, charging one of the inhabitants to take a mountain camel and serve as his guide. This country is full of a multitude of snow-covered streams and frozen rivers in which the traveler might fall and perish were he not accompanied at every step by native guides. They marched from morning till night through this region of ice-bound precipices. There remained at this time only seven religious, twenty servants, one elephant, ten donkeys and four horses. Next morning they came to the bottom of this mountain pass. Then, following a series of tortuous paths, they reached the top of a summit which had looked from afar as if it had been covered with snow, but as they approached the top they found that it was composed uniquely of white stones.

"So high was this peak that the frozen clouds and wind-driven snow did not even reach its tip. Night was falling as the travelers reached the summit but they were penetrated by such an icy wind as deprived them of the strength to stand up.

"This mountain showed not a trace of vegetation. There was nothing to be seen but chaotic piles of boulders everywhere and groups of soaring, arid peaks stretching as far as the eye could reach, like a forest of trees stripped of their foliage. It was so high and buffetted by such an impetuous wind that the birds themselves were unable to fly over it; only at a hundred or so paces to north and south beyond the summit were they able to take wing. Descending on the northwestern side the Master of the Law found after a few miles a small piece of even ground where he put up his tent and spent the night. The next day he resumed his journey."

Once north of the Hindu Kush, Hiuan Tsang, passing by way of

Andarab and Qunduz (in Chinese, Ngan-ta-lo-po and Huo) turned northeast through Tokharistan and Badakhshan (T'u-huo-lo and Pa-t'o-shan). These provinces, the reader will remember, constituted the fief of a *yabgu* or Turkish prince of the family of the khan of the Western Turks. Hiuan Tsang spent a month at this chieftain's camp and was then given an escort for the crossing of the Pamirs. With this protection he set off up the valley of the Pyandzh, which is in fact the upper Oxus or Amu Darya valley, along a precipitous trail between the Shugnan massif to the north and the Wakhan massif to the south (the "She-k'i-ni" and "Hu-mi" of the Chinese geographers). "These dark valleys and dangerous ridges," writes Hiuan Tsang, "are covered with perpetual snow and ice; a cold wind blows violently there." [1] At this altitude vegetation was becoming sparse: "The trees of the forests are few and far between and flowers and fruit rarely found." On the other hand the soil produced large quantities of onions, whence the Chinese name for the Pamirs—Ts'ung-ling or the "Onion Mountains." This description is borne out by what we are told of the Wakhan by another Chinese pilgrim, Sung Yun, who had crossed the Pamirs some hundred and twenty years earlier (in 522): "The country is so cold that the inhabitants dwell in caves. Animals and men live there huddled together to protect themselves from the wind and snow. Tall, snow-covered mountains bar the horizon; the snow melts in the morning and freezes toward evening; from afar these mountains look like peaks of jade. . . .

---

[1] In the memoirs of another Chinese pilgrim, Wu-k'ung (751–790), we find a romantic account of a storm in this region. The setting is the district of Ku-tu, the present-day Khottal; Wu-k'ung was on his way back from India to China, taking with him some sacred books and one of the Buddha's teeth which had been given him by the superior of a monastery in Gandhara. "As he was walking along beside a deep lake the *naga* or dragon of the waters found out that he was the bearer of a relic. The earth shook, black clouds gathered and piled up, the thunder roared and the lightning flashed and hail and rain poured down out of the sky. Not far from the lake's edge stood a tall tree. Wu-k'ung and all the caravan took refuge beneath it. The branches and leaves all fell. From the heart of the tree sprang a flame. The leader of the caravan then addressed his companions: 'One of you must be in possession of a relic, for otherwise why should the dragon of the waters try so angrily to get hold of it? Let he who has it throw it into the lake that all the rest of us may be delivered!' But Wu-k'ung began to pray, and his prayers touched the heart of the spirit of the waters. The storm abated and the relics were saved . . ." (Sylvain Lévi and Chavannes, "L'Itinéraire d'Ou-k'ong," *Journal asiatique*, 1895, vol. 2, p. 361.)

For ramparts the king's citadel has the mountains themselves. . . ."

Hiuan Tsang notes in passing that the inhabitants of some of these Pamir valleys had eyes of a bluish-green color; could they have been a tribe of the "Yoghnobi" whom Gauthiot visited in 1913 in order to study their language and who were closely related to the ancient Sogdians? In the Shugnan Hiuan Tsang was delighted to find a miraculous statue of the Buddha.

Farther to the east began the Pamir valley itself or the so-called Great Pamir, our traveler's "Po-mi-lo," which is actually the valley of the Pyandzh up to its source. "This valley," we read in Hwui-li, "is situated between two snow-covered mountains and forms the center of the Pamir or Ts'ung-ling Mountains. Gusty winds and snowstorms belabour the traveler endlessly, even in spring and summer. Since the soil is almost perpetually frozen only a very few poor plants are to be found; the whole landscape is one vast wilderness with no trace of human life." Hiuan Tsang's description, couched in almost the same terms, is as usual more precise: "The Pamir valley measures approximately a thousand *li* from east to west and a hundred *li* from south to north. In its narrowest parts it is no more than ten *li* wide. It is situated between two snow-covered mountains. An icy cold and a violent wind prevail there. Snow falls even in spring and summer; day and night the wind blows in furious gusts. The soil is impregnated with salt and covered with a mass of stones. Neither corn nor fruit will grow there and trees and plants are few and far between. Soon the traveler comes to uncultivated deserts with no trace of human habitation."

The reader should bear in mind that the Wakhan massif through which the Pamir valley wends its way lies at an average altitude of between 13,000 and 14,000 feet. "In the middle of the valley," Hiuan Tsang tells us, "there is a large lake—Lake Sar-i Kol or Victoria—which is situated at the center of the world (literally of the 'Jambudvipa') on a prodigiously high plateau." It is interesting to find the Chinese traveler's brush forming the equivalent of our expression, the "Roof of the World."

"The basin of this lake situated in the middle of the Pamir Mountains," continues Hiuan Tsang, "lies at a very great height. Its water is as pure and limpid as a mirror and none has ever been able to measure its depth. Its color is blue-black and it is sweet and pleasant to the taste. Sharks, dragons and turtles live in its abysses. On the surface are ducks, wild geese, cranes, etc. Eggs of enormous size are to be found in the wild plains of the region and also at times in the swampy fields and on the sandy islands." Hiuan Tsang did not fail to remark that Sar-i Kol Lake constitutes the water-shed between Kashgaria and Transoxiania, the water flowing to the east going down to the Yarkand Darya and the Tarim.

It is not uninteresting to compare Hiuan Tsang's account with that of Sung Yun, who crossed the Pamirs from the east more than a century before. "From the moment when the traveler enters the Pamir Mountains each step takes him gradually higher and higher. After four days he reaches the summit. There, as compared with the plain, it really seems as if one is halfway to heaven. On one side the rivers all flow toward the east; on the other they all flow toward the west. It is commonly said that this is the center of heaven and earth. Neither grass nor trees grow there. By the eighth month the temperature was already low, the north wind was driving away the wild geese, and the snow whirled and flew over a distance of a thousand *li*."

Farther east, after climbing precipitous ridges and negotiating paths covered with snow and ice, Hiuan Tsang came across some valleys with a better exposure, and some which were even quite sunny with a little wheat and some fruit trees growing, despite the altitude. These districts of the eastern Pamirs he calls "Kie-p'an-t'ö" and "Wusha." Probably, as Watters suggests, this is the region of Istigh, Bozai and Wakhjir. Before long, though, he was back in the wilderness. "On the mountainsides and in the valleys enormous masses of snow can be seen even in spring and summer, and gusty winds and an icy cold prevail. The soil is impregnated with salt and corn will not grow there. There are no trees at all and only a little poor scrub. Even at the height of summer there is a great deal of wind and snow. The traveler has hardly entered the region before he finds himself wrapped in mist and clouds." Hiuan Tsang was told about a caravan of several thousand merchants and camels which had perished to the last man and beast beneath the snowstorms.

These mountainous wastes were haunted by strange apparitions. As they passed a rock which loomed as sheer as a wall above the trail, travelers were informed by the caravan leaders that two *arhats* or Buddhist saints had been living up there in holes cut in the rock for the last seven hundred years. "Having extinguished every concrete thought and reached a state of total ecstasy they sit there in an upright posture without the slightest movement. One would take them to be exhausted by fasting, yet although they have been there for seven hundred years their skin and their bones show no sign of decomposition."

A little farther on the profane would tremble and the mystics be filled with wonder at another, similar legend. "At a distance of two hundred *li* to the west of Kie-p'an-t'ö the traveler comes to a mountain that is enveloped in clouds and vapors. Its sides rise extremely high. They appear to be on the point of collapse and remain as it were in a state of suspension. A number of years ago the thunder roared and a piece of the mountain fell away. In the caves which were thus exposed sat a religious with eyes closed. He was as tall as a giant; his body was wasted and his beard and his unkempt hair fell down to his shoulders and obscured his face." He was seen by some hunters or woodcutters who ran to inform the king. The king hurried to the spot and, the news having spread, he was soon joined there by the entire populace. A monk explained what had to be done: "The man who has entered a state of ecstasy can remain in this condition for an indefinite period. His body is supported through mystical power and escapes destruction and death. Exhausted as he is by his long fast, were he to emerge from the state of ecstasy abruptly he would die in that very instant and his body might crumble to dust. First his limbs must be moistened with butter and oil to make them supple again, then the gong can be struck to wake him." This was done, and when the saint heard the gong he at last opened his eyes and looked around him. Then, after a long pause, he asked those present: "You who are so small in stature, who are you?" Receiving a reply from one of the monks who was standing around he asked for news of his master, the Buddha Kasyapa, Sakyamuni's predecessor who had passed away hundreds of thousands of years before. The monks replied, "Long, long since did he enter the great Nirvana." "Hearing these words," Hiuan Tsang goes on, "the saint closed his eyes like a man in despair; then suddenly he asked, 'And has Sakyamuni appeared in the world?' 'He was incarnate,' they replied, 'he gave guidance to the age, and he entered Nirvana in his turn.' At these words the saint again lowered his head. Then he lifted his flowing hair with one hand and rose majestically into the air. By a divine miracle he was transformed into a fiery sphere which consumed his body and let his calcined bones fall back to the earth." The king of the country had a stupa erected to him in the heart of the mountains.

In the pilgrim's journey such miraculous legends alternated with dramatic alarms. In an icy gorge between the Pamirs and the Muztagh his caravan ran into a troop of brigands. The merchants accompanying him took to the mountains and fled. Several of the caravan's elephants, pursued by the brigands, fell into ravines and killed themselves. When the danger was over Hiuan Tsang and his companions made their way down another side of the mountain and laboriously continued on their way.

Hiuan Tsang was at this point following a trail which ran in a northwesterly direction. Very probably this trail passed through the post of Tash-kurghan and then ran along the western slopes of the Muztagh massif. He must thus have come, near the "Little Qara Kol," to the Gez, a tributary of the Qizil Darya or Kashgar River. Following the Gez in a northeasterly direction he came at last to Kashgar, or "Shu-lö" as it is called in the *T'ang Shu,* which he calls K'ia-sha after the Indians' Sanskrit name for the city, Kasha.

According to Hiuan Tsang the greater part of Kashgaria proper was already at this period a desert of sand and stones. But thanks to the mild climate and regular rainfall, the land still under cultivation—the oasis itself—still produced a great abundance of corn and a prodigious quantity of flowers and fruit. "Felt and cloth of excellent quality are manufactured in this country as well as fine woolens. Furthermore the inhabitants are skilled in the weaving of many kinds of soft, delicate carpet." Hiuan Tsang reports, as does also the *T'ang Shu,* that the people of Kashgar had green eyes, which seems to be a valuable piece of evidence as to the Sakan or Sogdian (i.e., "East Iranian") origins of a part of the population. He also mentions the Indian derivation of the local script (which probably came from Kharosthi). As regards religion the whole country was Buddhist, but to Hiuan Tsang's great regret it was the Buddhism of the Hinayana; there were a hundred or so monasteries in the area, housing almost ten thousand religious, but the teachings professed by these monks were those of the realist Sarvastivadin school. Consequently they drew this parting shot from the pilgrim: "They read the texts without studying the principles! " It should be added that, besides the Buddhism of the Little Vehicle, there must have been a considerable number of adepts of Persian Zoroastrianism in Kashgar since the *T'ang Shu* declares that tribute was paid to the "celestial god," i.e., the Zoroastrian Ormuzd or Ahura Mazda.

Leaving Kashgar, Hiuan Tsang crossed the Qizil Darya and its tributaries to the south and came to the kingdom of Yarkand. The capital of the country was not the oasis itself which today bears this name but a city lying a little farther south known then as Cho-kiu-kia, or So-kiu in the *T'ang Shu,* and known now as Kargalik. This, we are told, was an oasis protected by an amphitheater of mountain ranges and watered by a tributary of the Yarkand Darya which ensured a remarkable degree of agricultural prosperity, a land of corn, vines and fruit trees. Unlike the Kashgarians, the inhabitants of Yarkand professed the Buddhism of the Mahayana. Hiuan Tsang depicts them rather curiously as being "violent, impulsive, given to trickery and fraud and indulging openly in brigandage," while nevertheless "believing sincerely in religion and being fond of doing good works."

Furthermore the country was sanctified by the presence of supernatural beings. "On the southern frontiers of the country (that is to say at the foot of the Chung Kyr Mountains which form an extension of the K'un Lun Shan) lies a massif with very high passes and peaks piled one upon another. The plants and trees which grow there are dwarfed by the cold. From spring till autumn torrents course down the valleys and mountain-springs burst forth on every side. Niches can be seen in the flanks of the mountain and cells carved in the rocks. They are distributed regularly among the woods and caves. Many of the holy men of India, having attained arhatship, transport themselves through the air by virtue of their supernatural powers and take up residence here. Many have thus entered silence and extinction in this place. At this moment there are still three *arhats* abiding in these precipitous caverns who, having extinguished the mind principle, have entered a condition of total ecstasy. Since little by little their hair and beards grow longer, from time to time the religious of the country come and cut them." We have here the type of ageless and immortal ascetic lost in a trance for years and possibly for centuries up on the side of the Himalayas, a type which was to proliferate in Tibetan Buddhism and of which one of the most illustrious examples was Milaraspa.

Following the usual stations of the caravan route around the southern edge of the Tarim Basin, Hiuan Tsang next passed through Khotan, which he correctly calls Kiu-sa-tan-na, from the Sanskrit name Kustana. The site he refers to here corresponds to the town of Yotkan (in Chinese, T'ang Yu-t'ien) a few miles to the northwest of present-day Khotan.

The "kingdom of Khotan" was another fertile oasis set amid a desert of sand and stone. One of the country's assets was its plantations of mulberry trees, the origin of which we learn from the *T'ang Shu*. This was the period when China was keeping silk a jealously guarded secret.

The king of Khotan, however, having obtained the hand of a Chinese princess in marriage, obtained by the same token some mulberry seeds and a number of silkworms, which the princess brought with her hidden in her voluminous hair-style. Hiuan Tsang was shown one or two venerable old trunks which still bore witness to that first plantation of mulberries. Since that time the culture of silkworms had become one of the national industries of Khotan, and it was from there that, around 552, the industry found its way to Byzantium. Khotan also obtained a large income from the manufacture of woolen carpets and fine felts and taffetas and from the extraction of black and white jade. In this connection the *T'ang Shu* quotes the legend according to which Khotan jade was crystallized moonlight: "During the night the inhabitants watch for the places where the light of the moon falls at its brightest, and that is where they find the most beautiful jade." We might add that all these caravan halts east of the Pamirs were renowned for more voluptuous pleasures. The *T'ang Shu* ranks the courtesans of Khotan with those of Kucha, and the country was also famed for its music and dancing.

The population of Khotan or at least one of the elements of that population belonged as we have seen to the eastern group of Iranian peoples. At the same time the entire country was deeply Buddhist and the religious and literary language was Sanskrit. It contained some hundred monasteries accommodating about five thousand religious, the greater part of whom professed the Mahayana. The Khotanese attributed their conversion to Buddhism to the Mahayanist Bodhisattva Vairocana, who had come from Kashmir for that purpose. The dynasty itself claimed descent from the Celestial King Vaisravana, the Buddhist genius of the northern region. However, according to the *T'ang Shu,* Zoroastrianism was also practiced at Khotan, confirming once again that all these central Asian oases shared a mixed Indo-Persian civilization. Of all the countries and peoples which he visited on his journey, Hiuan Tsang gives a special place to the culture of Khotan. Clearly this

222 § IN THE FOOTSTEPS OF THE BUDDHA

was an ancient and thoroughly civilized country, worthy of the admiration of Confucian scholars. "The inhabitants," we read in his biography, "observe justice and its rites; they respect scholarship and love music. Their customs are upright and honest, in which they differ greatly from the rest of the barbarians. Although their language is very different the characters of their script are with the exception of a few changes the same as those used in India."

The *T'ang Shu* echoes the pilgrim's praise for the urbanity of the Khotanese. It also mentions the importance which, ever since the time of the Han, the kings of Khotan had attached to their traditional friendship with China. However, the advent of the T'ang found the ruling dynasty in the oasis (the Wei-ch'e dynasty, as the Chinese rendered it) not without their problems. Like all the oases of Kashgaria, Khotan had had to accept the suzerainty of the powerful khanate of the western Turks. But in 632 the king of Khotan, seeing Emperor T'ai-tsung establish his authority in China, had sent an embassy bearing gifts to the court of Ch'ang-an. Three years later he had sent his own son to enroll in the imperial guard. T'ai-tsung, however, did not remain content with such protestations of vassalage for long. In proportion as the Turks were defeated and scattered the great emperor laid an increasingly heavy hand upon the Indo-European oases which had once accepted alliance with them. The storm was to burst in 648. The imperial general A-she-na Shö-eul had just smashed another of the great principalities of the Gobi, Kucha, when his lieutenant Sie Wan-pei suggested to him: "After this blow all the lands of the West are terror-struck. Let us take our light cavalry and go and pass a halter round the neck of the king of Khotan that we may take him back and offer him to the emperor at the capital." It was no sooner said than done. Sie Wan-pei took Khotan utterly by surprise and King Fu-tu Sin lost his nerve. We learn from the *T'ang Shu* that the Chinese general "made known to him the prestige and supernatural power of the T'ang and exhorted him to come and present himself before the Son of Heaven." Fu-tu Sin complied. He was in any case to lose nothing by the episode, since after a stay of several months the Chinese court allowed him to return home, not without first presenting him with a ceremonial robe and five thousand pieces of silk.

When Hiuan Tsang reached Khotan around September 644 this *coup* had not yet taken place. It was already feared, however, and every Chinese passing through the country found himself showered with the most generous attentions. In fact the king and populace gave the pilgrim such a warm welcome that he spent some seven to eight months in the city, waiting while he had the manuscripts lost on the journey replaced in the Tokharian region, and waiting too for permission from the Chinese government to return to his homeland. He spent the time expounding to the king and the assembled religious of the country the texts of the idealist school and the teachings of Asanga and Vasubandhu.

Hiuan Tsang then resumed his homeward journey along the chain of oases that extend in a semi-circle between the K'un Lun Shan and the Akkar Chekyl Tagh to the south and the Takla Makan Desert to the north. Among the information which he gives us about this region, particularly outstanding is the large number of caves, hermitages and Buddhist statues which he either saw or heard about. We are reminded of what the *T'ang Shu* says about the king of Khotan living "in a house decorated with paintings."

In fact this region, so impoverished today, was once a considerable center of artistic activity. Not without reason does the list of the finest Chinese painters include the names of several artists from Khotan. This is confirmed by the paintings discovered by Sir Aurel Stein at Dandan Uilik to the east of Khotan, paintings on plaster, silk and wood dating some from the seventh and some from the eighth century and thus roughly contemporary with Hiuan Tsang. Moreover several of the characters depicted in these paintings might well be taken to illustrate the pilgrim's narrative. During the course of his peregrinations along the trails of central Asia he must surely have numbered among his traveling companions some of these curious, half-Turkish, half-Persian lords on their robust Kirgiz horses or their tall Bactrian camels. And what Hiuan Tsang tells us of the existence of a number of Buddhist communities within the Persian empire was corroborated in a curious way by the discovery, also at Dandan Uilik, of an authentic Bodhisattva (actually Vajrapani) represented in the guise of a Sassanid king with an aquiline nose and a black beard, wearing a tiara, a green top-coat and heavy leather boots—a complete Buddhist Khosrau, in fact. We could have no more appropriate reminder that from the point of view of material civilization and no doubt also from that of race the Khotan region remained up until the Turkish conquest a part of Greater Persia. And since from the religious point of view Khotan also formed an integral part of Greater India we find in these same works a definite Indian influence—a naked *nagi,* for example, emerging from a lotus pool, a delightful Khotanese Aphrodite and a worthy companion to the most charming figures of Ajanta.

A little farther to the east, at Niya and at Miran, Hiuan Tsang's contemporaries could perhaps still admire some works of a quite different inspiration, this time purely Greco-Roman. Among the Miran frescoes, which date from the fourth century at the latest and are astonishingly well preserved, we find a Buddha followed by his monks and surrounded by winged spirits who might equally well be from Pompeii. It is even possible that these "Roman" paintings tucked away in a forgotten corner of the Gobi, the now dead Lop Nor region, stem from the hands of Mediterranean artists, for Sir Aurel Stein found at Miran the signature of a "Tita" who might easily have been a Titus.

Arriving in the neighborhood of Lop Nor, in the outlying parts of what was then known as the kingdom of Shan-shan, the former Leulan, our pilgrim might possibly have met another great traveler, a desert rider like himself. I refer to the Sogdian who is known to us by his Chinese name of K'ang Yen-tien. His story has been pieced together by Pelliot—how he came from far-off Samarkand in the period 627–49 to found a trading colony at this junction of the caravan trails.

31. Paitava Buddha, Greco-Buddhaic. (*Musée Guimet*)

But this whole region to the east of Khotan, to whose one-time prosperity all these archeological discoveries attest, was already beginning to revert to desert. Hiuan Tsang mentions a large river a hundred *li* southeast of Khotan which had flowed in a northeasterly direction until the day it simply dried up. This particular story ends in a fairy tale, the waters reappearing after the marriage of the *nagi* of the river to a Khotanese nobleman, but the incidence of such wadis drying up must have been frequent enough in the region. Even as far back as the end of our classical period, as Sir Aurel Stein's discoveries proved, numbers of once fertile sites had had to be abandoned. Hiuan Tsang also mentions a former Khotanese city (he calls it in Chinese Ho-lao-lo-kia) which had been entirely buried beneath the sand. Farther east in the longitudinal Niya valley, where Sir Aurel Stein's excavations revealed that remarkable series of Greco-Roman Buddhist statues from the classical period, the waters of the Niya Darya were in the course of becoming a swamp, and desiccation was soon to follow. The ancient city of Niya, which for us is so interesting because of its intaglio-work and its Hellenistic seals, had had to be abandoned as early as the end of the second century A.D. bceause it was situated on the lower course of the river and the water had ceased to reach it. The medieval city, constructed three days' march to the south on the upper river nearer the mountains, was in turn threatened with the same fate.

"The city of Ni-jang," writes the pilgrim, "lies at the center of a great swamp. This swampland is hot and humid and is covered with reeds and wild rushes with neither track nor path across it. There is but one more or less practicable road leading to the city."

Even farther to the east the Gobi had dried up every drop of water and killed every scrap of vegetation. "Leaving Ni-jang," write both Hiuan Tsang and Hwui-li, "the traveler enters an immense desert of shifting sands. The sand forms into hills and then disperses again at the whim of the wind, which sends it flying in whirling clouds. This desert extends in all directions as far as the eye can see and none can find his way in it. To guide his steps the traveler has no other resource than the heaps of human and animal bones left by the caravans that have gone before. Nowhere is there a single water-hole or grazing place. Often the desert wind blows with scorching heat, and then man and beast fall senseless to the ground. Sometimes a kind of singing or whistling can be heard, sometimes agonized cries. After looking about him and listening the traveler loses all sense of direction. Many men lose their lives there."

32. Avalokitesvara, Tibet. (*Musée Guimet*)

However, Hiuan Tsang's caravan arrived without mishap at Chö-mo-t'o-na, the present-day Cherchan. Then, passing by way of Char-khlik and the sands of the Qum Tagh, between the Lop Nor Depression and the mountains of the Altin Tagh, they came to Tun-huang or Sha-chou, the first Chinese post toward the West.

Hiuan Tsang spent some time at Tun-huang, waiting for a favorable response to the plea he had dispatched to the emperor. The city was an important center where travelers from the Great West might recover from the ordeal of their journey. It was also an extremely important Buddhist center, as we know from the series of frescoes and painted silk banners in the Musée Guimet, Paris, and the British Museum which were brought back by Pelliot and Sir Aurel Stein, respectively, and which were found in the "Caves of the Thousand Buddhas" or Ts'ien Fo-tong about eight miles southeast of the city. Looking at these venerable works, which date for the most part from the T'ang dynasty or the period immediately following, we can fully appreciate the fascinating place which Hiuan Tsang's journey occupies in the history of civilization. From that decisive era in the development of Chinese thought and culture, in an outpost frequented by all the caravans from India and Persia, we catch a vivid glimpse of the way in which T'ang China absorbed, interpreted and adapted influences from abroad. Beside one Bodhisattva with his naked torso draped in transparent Indian scarves we find another who is already completely Chinese in physique and costume. Many of the banners are no less interesting from the aesthetic point of view. What a riot of imagination for example is the depiction of the "Assault of Mara" with its armies of multicolored demons and naive "pre-Raphaelite" illumination; it is as fantastic as Western medieval depictions of hell. And how majestic, on the other hand, are the great Mahayanist paradises where amid vibrating harmonies of old golds, muted blues and fiery reds the Bodhisattva bestows upon us as he did upon the supplicants of the year one thousand his gesture of tender mercy. These works prompt us to evoke the pages in which Hiuan Tsang describes the processions organized for his homecoming with their icons and streaming banners. And how vividly the ancient text reads now that those very banners with their flamboyant imagery hang upon the walls of our museums.

The intellectual link which Hiuan Tsang had set out to establish between the mystical land of Magadha and the great China of the T'ang emperors was assured once and for all in their domain by the artists and artisans of Tun-huang.

In art as in thought the Far East was bound to Indian culture.

Hiuan Tsang must have experienced a certain anxiety on arriving at Tun-huang. What sort of welcome lay in store for him from the imperial government, whose orders he had deliberately flouted in leaving the country originally? Emperor T'ai-tsung, however, was too broadminded a man to hold such a technicality against him. Moreover sixteen years had passed since that day when an obscure young monk had slipped by night across the frontiers of China. The ill-temper of the court had had time to subside, and besides the pilgrim was returning from his prodigious journey covered in glory, having been received on terms of friendship by the mightiest rulers of foreign lands, and his fame naturally redounded to the credit of his country.

The news of Hiuan Tsang's arrival had spread throughout the Empire, where his extraordinary odyssey was the subject of general curiosity and admiration. In the expansionist and receptive China of the T'ang dynasty the intrepid pilgrim who had crossed the Gobi, the T'ien Shan, the Hindu Kush, the Indus, the Ganges and the Pamirs became the hero of the hour. And when, one spring day in the year 645, he approached Ch'ang-an, the imperial capital, "the rumor of his arrival spread like lightning and the streets were filled with an immense multitude of people eager to set eyes upon him. Disembarking, he attempted in vain to make his way through the crowd, and decided to spend the night on the canal."

On the orders of the court, which was absent from the capital at the time, the magistrates of Ch'ang-an had prepared for the pilgrim a reception worthy of his accomplishments. The governor invited the city's religious to gather in the Street of the Red Bird and solemnly convey to the Monastery of Supreme Happiness (Hung-fo-ssu) the relics, statues and manuscripts which the pilgrim had brought back with him.

"All redoubled their ardor and enthusiasm and made preparations of great magnificence. They emerged from every monastery bearing banners, carpets, daises, costly tables and richly adorned palanquins which they arranged in order. The monks and nuns wore their ceremonial robes. Religious chants were sung at the head of the procession, and monks bearing incense-burners filled with perfumed incense brought up the rear. The procession soon arrived in the Street of the Red Bird. The books and statues were distributed here and there amid the procession, which advanced with calm and majestic step. Girdles loaded

33. "Assault of Mara," from Touen-Houang. (*Musée Guimet*)

with precious stones were heard to clink and resound and a mass of golden flowers spread their dazzling light. The monks who marched in front or formed the escort celebrated this extraordinary event in song and a crowd of lay people shared their joy and admiration.

"The procession began in the Street of the Red Bird and extended as far as the gate of the Monastery of Supreme Happiness, covering a distance of several leagues. The inhabitants of the capital, scholars and magistrates lined both sides of the street, standing in postures redolent of both love and wonder. Men and horses formed a dense mass extending over an enormous area. The magistrates in charge of the ceremony, fearing that many people would be crushed to death in the crowd, ordered everybody to remain where he was, and to burn incense and scatter flowers. A perfumed cloud hung over the procession, and along its whole length could be heard the rhythmical sound of religious chanting. On that day the whole multitude saw simultaneously clouds of five colors shining in the sun and unfolding in sparkling sheets over a distance of several *li* above the books and statues, seeming now to go before them, now to accompany them."

Several days after this ceremony the Master of the Law was permitted to pay his respects to the emperor. The reception took place at the Phoenix Palace at Lo-yang, the second imperial capital, where the court was in residence at the time.

T'ai-tsung asked Hiuan Tsang why he had once left China without letting him know, a euphemistic reference to the contravened decree. This was the delicate question. Hiuan Tsang acquitted himself as a good Chinese scholar should by pointing out that he had addressed a number of pleas to the court but that on account of the obscurity of his name they had failed to reach the emperor himself. He added with his usual frankness that he had been unable to restrain the impulse of his passionate enthusiasm for Buddhism.

T'ai-tsung, a man of superior character, was pleased with such sincerity. Far from reproaching the pilgrim, the emperor congratulated him on having risked his life for the salvation and happiness of mankind "and expressed to him his astonishment that, despite the obstacles placed in his way by mountains and rivers, the great distance of the places visited and the strangeness of their customs, he had succeeded in achieving the purpose of his journey."

Indeed the trip the pilgrim had made could not but excite the interest of the Chinese conqueror. It could prove singularly useful, as providing both information and a precedent, in view of the designs of the Chinese protectorate on the Indo-Iranian borderlands. But at this point we must turn back and review some recent developments in Chinese history.

CHAPTER 13

The Glory of
the T'ang

Hᴵᵁᴬᴺ ᴛsᴀɴɢ came back in 645. A number of serious developments had taken place since the pilgrim's departure, and the Far East to which he returned was not the same as that which he had left. The authority of the T'ang, which at the time of his departure had been quite new and still fairly precarious, was now definitively established at home, and abroad the prestige of the dynasty had grown prodigiously. While the Master of the Law had been in the Buddhist holy land gathering the heritage of the Buddha's Wisdom, T'ai-tsung the Great had been conquering central Asia. The history of this epic conquest is so closely linked with that of Buddhism that we must pause here to recall briefly its principal phases.

The reader will remember that as early as 630 the Chinese legions had thrown the redoubtable northern Turks back into the Mongol plains to the Onon and the Kerulen, and in two encounters had destroyed their empire. A hundred thousand Turks had been massacred and the herds which constituted the wealth of the hordes had been scattered or captured. It had been the end of an entire world.

The Indo-European cities of the Gobi had yielded in their turn, whether of their own free will or as the result of force. Kashgar had acknowledged itself a tributary in 632 and Yarkand in 635. Then it was the turn of the king of Turfan, K'iu Wen-t'ai, the man who had been so hospitable to Hiuan Tsang.

For long a faithful vassal of China, in 640 this ruler committed the folly of entering into an alliance with the Turks to cut off the caravan route between China, India and Persia. He was banking on the protection of the sands of the Gobi, but the imperial general Hou Kiun-tsi crossed the desert with his cavalry and appeared unexpectedly before Turfan. K'iu Wen-t'ai died of a seizure as soon as he received news of the raid. After a bloody battle the Chinese laid siege to Turfan. "Hou Kiun-tsi ordered the war-engines forward and the flying stones fell like rain." The new king, a very young man, came to the Chinese camp to ask for terms. "Before his explanations reached a level of total abjection" one of the Chinese generals stood up and said, "The first thing to be done is to take the city; what is the point of discussing matters with this child? Give us the signal and let us march to the attack!" The young king, "drenched in perspiration," prostrated himself on the ground and agreed to anything. The Chinese general took him prisoner, brought him back and "offered him" to T'ai-tsung in the Kuon-ti Hall. "The ritual of the libations of return was performed and for three days wine was distributed." The king of Turfan's jeweled sword was given by the emperor to the Turkish *condottiere* A-she-na Shö-eul.

In the whole Tokharian region of the northwestern Gobi only the kings of Qarashahr and Kucha still held out. We are familiar from Hiuan Tsang's account with the high culture and fierce pride of these two Indo-European oases which had for so many centuries defied both the might of China and the Turkish threat.

The people of Qarashahr, however, had helped China to crush Turfan, their enemy. When Turfan was annexed they began to be afraid. On the morrow of the disaster we find the king of Qarashahr, Tu-k'i-che, giving his daughter to a Turkish chieftain and concluding a close alliance with the western hordes. Affairs had taken a serious turn. T'ai-tsung dispatched to the Gobi a fresh army under the leadership of General Kua Hiao-k'o, an extremely resourceful warrior. "The site of Qarashahr," we read in the *T'ang Shu,* "had a circumference of thirty *li*. On all four sides tall mountains and the waters of the lake (Bagrash Kol) surrounded it entirely. For this reason the inhabitants were sure that they could never be taken by surprise. But Kua Hiao-k'o advanced by forced marches and, crossing the river, arrived by night beneath the ramparts. He waited until dawn broke before giving the order to attack amidst the cries of the multitude. The drums and trumpets rang out with a loud noise and the soldiers of the T'ang unleashed the full force of their fury. The inhabitants were seized with panic. A thousand heads fell." T'ai-tsung had directed the whole operation from his capital: "One day the emperor said to the ministers standing at his side, 'Kua Hiao-k'o left for Qarashahr on the eleventh day of the eighth month. He will have arrived on the twentieth and must have destroyed the kingdom on the twenty-fourth day; his messengers will be arriving at any minute.' Suddenly a courier entered the room with news of the victory (644)."

As soon as the imperial army had withdrawn, however, the anti-Chinese party again got the upper hand and its candidate, Sie-p'o A-na-che, overthrew the prince invested by the T'ang and seized power.

T'ai-tsung decided to terminate the independence of the Tokharian cities once and for all, for besides Qarashahr he also had occasion to punish Kucha. The old king of Kucha, Swarnatep, who had played host to Hiuan Tsang, had at first shown himself to be an obedient vassal. In 630, for example, he had presented the court with a herd of the Kuchean horses that were so highly valued in the Far East. Subsequently, however, alarmed by the power of the T'ang, he had placed himself under the western Turks. In 644 he had refused tribute and had assisted the people of Qarashahr in their revolt against the Chinese Empire.

From that moment T'ai-tsung had vowed to punish them. Meanwhile Swarnatep had died (646) and been replaced on the throne by his younger brother Ho-li Pu-she-pi—in Sanskrit, Haripushpa or "Divine Flower." The new king, feeling that the storm was about to burst, hurriedly dispatched an embassy to the court protesting his devoted obedience (647). It was too late. A-she-na Shö-eul, the Turkish *condottiere* now in the service of China, was already setting out for the West with an army of Chinese regulars and Tatar mercenaries.

The inhabitants of the two Tokharian cities were expecting the attack to come from the southeast out of the Gobi. It actually came from the northwest. A-she-na Shö-eul in fact began his campaign by hunting down in their plains and mountains the nomadic Turkish tribes, allies of the rebels who lived one of them in the vicinity of Gushen and the other on the Manass not far from presest-day Urumchi. Then, following the trail down from Urumchi to the Lesser Yulduz, he fell on Qarashahr and Kucha unawares. A-na-che hurriedly fortified Qarashahr and attempted to put up some resistance, but he was captured by A-she-na Shö-eul who, "to set an example," cut off his head (648). A-she-na then pounced on Kucha.

Instead of the expected allies from Qarashahr and Turkish reinforcements the terrified Kucheans were offered the spectacle of the Chinese squadrons deploying in the stony desert which stretched away to the north of the town. A military ruse completed their defeat. When King Ho-li Pu-she-pi emerged from the walled city to face the invaders the Chinese adopted the old tactics of the Mongol wars and pretended to fall back, thus drawing the Kuchean cavalry out into the desert where they promptly destroyed it. It was the combined Crécy and

Agincourt of those handsome lords of the Qizil frescoes. A-she-na Shö-eul entered Kucha in triumph; then, since King "Divine Flower" had fled with the remnants of his army to the town of Yaqa Ariq, he pursued him there and took the town after a forty-day siege. Meanwhile one of the Kuchean generals, having rounded up a handful of fugitives, launched a return blow against Kucha. A Chinese general was even killed in this foray. This time the repression was merciless. A-she-na Shö-eul felled eleven thousand heads. "He destroyed five large cities and tens of thousands of men and women. The countries of the West were stricken with terror. . . ."

It was the end of the Tokharian world, the end of a world of charm and refinement, belated survivor of the races of old. The brilliant civilization of Qizil was never to recover from this catastrophe. And when China, after a century of direct rule, again lost interest in Kucha in the second half of the eighth century, it was not the Tokharian aristocracy of former days that resumed power but, as at Turfan, the Uigur Turks. The former Tokharia became eastern Turkistan.

After northern Kashgaria it was the turn of the southern Gobi. As we saw earlier, a detachment of A-she-na Shö-eul's Chinese army swept down from Kucha to Khotan and obliged its king to pay a visit of vassaldom to the court of Ch'ang-an, followed by an enforced stay of several months (648).

Even before he had finished with the Tokharian cities T'ai-tsung had settled accounts with the western Turks. We recall the might of these masters of the steppe and the deep impression which Hiuan Tsang brought back from his stay among them. T'ai-tsung, with his hands full combating the Turks of Mongolia, had for a long time treated them with respect in accordance with the wise maxim that "one must join with those that are far off in order to dominate those that are nigh," and as the object of these advances the khan of the western hordes had come to believe himself the equal of the Son of Heaven. As soon as the Mongolian Turks were *hors de combat,* however, the might of China fell upon the Turks of the West. In 641 they were crushed by the T'ang army in a tremendous battle at Khatun Bogdo-Ola, in the vicinity of present-day Urumchi. Imperial diplomacy completed what had been begun by force of arms, and brought about the division of the empire of the western Turks into several rival hordes which it then manipulated at will. It was with the backing of China that one of those hordes, the Uigurs of Barkol, began at that time to play a major role in the Gobi. For two centuries the Uigurs, who were the most organized of the Turkish peoples, were the devoted collaborators of Chinese foreign policy. China, by way of reward, encouraged or tolerated their settling in the Turfan oasis in the middle of the eighth century, where their period of rule was to be marked by a renaissance of the old schools of Tokharian painting.

Even the king of Tibet, the enterprising Sron-btsan-sgampo, had come within the imperial orbit. In 641 he had obtained from T'ai-tsung the hand of an imperial princess, the Princess of Wen-ch'eng whom we shall find in the next chapter so successfully patronizing the travels of Buddhist pilgrims. Even the states of the Indo-Persian borderlands had bowed to the rising might of the great emperor. The Turko-Iranian princes of Bukhara, Samarkand and Kapisa henceforth sent their tribute to the court of Ch'ang-an.

From this rapid survey we can appreciate the importance which Hiuan Tsang's journey assumed in the eyes of Emperor T'ai-tsung. Religious expeditions like that led by the Master of the Law extended the zone of Chinese influence into places which armed force could not reach. T'ai-tsung questioned the pilgrim at length on the observations he had made of the climates, national products and customs of the countries to the south of the Pamirs. So satisfied was the statesman with the information supplied by the missionary that he wished immediately to make him a minister. We need feel no astonishment at this proposition if we reflect that around this time T'ai-tsung, whose empire now extended to the Pamirs, was doubtless entertaining desires of drawing northern India into his sphere of political influence. As early as 643, as we have seen, he had sent an initial embassy to the court of the Indian emperor Harsha in the persons of Li Yi-piao and Wang Hiuan-ts'ö. In 647, not long after Hiuan Tsang's return, he was again to dispatch Wang Hiuan-ts'ö to India.

The imperial offer of a ministerial position in any case met with the Master of the Law's refusal. "Having entered by the Black Door (of a monastery) as a child and having ardently embraced the Law of the Buddha he had never heard of the teaching of Confucius which forms the heart and soul of the administration. If he had abandoned the principles of Buddhism to follow a temporal call he would have been like a ship sailing under full canvas leaving the sea to voyage on dry land: not only would he not have succeeded in the attempt but he could hardly have avoided being broken and perishing. . . ."

On the other hand it was no mere courtier's flattery that prompted Hiuan Tsang to reply to the emperor's congratulations by saying that the imperial victories had facilitated his journey: "Since Your Majesty has occupied the throne He has brought peace to the Four Seas and His might has even reached the realms beyond the Pamirs. Therefore whenever the princes and chieftains of barbarian tribes see a bird coming out of the East, borne upon the wings of the clouds, they imagine that it comes from Your Majesty's empire and they salute it with respect. Hiuan Tsang, protected by the Power of Heaven (Your Majesty), could similarly come and go without difficulty." Indeed we cannot dispute the fact that, in countries like Samarkand for example, it was the pilgrim's Chinese citizenship that earned him the protection of the local ruler. And the ambassadors which the northern Indian emperor Harsha received from the Chinese conqueror must for their part have been familiar with the particularly warm and attentive welcome which the pilgrim had received in India.

The task to which the Master of Law was henceforth to devote himself was the translation of the six hundred Sanskrit works which he had brought back from India. For this purpose he would have liked to retire to the Monastery of the Little Wood or Shao-lin-ssu in a rural setting on the southern slopes of the Song Shan, "a monastery lying far from the clamor of markets and villages, where cypress, pine and willow threw their shade over silent caves and limpid fountains." T'ai-tsung, however, having conceived a great liking for the pilgrim and wishing to be able frequently to enjoy his company, preferred to have him settle nearer at hand in the Monastery of Great Beneficence (Ta-ts'u-ngen-ssu) which had just been completed in the capital, Ch'ang-an.

Once in residence there Hiuan Tsang gathered around him a veritable team of translators, all of them well versed in Sanskrit. For several months this industrious band worked silently away at creating correct equivalents for the subtle terminology of Indian metaphysics. The first collection was completed in the autumn of 648 and immediately presented to Emperor T'ai-tsung who, "lowering his divine brush, wrote a preface whose sublime ideas will shine as the sun and moon and whose calligraphy, precious as silver and jade, will endure as long as heaven and earth." Hiuan Tsang delivered to T'ai-tsung at the same time the account of his travels which the emperor had enjoined him to write.

So fond indeed had T'ai-tsung become of the Master of the Law that at his request he authorized fresh monastic ordinations (ordinations had always been controlled by the state). During the day the emperor frequently summoned him to his side, and in the evening the monk would return to his monastery to translate a fresh batch of the philosophical texts of the Yogachara school.

As we have seen a new monastery, the Monastery of Great Beneficence, had just been completed for Hiuan Tsang and his companions. Their installation was the occasion for a great and solemn ceremony in which the emperor himself took part: "In the twelfth moon, on the day of Mou-shin, the emperor gave orders that the various bands of musicians should be assembled, that banners and carpets should be prepared, and that all should gather the next day at the Ngan-fo-men Gate, the Gate of Peaceful Happiness, to head the procession of monks. The procession spread out through the streets of the city. There were fifteen hundred carriages adorned with brocade canopies and with banners painted with fishes and dragons and three hundred sunshades made of costly material. Two hundred images of the Buddha, embroidered or painted on silk, two statues of gold and silver and five hundred banners woven of silk and gold thread had been taken out. The sacred books, statues and relics which the Master of the Law had brought back from India had also been taken out and placed on pedestals borne by several carriages in the midst of the procession. On either side of the statue were two large carriages, each of which bore a mast topped by a splendid banner. Behind the banners floated the image of the 'Lion of the Sakya' which headed the procession. A further fifty carriages had been decorated with great magnificence and upon them were seated fifty persons of high rank. There followed all the religious of the capital, carrying flowers and intoning religious hymns. After them, marching in good order, came all the civil and military magistrates; and the nine divisions of the imperial band, disposed on both sides, brought up the rear. The sound of bells and drums was heard and the splendid standards could be seen blowing in the breeze. All the inhabitants of Ch'ang-an were in attendance. An imposing escort was provided by a thousand men of the palace guard. The emperor, accompanied by the crown prince and all the women of the harem, watched from the top of a pavilion overlooking the Ngan-fo-men Gate; holding an incense burner he followed with joyous gaze the deployment of the huge procession.

"At last the statues reached the gate of the monastery. They were there set down amid a cloud of incense to the sound of harmonious music. Afterward the whole multitude dispersed in silence."

During the months that followed Emperor T'ai-tsung grew increasingly fond of Hiuan Tsang. Sprung from such different origins, one from the life of the army camps, the other from the world of prayer; one having brought half of Asia into subjection, the other having completed a successful journey through the fabled "Western Lands," they had both now entered the twilight of their careers. T'ai-tsung took great pleasure in listening to the monk as he told him about the teachings of Buddhism, about the life beyond, and especially about India and the sights and monuments he had seen there.

On 10 July 649, after a twenty-three-year reign devoted to subduing the barbarians and restoring the empire, T'ai-tsung died in his palace at Ch'ang-an and was buried at Li-ts'iuan Hien in Shensi. A detail which nicely characterizes the conqueror—he had his tomb "guarded" by the statues of fourteen vassal kings from the khans of Turkistan to the king of Champa in Indochina. Such was the devotion of his veterans that one of them, the old Turkish chieftain A-she-na Shö-eul, wanted to kill himself over the corpse in the ancient Scytho-Tatar manner "to guard the emperor's funeral couch."

After the death of his protector, notwithstanding the affection in which the new emperor Kao-tsung held him, Hiuan Tsang shut himself away in the Monastery of Great Beneficence and devoted all his efforts to the translation of the sacred books. "Each morning he set himself a fresh task, and if some business prevented him from completing it during the day he would continue working into the night. Whenever he encountered a difficulty he laid the book aside and then having worshipped before the Buddha and accomplished his monastic duties until the third watch, he got up, read aloud the Indian text and noted successively in red ink the portions he was to read at sunrise. Each morning he got up at dawn, partook of a slender meal, and for four hours expounded a fresh holy book. His disciples who came to ask for his instructions filled the galleries and adjoining rooms. In spite of the multiplicity of his activities his soul preserved the same energy at all times and nothing could trouble it or bring it to a halt. Often, too, he would converse with the religious upon the sages and holy men of India, upon the systems of the various schools and upon the distant journeys of his youth."

The life of the Master of the Law continued thus in incredible industry among his translations and his commentaries, interrupted only by a few brief visits to the palace at the request of Emperor Kao-tsung.

But he felt himself growing old, and he had a recurrence of the illness which he had contracted while crossing the Pamirs. He wished to see the village of his birth again and the old family home. "He inquired about his parents and about his old friends who were almost all gone, for he was left with only one sister. He went to visit her and was filled with both sadness and joy at seeing her again. He asked his sister where were the tombs of his father and mother. He went there himself with her and tore up with his own hands the weeds that had been growing there for many years. He chose a place with a better outlook and prepared a double coffin for their final rest."

In 664, having just completed the translation of the *Prajña Paramita* (*Perfection of Wisdom*), he felt his strength declining and realized his end was near: "I feel that my life is drawing to its close. When I die you will take me to my last resting-place. It must be done simply and modestly. You will wrap my body in a mat and lay it in the bowels of some valley in a calm and solitary place." He decided to make a final pilgrimage to the Lan-chi valley to pay his respects to the statues of the Buddha and the Bodhisattvas. On his return to the monastery he gave up his translation work and attended solely to his religious duties.

A few hours before his death he cried out as if emerging from a dream: "I see before my eyes an immense lotus flower of delightful purity and freshness." He also saw in a dream a number of tall men dressed in brocades who emerged from the Master of the Law's room bearing silk hangings embroidered with beautiful flowers and gems of the highest value which they used to decorate, within and without, the room devoted to the translation of the holy books. He then called upon his disciples "to say a joyous farewell to this impure and contemptible body of Hiuan Tsang which, having played its part, deserves to exist no longer. I desire," he added, "to see the merit that I have acquired by my good works devolve upon other men, to be born with them in the Heaven of the Blessed Gods (*Tushita*), to be admitted into the family of Maitreya and there serve that Buddha who is so full of tenderness and affection. When I return to the earth to pursue further existences I desire in each rebirth to fulfill with boundless zeal my duties toward the Buddha and to achieve transcendent knowledge." After saying his farewells he fell silent and entered into meditation. He uttered this final orison which he made those who were present repeat after him: "Adoration be thine, o Maitreya Tathagata, endowed with sublime intelligence; I desire as do all men to see your loving face. Adoration be thine, o Maitreya Tathagata! I desire, on leaving this life, to be among the number of those that surround you." Shortly afterward his spirit passed away. "His face retained its pink complexion, with every feature expressive of joy and happiness in the highest degree. . . ."

Emperor Kao-tsung mourned his passing and had him buried with exceptional honors in the Monastery of Great Beneficence.

CHAPTER 14

Pilgrims of
the Southern Seas

Hiuan tsang's pilgrimage was far from being an isolated event. A contemporary of his, Yi Tsing (634–713), also a monk, has left us an account of the journeys made in his day by other "eminent religious who went to seek the Law in the Western Lands," that is to say in India.

It is a melancholy list. "There were some who crossed the Crimson-Colored Barrier (the Great Wall) and marched alone into the West; others, crossing the vast ocean, voyaged without companions. There was not one of them but bent all his thoughts upon the Holy Vestiges, prostrating himself full-length upon the ground to perform the ritual honors; all believed they would return and, by spreading hope, discover the Four Blessings.

"Yet the triumphal way was fraught with difficulties and the Holy Places vast and distant. For the dozens who budded and flowered and for the few who made the attempt there was scarce one who brought his work to fruition and gave any real results, and few who completed what they set out to do.

"The reason for this was the immensity of the stony deserts of the Land of the Elephant (India), the great rivers and the brightness of the sun that spits down its heat, or the vast waves raised up by the giant fish, the troughs and waves that lift and swell right up to the sky. Walking alone beyond the Gates of Iron (between Samarkand and Balkh), the traveler wandered among the ten thousand mountains and fell to the bottom of steep precipices; sailing alone beyond the Pillars of Copper (south of Tongking), the voyager traversed the thousand deltas and lost his life. . . . Therefore although more than fifty went forth those who survived were but a handful of men."

One of the earliest of Hiuan Tsang's successors and emulators was the monk Hiuan Chao. A native of what is now Shensi province he came, as did Hiuan Tsang, of an ancient Mandarin family. Like him he entered a monastery at a very early age. "At the age when the child's hair is tied up he removed the hair pin and left the world behind him." As soon as he reached manhood he decided to go and worship the Holy Vestiges of the Buddha. After a stay in Ch'ang-an to improve his knowledge of the Sanskrit texts "he took up the stick that is adorned with bronze and set out for the West." The time was about 651. As Hiuan Tsang had done twenty years before him he plunged into the "Shifting Sands" (the Gobi), negotiated the Gates of Iron and climbed the "Snowy Mountains" (the Hindu Kush). He appears at that stage either to have lost his way or to have gone back on his tracks because Yi Tsing has him traveling through Tokharistan and then arriving at the Tibetan frontier. By great good fortune this country was governed at that time by a Chinese regent, the widow of King Sron-btsan-sgampo, the Princess of Wen-ch'eng. The princess, an extremely devout Buddhist, set the pilgrim on the right road again and gave him an escort as far as the Punjab.

As he was coming down from the mountains and approaching Jalandhara (Shö-lan-t'o-lo) his caravan was stopped by brigands. He and his companions found themselves in a precipitous valley which offered no hope of assistance. "He however called upon the gods to help them. He wrote a vow and, prostrating himself before the saints, laid bare his heart. In a dream he received a premonition; he got up and found all the brigands asleep. With secret guidance he emerged from their circle and made his escape."

Hiuan Chao spent four years at Jalandhara perfecting his knowledge of Sanskrit. He then proceeded to Magadha and the Holy Places and spent four years at Bodh Gaya in the vicinity of the Bodhi Temple and then three years at Nalanda. Whereas Hiuan Tsang had spent most of his time at Nalanda studying Yogachara idealism, Hiuan Chao studied first the radical critical philosophy of the Madhyamika under the direction of the master Jinaprabha and then the mystical union and ecstasy of the *yoga* and *dhyana* with the master Ratnasimha.

From the political point of view the situation in northern India had changed a great deal in the last twenty years. Harsha had died c. 647. His place had been taken by a usurper who had been unwise enough to attack the Chinese embassy sent to the deceased monarch by Emperor T'ai-tsung. Ambassador Wang Hiuan-ts'ö, determined not to let this insult go unpunished, asked for the assistance of the kings of Nepal and Tibet, both clients of the T'ang dynasty. With the reinforcements they gave him he returned to the Ganges Basin, defeated the usurper, took him prisoner and led him in chains back to the court of Ch'ang-an. It was this same Wang Hiuan-ts'ö who enabled Hiuan Chao to return to China, once he had completed his pilgrimage. His return route passed through Nepal where the king lent the pilgrim an escort to accompany him as far as Tibet. In Tibet the excellent Princess of Wen-ch'eng, who was still regent, lavished gifts upon Hiuan Chao and gave him an escort back to China.

Hiuan Chao had intended to do as Hiuan Tsang had done on his return and devote himself to the translation of Sanskrit texts, but he had no sooner installed himself (around 664) in Lo-yang with a team of pupils about him than a decree arrived from the emperor ordering him to return to India on behalf of the court and find there a celebrated healer and certain medicinal drugs. He had to leave his Sanskrit books in Lo-yang and set out once more. "Again he crossed the Shifting Sands and a second time passed through the Stony Desert. In the precipitous mountains he walked upon the edge of wooden foot-bridges; throwing but the shadow of his profile he passed sideways across. He swung upon bridges of rope; by twisting his body around he was able to reach the other side. He encountered some Tibetan robbers who deprived him of all he had, even his head-piece, though they left him his life. . . ." Finally he reached India and there met the healer whose reputation had caused such a stir at the Chinese court. The healer set out for China but told Hiuan Chao to go on into India to gather fresh medicinal plants for his august clients. The pilgrim took advantage of his mission to pay a second visit to the relics of Balkh and Kapisa. He then traveled through the Deccan collecting the plants ordered by the court. Before setting out to return to China he went to rest for a while at the monastery of Nalanda.

The way home, however, was now closed both by the Tibetans, who had recently rebelled against the Chinese Empire and cut off the road from Nepal, and by the Arabs, whose front line had since 664 advanced as far as Kapisa. The traveler was obliged to wait in Magadha until history should take a more auspicious turn. "He reposed his will upon the Vulture's Peak and buried his feelings in the Bamboo Grove. Yet he ceaselessly retained the hope of being able to go and spread the light of religion." He hoped in vain, for he fell ill and died on the banks of the Ganges, his age over sixty.

The Chinese were not the only ones to make the pilgrimage to the Holy Places. Not long before, during the reign of T'ai-tsung, several

Korean monks had journeyed to India, most of them taking the route across central Asia but a few using the sea route via the Indo-Malay state of Sri Vijaya, whose capital corresponded to the present-day Palembang, on the island of Sumatra. The entries which Yi Tsing devotes to them end almost invariably with the same formula: "They perished in India and failed to return home."

Indeed as we see from the example of Hiuan Chao the journey from China to India was now becoming more difficult. The might of China, so formidable under T'ai-tsung, entered a period of conspicuous decline under his successor. At any rate it was incapable of ensuring the safety of the central Asian trails. Quite apart from the Arabs, who had been installed in Persia since 642 and whose forays now reached as far as Kabul, there was a fresh contingency: the revolt of the Tibetans against Chinese suzerainty. The Tibetans (or T'u-fan, as the Chinese called them), retaining all the fire of their barbarian temperament which their conversion to Buddhism was too recent to have assuaged, were in a state of ferment and had since 660 been challenging China for the hegemony of central Asia. Around 670 they even succeeded in robbing the Chinese Empire of the oases of Khotan, Yarkand, Kashgar and Kucha, which China was not able to reconquer until c. 692.

At the very gates of China itself the marchlands of Shensi and Ssuch'uan had become a battlefield. "My prince," the poet Tu Fu was to protest to Emperor Ming Huang, "have you seen the shores of the Koko Nor where the unburied bones of the soldiers lie bleaching, and where the spirits of those lately killed importune with their cries those whose bodies perished long ago? The sky is dark, the rain beats coldly upon that cheerless beach, and voices are raised in moaning on every side." It was the beginning of those terrible Tibetan wars that were to drain the strength of the T'ang dynasty.

The trails of central Asia, infested by the Tibetans in the Kashgaria region and by the Arabs in the region of Bactriana, became virtually impassable. Buddhist pilgrims, abandoning the traditional route once followed by Hiuan Tsang, preferred henceforth to travel by sea.

The maritime route, however, was itself by no means lacking in danger, as we learn from the dramatic story of Ch'ang-min. This monk, who belonged to the Dhyana school, sailed for India by way of Java (Holing) and Sumatra (Malayu). From the latter he set sail for the coast of the Deccan. "Now the merchant ship on which he had embarked was carrying a very heavy cargo. They were not far from their port of departure when suddenly an enormous sea got up and in less than half a day the ship foundered. As it was going down the merchants made a rush for the lifeboat and began fighting among themselves. The owner of the ship, however, was a believer. He cried out, 'Master, get into the boat!' Ch'ang-min replied, 'Let others get into it!' Then, placing the palms of his hands together toward the west, he called upon Amida Buddha. As he was intoning his prayer the ship plunged and disappeared. When silence returned he was dead." The reason for his behavior, adds his biographer Yi Tsing, was that "in scorning one's own life for the benefit of other creatures one revëals a heart obedient to the Bodhi; to forget oneself to save other men is to act like the Buddha."

Others, however, were more successful, and voyages through the southern seas, notwithstanding the risks involved, were fairly frequent during this period. The coasts of Vietnam and Cambodia and of the East Indies had long been civilized. What is now North Vietnam constituted a properly administered Chinese province. South Vietnam was then occupied by the ancient kingdom of Champa which was racially Malayo-Polynesian and Indian in its culture and religions; despite its inhabitants' inveterate habit of piracy, it remained a kind of dependency of India. In the capital of the country, Indrapura, corresponding to the present-day Tra Kieu, near Tourane (Da Nang), and at the Sivaite sanctuaries of Mi-so'n the combination of Indian influence and Cham originality gave rise to a most distinctive idiom in architecture and sculpture which reached its height precisely in this seventh century. It is to this period that we owe the thrillingly powerful statues of the Tourane Museum, which bear immortal witness to the genius of the Cham people.

Farther on, Cambodia was the seat of another deeply Indianized kingdom, "Chen-la" as the Chinese called it, which had recently taken the place of the former Fu-nan and constituted the prototype of the great Khmer Empire of the ninth century. The maritime portion of Chen-la or "Water Chen-la," the capital of which was Vyadhapura or Angkor Borei on what is now the frontier with South Vietnam, lay like Champa on the sea route between China and India. It was moreover at this period that the robust "pre-Angkorian" school of sculpture was developing in Cambodia; it had already found an original form and was in the process of enriching the treasure-house of the Indian aesthetic with a new art.

Lastly, on the island of Sumatra to the south, a third Indianized kingdom had been established, that of Sri Vijaya, today's Palembang, which had ousted the sister kingdom of Malayu in 670. This Indo-Malay state, ruled by the great Sailendra dynasty, was to extend its hegemony at one point over all the southern seas from Java to the Gulf of Siam. Simultaneously with establishing a veritable thalassocracy over this region the Sailendra infused it with Indian culture, and they did so with incomparable brilliance for it was they who, toward the end of the eighth century, were responsible for the Buddhist reliefs of Borobudur on the island of Java. In fact it is interesting to observe that it was here in this farthest province of Greater India that Indian art produced its purest masterpieces and worked out its canon to the fullest extent. The Chinese pilgrim who traveled by sea found India come out to meet him. Those who wished to study the Sanskrit scriptures had no need to push on to Nalanda; they need go no farther than the Sumatran monasteries of Sri Vijaya. Those who sought the revelation of Indian Buddhism could if the worst came to the worst forgo a visit to the Buddhas of Mathura and Sarnath and the frescoes of Ajanta; they had only to stop at Java and admire the reliefs and statues of Borobudur. In them all the soothing harmony, all the spirituality of Buddhism, already found expression.

We need not be surprised, then, to find our pilgrims traveling these ancient maritime routes. In spite of the dangers they were now safer than the trails of central Asia with their Tibetan marauders. Moreover the control which the Sumatran emperors of Sri Vijaya exercised over the southern seas gave this area a security which it was later to lose and never find again.

One of the first pilgrims to take this route was Master of the Law Ming-yuan. Starting from southern China he traveled overland to the Gulf of Tongking and there took ship. Having survived a typhoon he called in at Java and then went on to Ceylon, where he was given a friendly reception by the king and his court. His response was most unworthy: having secretly gained access to the stupa in which it was kept he attempted to make off with the relic of relics, the Buddha's Tooth. "The people of Ceylon," writes Yi Tsing, "guard this tooth of the Buddha with quite exceptional precautions. They keep it in a tall tower with multiple doors each of which is locked with intricate locks. On each lock they make a seal and this is stamped with the signet of five officials. If one of the doors is opened the city is averted by a loud noise. Offerings are made to the relic daily and fragrant flowers are heaped up all around and upon it. If the people pray with great faith the tooth appears above the flowers or shines with supernatural brightness. There is a tradition according to which, if Ceylon were to lose the tooth, the island would be swallowed up and devoured by the demons. It is to prevent such a calamity that the relic is guarded with such exceptional diligence." According to another tradition, however, the tooth was destined to finish up in China. "That will be a remote result of the power of the saints," writes Yi Tsing mysteriously. "Given faith, it will come to pass."

Ming-yuan no doubt believed himself to be the chosen instrument for his purpose in stealing the relic was to take it back to China. But he was spotted, a crowd gathered, the tooth was recovered, and the monk came close to getting a very rough handling. "The affair," writes Yi Tsing delicately, "did not go as he had wished, and he was covered with shame and disgrace."

Shortly after this unfortunate episode the monk Yi-lang from Ssu-ch'uan embarked with his brother from a port near Canton and sailed via Cambodia, or Fu-nan as it was then still called, to Ceylon and on to the Deccan, where he disappeared. Another monk from Ssu-ch'uan, Huei-ning, traveled to Java around the same time and there studied the Sanskrit scriptures for three years under the direction of the Indian monk Jñanabhadra; he then embarked for India where subsequent pilgrims were unable to find any trace of him. He must have perished at sea during the crossing. The Tongking monk Yun-k'i also went to Java to study under Jñanabhadra. Like Yi Tsing we note with interest that he could speak both Sanskrit and Malay (or "Fan" and "Kunlun" as the Chinese called them) equally well, with the result that he eventually settled in Sri Vijaya.

Sometimes one of the pilgrims would make a dramatic discovery as Ta-ch'eng-teng did. A monk of the Dhyana school, he had already traveled a great deal. While still a child he had embarked with his parents for Dvaravati, a country then inhabited by the Indianized Mon people and corresponding to the southern part of modern Thailand. Having returned to China and taken orders, he conceived a desire to see India. He sailed for Ceylon and crossed the Deccan from south to north. At the port of Tamralipti (Tamluk) in Bengal his boat was pillaged by corsairs who left him with nothing but his life. After a stay of twelve years in that part of the country he went to visit the Holy Places, Gaya and Nalanda, Vaisali and Kusinagara. It was during the course of this journey that he came across the hermitage of another Chinese pilgrim and fellow-student of his, Tao-hi. But Tao-hi had died not long before. "His Chinese books were in the same condition as during his life. His Sanskrit tablets were still in order. Seeing them, Ta-ch'eng-teng was unable to contain his tears: 'Once upon a time at Ch'ang-an we used to sit together upon the mats in the hall where the Law was taught; today, in a foreign land, I find only his empty dwelling.' "

The same fate awaited another celebrated monk, Tao-lin. Sailing by way of Java and passing on the way the "Land of the Naked Men" (probably the Nicobar Islands) he disembarked at Tamralipti in Bengal. He then traveled the length and breadth of India, from Na-landa, where he spent a number of years, to the Deccan and thence to Kashmir and Kapisa. After that we lose track of him. His biographer is of the opinion that he tried to get through to Persia and was ambushed by brigands, possibly a band of roving Arabs.

How many more names do we read in Yi Tsing's memoir—of how many shadowy figures do we catch a glimpse! The melancholy account of their travels and mysterious deaths somewhere in the jungles of Bihar or the forests of the south is almost always the same. We can only poorly distinguish the personalities of these seekers after truth who left their homeland in droves to tramp the dangerous roads of India. Yet even the very mention of these journeys is thrillingly evocative. The ease with which people could travel about in those far-off days! And, realizing this, how much better we can understand the similarities and points of comparison between the treasures of our museums. From India and Ceylon to Java, Cambodia, Champa and the Cantonese ports there was an incessant interchange of ideas, books and works of art. In this respect the southern seas played the same role as once the chain of oases across the Gobi had done, and as a center of Indianism, Sri Vijaya on the island of Sumatra could only be compared with what Kucha in central Asia had formerly been.

Among these pilgrims Che-hong and Wu-hing deserve a place of their own; their faces stand out in greater relief for us and their journeys appear to have been more fruitful in results.

Che-hong, as it happened, was the nephew of ambassador Wang Hiuan-ts'ö whose diplomatic and military missions in India we have already mentioned. Doubtless Che-hong's Confucian background and his contacts in the administration would have brought him rapid promotion had he decided on a professional career. Being of a contemplative and serious nature, however, the young man evinced quite other inclinations. In any case the spectacle of the court of Empress Wu Tsö-t'ien with its crimes and upheavals was understandably repellent to a delicate soul. "Discerning that the court and the city offered nothing but clamor and tumult" and "holding in honor the purity and tranquility of Buddhist wisdom," he retreated to the mountains of Kuangsi and there spent several years in meditation. "He contemplated the picturesque beauty of mountain and stream and walked in the quiet solitude of the forests and groves. He took up his brush to write of the desire he felt to leave on that distant voyage." At that point he made the acquaintance of another monk who shared the same feelings, Wu-hing.

Like him, Wu-hing had withdrawn to the mountains of southern China where, wandering among the peaks and beside the streams of this landscape of distant views, of mists and jutting pinnacles which the Sung artists were later to popularize, he gave himself up to the synthetic ecstasy preached by the Dhyana school and communed at length with the essence of things. He too dreamed of traveling to the Holy Land. In his mountain retreat he had just finished reading the *Lotus of the Good Law*. "He said then with a sigh: 'If a man seeks out a net it is because he intends to catch fish; if a man inquires into language it is because he desires to turn his attention to the Teaching. It would be good to be able to question a master, to see in him as in a mirror my heart and my soul, to open the door to peace and set a term to trouble and doubt." The meeting with Che-hong finally made up his mind, and the two friends left together on the pilgrimage to India.

They set sail from what is now Lei-chou in the Kuang-tung Peninsula. After a month at sea they reached Sri Vijaya on the island of Sumatra. The reigning Sailendra monarch loaded them with favors—as Buddhists first of all, and secondly as subjects of the T'ang—and it was on a royal ship that they embarked for India. An interesting detail is that they first put in at Negapatam in India proper but immediately set sail again for the island of Ceylon. This order of travel shows what an important place Sinhalese Buddhism had assumed as far as Chinese religious were concerned and how little restriction the quarrel between the two great Buddhist schools, the Hinayana and the Mahayana, placed upon personal relationships. The gulf which today separates the Little Vehicle of Ceylon and Thailand from the Sino-Japanese Great Vehicle did not as yet exist. All the pilgrims from China went first of all to Ceylon to look at the Tooth of the Buddha, and the reader will remember that it was only the outbreak of some temporary local unrest which prevented Hiuan Tsang himself from visiting the island.

From Ceylon Che-hong and Wu-hing embarked for the coasts of Orissa and Bengal, where they stayed for a year. They then settled down in the monastery of Nalanda, where the king of Magadha honored them with the title of "Superior" (Viharasvamin), and there they saw arrive the man who was to be their chronicler and the chronicler of all the Chinese pilgrims, Yi Tsing, the most illustrious of the successors of Hiuan Tsang.

CHAPTER 15

The Voyages of Yi Tsing

Yi TSING, who was to be the historian of the other Buddhist pilgrims, has also left us an account of the vicissitudes of his own pilgrimage. He was born in Che-li in 634. At the early age of seven he was admitted to a monastery. His master, the monk Shan-yu, died when he was only twelve years old. "This event," writes Chavannes, "made a deep impression on him. When twenty-five years later he resolved to depart for India it was to the tomb of his former master that he went to seek the supreme encouragement he needed. It was a grey day in autumn when he came to visit the burial mound; the shrubs which had been planted at the time of the funeral had become young trees, and their growth testified to the age of this grief still present in the disciple's heart; a fog descended upon the region, which was covered with yellowed grass;

there was something mysterious in the calm melancholy of the scene, as if the spirit of the dead man had awoken to bestow his blessing upon the pilgrim. Yi Tsing told him of his forthcoming journey and begged his protection."

In the autumn of 671 Yi Tsing embarked at Yang-chou in Kiangsu province on a Persian ship. The season was propitious; it was the start of the northwest monsoon. "The wind was beginning at that time to blow into the vastness of space and the thousand-foot-long ropes were suspended two by two. It was the beginning of the time marked by the constellations; we left the north behind us and the vane of feathers floated in lonely isolation. For a long time were we engaged upon the massive deep; huge waves as high as mountains barred the surface of the ocean, sweeping right across the vast abyss; the spray, like clouds, rose full up to the sky."

Twenty days later Yi Tsing's ship sighted the island of Sumatra. Yi Tsing spent eight months there, six at Sri Vijaya and two at Malayu. Then a Sumatran ship took him across the Bay of Bengal. On the way he saw the "Land of the Naked Men" which as we have said was probably the Nicobar Islands. "Looking shorewards the traveler sees a luxuriant vegetation of coconut trees and areca palms. As soon as the natives sight a ship approaching they vie with one another in getting out their little boats, more than a hundred of which come out to meet the ship. They all bring coconuts and bananas and cane and bamboo objects which they seek to exchange against iron. A piece of iron the size of two fingers will purchase between five and ten coconuts. The men are all completely naked; the women hide their sex with leaves. Should the merchants in jest offer them clothes they make signs with their hands to the effect that they do not use them. These natives live exclusively on coconuts and yams. Whenever a ship refuses to trade with them they immediately let fly with poisoned arrows."

From the Nicobar Islands to the Bengal coast took Yi Tsing a further fortnight. In the second moon of the year 673 he disembarked at the port of Tamralipti or Tamluk where he remained for a year perfecting his Sanskrit before pushing on to the interior. He then set out on the pilgrimage to Magadha, the principal "holy land." "Ten days away from the temple of Bodh Gaya the traveler enters a region of mountains and lakes. The perils of the road are not easily overcome. Only a party of several persons traveling together can get through because the various members can all help each other; no one should proceed alone. At that time I fell victim to a bout of illness. My body ached all over and I was at the end of my strength. I tried to take advantage of the passage of a caravan of merchants, but in a short while my exhaustion was such that I was no longer able to keep pace with them. Though exerting myself to the full in my desire to push ahead, for every five *li* that I traveled I was obliged to halt a hundred times. There were more than twenty monks from the temple of Nalanda with me then who had all gone on ahead. I was left behind alone in the rocky defiles. Toward evening, between three and five o'clock, some mountain brigands approached with bows strung, shouting at the tops of their voices. They drew near to inspect me, laughing at me amongst themselves. They began by stripping me of my clothing. All my straps and belts too they tore from me. I thought in that moment that I should soon be saying farewell for a long time to come to the generations of men, that I should be disappointed in my desire to make the pilgrimage and that my limbs would be scattered upon the points of their lances." No doubt recalling the tragic fate that had so nearly befallen Hiuan Tsang on the Ganges, Yi Tsing believed that these savages were on the point of cutting his throat on account of his pale skin and offering him as a sacrifice to some Sivaite idol: "I then went down into a muddy hollow and covered myself from head to foot with slime; afterward I covered my body with leaves and then, supporting myself on my stick, I went slowly on my way. The sun went down and our stopping-place was still far off. In the second watch of the night (between nine and eleven o'clock) I was fortunate enough to rejoin my companions. I heard the venerable Ta-ch'eng-teng calling to me over and over again from the village; as soon as we were reunited he began busying himself with fetching me a robe and washing my body in a pool."

At last Yi Tsing reached Nalanda and Gaya and was able to adore the holy places for himself and also on behalf of his friends back in China who had asked him to say a prayer for them before the Bodhi Tree. "I prostrated my whole body upon the ground. In my mind was but one thought, a most respectful sincerity. For China I asked the Four Blessings; then, for the whole Buddhist world, knowledge of the Holy Tradition, the universal meeting beneath the Dragon-Flower Tree, the meeting with the venerable person of the Compassionate One (Maitreya, the Buddha-to-be) and the acquisition of Perfect Understanding. Afterward I performed in their entirety the series of adorations before the holy relics."

Yi Tsing also paid a visit to the sacred spot at Kusinagara where the Buddha had entered Nirvana, the Deer Park at Benares, site of the first sermon, and all the places celebrated in the scriptures. He remained at Nalanda for ten years, receiving instruction from the doctors of the Law and collecting together copies of the holy books.

Eventually, however, the time came for him to return home. He decided to take the sea route again so that he could edit his Sanskrit texts in the scholarly atmosphere of Sri Vijaya. His compatriot Wuhing, whom he had found at Nalanda, was also going back to China but he wanted to travel by way of the Gandhara region. The two friends bade each other a sad farewell. "We traveled together for a distance of six *yojana* from Nalanda. We were both deeply grieved to be thus parting from one another during our lifetime. Both of us nurtured the hope that we would meet again. Contemplating the immensity of the task which still lay before us, we wiped away our tears upon our sleeves." They went for a last walk together on the Vulture's Peak to the northeast of ancient Rajagriha. "When we had completed our adorations and made our offerings we looked out over the countryside and the mountain gorges and were unable to master a great feeling of sadness." It was then that the pilgrim composed this melancholy poem:

"I went to contemplate the transformation of things at the summit of the Jetavana and looked out over the former royal city. The pool, ten thousand years old, is still in good condition. The thousand-year-old park is still cool and green. But the path laid down by King Bimbisara is vague and uncertain; on the flank of the mountain it is quite destroyed. The holy terrace of the Seven Jewels has lost its former vestiges. The celestial flowers of four colors no longer rain down with melodious harmony; both harmony and flowers long ago passed away."

Then come these lines with their moving piety: "How I regret having been born so late. In the world of today I cannot make out the Gate; I cannot see the Way that leads to Nirvana. I climbed on foot to the height overlooking the city and I gazed into the distance. My heart journeyed out over the Seven Seas. The Three Worlds, a prey to confusion, were as if engulfed; in the ten thousand orders of beings there was not one heart that was sincere. Only the Compassionate One had complete understanding; he scattered the dust and calmed the waves; he opened up the Ultimate Path. Meeting a famished tigresss he surrendered the rampart of his body; he let his pity fall upon creatures in distress. In the river whose waves were stilled he dissolved his ancient ties. With the sword of Understanding, frozen like rime, he divided the fogs as they gathered. In all the endless *kalpas* there is not one in which he has not practiced virtue. Throughout the six divisions of the day he takes pity upon living creatures. He has transcended the current of existence and the glory of Nirvana is his. . . ."

Yi Tsing goes on to evoke the toils which still faced the two pilgrims on their hazardous journey home: "In the river of sand and in the snowy mountains in the morning the traveler cannot make out the road. On the vast ocean and hard by sudden shores he is lost while crossing at night. He risks ten thousand deaths to save one single life. . . . But we pilgrims have renounced pleasure for our own persons; we ask not heaven for fame among posterity. We have made a vow to sacrifice this body that is exposed to danger in the search for the victorious Teaching. We hope, all of us, to be able to satisfy our passion for spreading the Light."

He continues with this final farewell to the soil of India, to the hills and forests and villages of Bihar, the countryside which provided the setting for the life of the Blessed One: "This song of sadness I will not sing again. I look from afar upon the places I visited in the morning. To the east I meditated upon the two Footprints left upon the hill; to the west I galloped to the Deer Park where the three revolutions of the Law began. To the north I have seen the still unsullied pools of Kusa-garapura; to the south, the cave which is still there in the holy mountain. The five peaks are still beautiful, the hundred pools can still be clearly seen. In their great purity fresh flowers cast their light on every side; with great brilliance the Tree of Wisdom shines through the three months of spring. Leaning on my pilgrim's staff I made my way to the steep mountainside. Supporting my steps I have climbed the Jetavana Mountain and seen the stone on which the Blessed One once laid his folded robes. . . . In gazing and meditation I am as if united with that which is divine."

Finally there comes this more human and very personal note: "I am sad; China is far from here. . . . While in my youth I enjoyed the pleasures of listening, day followed upon day until, without my realizing it, I have reached the years of my decline, autumn having ever followed upon autumn. I have already accomplished my original intention of visiting this mountain (i.e., of visiting the Holy Land). Oh, that I might take with me the holy books and set out on my way back to China!"

Taking leave of his companion, whom he was never to see again, Yi Tsing went back to Tamralipti and re-embarked (685). He had with him more than ten thousand rolls of Sanskrit texts. He stopped at Sri Vijaya, as he had planned to do, and spent four years there translating, in a Sanskrit *milieu,* a part of this enormous booty. The task, however, was too great for one man and in 689 he traveled to China to enlist help. He disembarked at Canton, recruited his disciples, and four months later re-embarked with them for Sumatra.

Yi Tsing spent a further period of more than five years in Sri Vijaya, writing up his own notes and translating his Sanskrit texts. He finally returned to his homeland for good in 695, and in the middle of that summer he entered Lo-yang, the second imperial capital. The court was interested in his travels as it had been in Hiuan Tsang's, and granted him an official reception. On this occasion, however, the imperial throne was occupied by a woman, one of the most extraordinary figures in Chinese history—the Empress Wu Tsö-t'ien. The reign of this Chinese "Agrippina" is of such interest to the historian of Buddhism that we must here attempt to evoke something of her disturbing personality. Indeed by a curious paradox this immoderate woman proved to be one of the most zealous protectors of the faith of Sakyamuni.

Wu Tsö-t'ien was a former favorite of Emperor T'ai-tsung. She had entered his harem in 637 at the age of fourteen and distinguished herself there as much by her wit as by her beauty. Kao-tsung noticed her among his father's women when he was still crown prince, and from that day on secretly loved her. When T'ai-tsung died all the women of his harem had to crop their hair and enter the convent of Kan-ye-ssu. As soon as the official mourning period was over Kao-tsung, now himself crowned Son of Heaven, brought the young woman out of her retreat and restored her to her place at court.

The ambitious concubine, however, was not content with a subordinate role. As the poet Lo Pin-wang, her enemy, put it, "with her eyebrows arched like a butterfly's antennae she consented not to take second place to other women. Hiding behind her sleeve she applied herself to spreading slander. Her foxy charm was peculiarly able to bewitch the master." She did not hesitate to stoop to the most heinous of crimes to gain her ends, strangling with her own hands the child she had just had by the emperor and charging the legitimate empress with the deed.

The Chinese historians have left us an account of this drama which again puts us in mind of Tacitus, though in a setting of specifically Chinese courtesy and hypocrisy. Soon after the birth of the child, a girl, the empress came to pay Wu Tsö-t'ien a visit. She took the child in her arms and fondled it, congratulating the young mother. As soon as she had left Wu Tsö-t'ien strangled the new-born infant and afterward replaced it in its cradle. The emperor was then announced. Wu Tsö-t'ien received him with her face radiant with joy, uncovering the cradle to show him their daughter, and revealing to their horror the little corpse. She burst into a fit of sobbing in which she was careful to avoid directly accusing the woman she had resolved to ruin. Finally, in reply to the emperor's urgent questions, she placed the blame upon her attendants. The latter, in attempting to clear themselves, naturally mentioned the visit of the empress a few moments before. And so cleverly had the scene been handled that Kao-tsung became convinced of the empress' guilt. He stripped her of her rank and raised Wu Tsö-t'ien in her place (655). Despite the reproaches of his father's former companions in arms he soon fell under the yoke of his new consort. Like Nero's mother, she too attended the deliberations of the Council concealed behind a curtain. When Kao-tsung continued in secret to visit the empress he had repudiated, Wu Tsö-t'ien had the unfortunate woman's hands and feet cut off.

From 660 onward it was Wu Tsö-t'ien who directed all affairs of state in Kao-tsung's name. By means of a network of informers she was able to terrorize the entire court with impunity and even decimate the imperial family of the T'ang. After putting to death the mandarins who opposed her she forced their wives and daughters to enter her service as slaves. The timorous emperor, aware of her victims' innocence, dared do nothing to save them. Remorse undermined his health and he died of grief in 683 after seeing his favorite son poisoned by Wu Tsö-t'ien. Continuing to reign in the name of her own son she remained absolute mistress of the Empire for a further twenty-two years.

Her crimes apart she was a woman of considerable ability and knew a great deal more than her late husband about the handling of affairs. Under her energetic leadership T'ai-tsung's administrative machine continued to function effectively, and despite the tragedies which beset the seraglio the great emperor's veterans contained the barbarians on all fronts. Indeed it was during Wu Tsö-t'ien's period of personal rule that China recovered from the Tibetans what were known as the "Four Garrisons," that is to say the four Kashgarian cities of Kucha, Qarashahr, Kashgar and Khotan (692).

All things bowed before this indomitable woman. Her audacity did not stop at deposing her own son, the young Chung-tsung (684), nor, finally, at proclaiming herself "emperor" (690). In vain had the princes of the blood, ashamed at having a former concubine lord it over them, flocked to the standard of revolt raised by the old legitimist General Siu King-ye and the poet Lo Pin-wang. They had been crushed and their heads brought to the empress. As mistress of the reins of power she manipulated them to satisfy her every whim, even going so far as to take a young bonze for her favorite, appointing him superior of one of the monasteries of Lo-yang and "granting him official permission to enter and leave the palace at any hour of the day or night."

For in the character of this extraordinary woman, with all her excesses of cruelty and voluptuousness, there lay embedded somewhere a concern for religion. Though clearly incapable of appreciating the tremendous gentleness of Buddhism she did nevertheless show signs of the most sincere piety. We thus find her between 672 and 675 patronizing the sculpture of the famous rupestral Great Buddha of the Lung-men caves with his entourage of Bodhisattvas, monks and *lokapalas*. And it is doubtless precisely such works as this, in which the mysticism and idealism of a former age are replaced by a realistic violence which is almost shocking, that can enlighten us as to the variety of Buddhism which Wu Tsö-t'ien found to her taste. Still, they do testify to the brilliant era of patronage which the faith enjoyed under the empress.[1]

When Yi Tsing arrived in Lo-yang the empress, evincing the same sentiments, came in person to greet him at the eastern gate of the city at the head of an enormous procession.

Yi Tsing, however, could hardly entertain with regard to Wu Tsö-t'ien the same relationship of trusting friendship which had united Hiuan Tsang and Emperor T'ai-tsung toward the end of their lives. Having no doubt little desire to frequent a corrupt court, the saintly monk devoted himself entirely to his translation work. He was given a number of mandarins and Chinese scholars to help him in this task, as well as several Indians who had settled in China. For a time his principal collaborator was a Khotanese monk named Sikshananda. With the aid of these various helpers he completed the translation of no less than fifty-six works, quite apart from his own original productions.

While he was thus absorbed in his work a palace revolution finally brought down his redoubtable protectress. In the face of public discontent she had decided to restore to the throne at least nominally the young emperor Chung-tsung. In reality she continued to govern alone with her new favorites, the Chang brothers. A plot was hatched against

---

[1] It was the same story with another celebrated Chinese empress, the dowager Hu of the Wei dynasty, a former concubine who became mistress of northern China (516–28). "She was described in terms that made her both feared and admired. One day she invited the courtiers to take part in an archery contest. The majority showing themselves to be incompetent bowmen, she stripped them of their rank on the spot. When she took up the bow herself her arrow pierced the eye of a needle. But this energetic woman put into the exercise of her passions the same ardor that she put into her work, taking one lover after another and raising him on the instant to a position of supreme power. The people and officials began to grow weary of these debauches which threw the court into upheaval. As her son grew older the empress became anxious lest he turn against her. Then, when he reached the age of eighteen and showed signs of desiring his independence, he suddenly died. Public opinion accused his mother of having poisoned him. In order to calm the storm which she felt was gathering about her she pretended to place upon the throne a little prince of three years of age, cousin to the deceased. But her time was come. With the backing of all the malcontents a general raised the revolt at the head of the army. In vain did the panic-stricken empress attempt to escape with her life by shaving her head and taking refuge in a temple as a nun; the triumphant insurgents drowned her in the Huang-ho." Yet that same empress, like her later emulator, was an extremely devout Buddhist and was responsible for sending the pilgrims Sung Yun and Huei-sheng to the Gandhara region to bring back Mahayanist texts (518–522). The piety of these Chinese empresses recalls that of Brunhilda and Fredegund, and of Irene of Constantinople.

her, however, and one night in 705 the conspirators broke armed into the palace. Encountering the feeble Chung-tsung, the emperor without authority, they acclaimed him and dragged him forcibly along with them as they burst into Wu Tsö-t'ien's apartments. The former empress, woken up out of sleep, alone and defenseless, her favorites lying at her feet with their throats cut, still stood up to the rebels. She tried one last time to intimidate Chung-tsung and might possibly have succeeded had the conspirators left her time. Holding a dagger to her throat, they forced her to abdicate. She died of vexation a few months later, at the age of eighty-one.

Chung-tsung, once restored to power, showed himself a no less zealous protector to Yi Tsing than the deceased sovereign had been, and one no doubt very much more to the pilgrim's taste. He took a particular interest in his work and one day even went in person to the western gate of Lo-yang to announce to all the officials that the holy books had just been freshly translated.

Moreover Chung-tsung recollected that in the days of his persecution and banishment from the court by Wu Tsö-t'ien he had prayed at length to the Bodhisattva Bhaishajyaguru, kind doctor of bodies and souls, and that his prayers had been granted. When the events of 705 replaced him on the throne he had no wish to appear ungrateful to his celestial guardians. As a result the most saintly monks of the capital were frequently summoned to the palace, notably among them Yi Tsing, who spent the summer of 707 with the emperor. Chung-tsung himself paid many visits to the pilgrim, sitting down on his mat and participating personally in the work of translating the scriptures.

But this affectionate collaboration between the saintly monk and the gentle emperor was destined to be interrupted by a fresh palace drama. Chung-tsung's wife, the young Empress Wei, had taken a lover in the person of one of the deceased empress' nephews, the handsome Wu San-ssu. The cuckolded emperor was quite unaware of his condition. One of the princes of the blood, outraged by these depraved goings-on, stabbed Wu San-ssu to death (707); in vain, as it turned out, for Chung-tsung repudiated the man who had done him justice. Finally this "Messalina," finding her phantom husband still in her way, poisoned him in order to reign alone. But she did not have Wu Tsö-t'ien's terrible authority. Her crime, as soon as it was discovered, provoked members of the imperial family to revolt under the leadership of the young Prince Li Lung-ki. In 710 the conspirators repeated the drama of five years before, invading the palace by night and bringing down the usurping empress under a hail of arrows. Her head was stuck on the end of a pike and displayed to the crowd. Li Lung-ki then had his own father, Jui-tsung, appointed emperor (711), and the next year ascended the imperial throne himself, becoming, under the names of Hiuan-tsung and Ming Huang, the greatest sovereign of the T'ang dynasty after T'ai-tsung (712–55).

As for Yi Tsing, he lived on in studious retirement far removed from these alarms, completing his great work of translation and finally reaching the term of his industrious life. A son of the king of Kashmir, who had traveled from India to bring his country's homage to the imperial court, assisted him for a while with his knowledge. He died a pious death in 713 at the age of seventy-nine.

Though lacking Hiuan Tsang's powerful personality, this less colorful, less distinct figure nevertheless merits the space we have devoted to him. A certain melancholy turn of thought, the nostalgia which he brings even to his descriptions of the Indian landscape, lend a particular charm to his physiognomy. His whole book, right down to the specifically Chinese poems with which he punctuates the narrative, breathes an atmosphere of gentleness and tenderness. Nor do we find the Confucian rhetoric which shows through here and there displeasing for it helps us to complete our picture of this pious monk and assiduous scholar who accomplished the most astonishing journeys without appearing to have had the least idea of his own historical importance.

And so the Chinese pilgrims of the great T'ang dynasty, both by their travels and by their translations, brought the Far East daily closer to India. It was a unique moment in the history of Asia. Thanks to the T'ang peace the continent lay as open to missionaries as to embassies and merchant caravans. Much more—it enabled Japan, the new born child of Sino-Buddhist culture, to share in its turn this great world current. One of Hiuan Tsang's chief disciples was in fact Japanese; this was the monk Dosho who went to China with an embassy in 653 and on his return home spread the Master's doctrine of Yogachara idealism, known in Japan as the Hosso doctrine. At about the same time a second Japanese, Shitsu, visited the T'ang Empire in order to study Buddhist philosophy (658).

These Japanese pilgrimages of the early Middle Ages, the consequence and the complement of the travels of the pilgrims from China, are conjured up for us in a charming T'ang poem by Ts'ieu K'i, "The Japanese Bonze Returning to his Country":

> His vocation brought him to the Higher Empire.
> His voyage is like a dream.
> As he arrives from the far-off ocean, is it the heaven he has sailed?
> Light is the ship in which he returns, yet heavy with learning.
> The vastness of the sea and the moon's clearness recall the virtue of
> the Buddha.
> The fishes and dragons would leave the water to hear the Indian
> prayers.
> Does it not shine sweetly, this lamp that lights the world's eyes?

For this indeed was that supremely memorable epoch in which Japan, under the influence of Chinese missionaries, made her definitive entry into the way of Buddhism and, through Buddhism, into the company of the ancient civilizations. It was the work above all of two politicians of genius who also proved to be two great minds, the regent Shotoku Taishi and Prince Nakanoe, the first of whom governed Japan from 592 to 621 and the second from 645 to 671. The foundation of the historical Japan was the 604 Constitution of Shotoku, the second clause of which read: "The *Three Jewels* (the Buddha, the Law, the Order),

are the supreme refuge of all creatures and the ultimate end of all existence. . . . Few men are fundamentally wicked. All men are capable of
realizing the truth when instructed in it." Shotoku Taishi, acting on the
first of these maxims, erected on the shores of the Inland Sea monastic
colleges where the Sino-Sanskrit scriptures were taught, and hospitals
for the aged and infirm.

The true witness of this transformation, however, is the Horyuji
temple founded by Shotoku Taishi at Nara in 607. Whereas everything
else in Asia has changed, India having forgotten the very name of the
Buddha and China barely remembering the great flowering of intellect
which took place under the T'ang dynasty, the Horyuji temple still
preserves in all its purity the doctrine of mystical idealism that Hiuan
Tsang and Yi Tsing went to India to study thirteen hundred years ago.

CHAPTER 16

The Peace of
the Pagodas

How MARVELOUS if we could know what the meditations of these great travelers were once they had returned to their homeland. One or two of them, of course, such as Hiuan Tsang and Yi Tsing, have left us pragmatic accounts of their journeys, and we have their translations and the religious or metaphysical treatises which they wrote, inspired by what they had learned from their Indian masters. But what we should like to know about these Far Eastern sages, these discerning scholars and sensitive poets, is what they dreamt in the privacy of their hearts. Back in the silence of their monasteries after voyaging so far and seeing so much they must sometimes have conjured up once more the great silent lands which, as they stood at the summit of the Pamirs, had lain stretched out at their feet. They must have recalled those evenings at Benares, or heard in the depths of memory the song of the sea that had accompanied them from Along Bay to the ports of Sumatra and on to the paradise island of Ceylon. As the doors of their monasteries swung to behind them these pilgrims of wisdom were shut in with the dream of a whole world.

It was this atmosphere of nostalgic reverie that was the most charming feature of the Buddhist monasteries of the T'ang period, those havens of learning, contemplation, recollection and silence. So deep was the impression that emanated from their walls that the entire Chinese poetry of the period is imbued with it. There is a whole series of T'ang poems on the subject of "A Visit to the Monastery":

> I made my way to the abode of holiness
> Where it was my good fortune to receive a kindly welcome from a
> venerable bonze.
> I entered deeply into the principles of sublime reason
> And broke the tyranny of worldly preoccupations.
> The monk and myself were united in a single thought.
> Having exhausted the capacity of words we remained silent.
> I looked at the flowers, as still as ourselves.
> I listened to the birds that hung in the air and I understood the
> Great Truth.

So wrote Sung Che-wen, favorite poet of the pious Emperor Chung-tsung. We find the same sentiments expressed by Li Shang-yin in this depiction of a hermitage which is also a spiritual landscape, the landscape of the Buddhist soul itself:

> The sun is setting behind the hills of the West.
> I have come to visit the solitary bonze in his hermitage.
> The dead leaves are flying about his domain but where is the owner?
> Cold clouds encroach upon the paths.
> Alone in the first hour of the night he will sound his bell.

He will lean, musing, as he does every evening, against the single
        trunk of his wisteria plant.
In this world no bigger than a speck of dust
What is the use of loving and hating?

All the detachment, all the immense peace of Buddhism are contained in these lines. And in the following poem, from the brush of the eighth-century poet T'ao Han, we have the whole mystic dream of the Mahayana:

Pines and cypresses conceal the mountain gorge,
But in the West I find a narrow path.
The sky opens up, a peak looms,
And, as if formed from the void, a monastery appears before me.
The building seems to perch upon a terrace of cloud,
Launching its pavilions into the air amid the sheer rocks.
Night comes; monkeys and birds fall silent.
The sound of the bells and the chanting of the bonzes reach me
        through the clouds.
I contemplate the blue peaks and the moon's reflection in the waters
        of the lake.
I listen to the sound of the springs and the wind troubling the leaves
        beside the rushing torrent.
My spirit has gone forth beyond visible things,
Captive, yet roaming free . . .

Here the poetic impulse reaches the sublime heights of metaphysics. The pilgrims and the poets have brought us to the threshold of Buddhist thought, which we must now enter and examine a little more closely.

CHAPTER 17

The Soaring Metaphysics of the Mahayana

We have followed the Buddhist pilgrims on their long journeys from the marshlands of Tun-huang across the sands of the Gobi to the Ganges and the holy land, and from the South China Sea to the coast of Ceylon. Surely we are now entitled to ask what it was that drove these men to set out from all over the Far East and undertake this immense pilgrimage, braving every danger? Certainly they were moved by a desire to venerate the Holy Places of Buddhism; both Hiuan Tsang and Yi Tsing speak at length and with tremendous feeling of the sacred spot in the Nepalese jungle where the Blessed One was born, of the clearing in Bihar where stood the Bodhi Tree beneath which he had attained Enlightenment, of the monastic parks in which he had preached and the grove of sala trees where he had waited for death.

Yet it would be wrong to think of the majority of these travelers as naive pilgrims prompted only by a sentimental piety. On the contrary most of them were prodigiously learned philosophers and powerful metaphysicians; pious they certainly were, but they were also men of genius and in that respect far superior to the ordinary votary. What they came in search of, over and above the opportunity of contemplating the sacred sites and relics, was the Teaching. Now, at this period the Teaching no longer consisted of the ancient *Sutras,* the poetic *Jatakas* and the honeyed words of the parables, that golden legend which had once alone sufficed to convert the multitudes. Under the mantle of the traditional religion there had slowly and surely been built up a constructive metaphysics, and what the Chinese pilgrims came to India in search of was nothing less than the truth in its entirety. Hiuan Tsang and Yi Tsing refer continually to the purpose underlying their efforts and it is invariably a question of translating philosophical texts. The reader will not be surprised, then, if we round off our tableau of Indian and Chinese Buddhism during the T'ang period with a few pages dealing with the religious philosophy of this great age. To study the actions of these men without trying to understand the spiritual reasons behind them would be to condemn ourselves to the world of mere appearances.

The first of the Mahayana doctrines that Hiuan Tsang and the other Chinese pilgrims came across in India was that of the Madhyamika or Middle Path school, founded in the southern Deccan around the first century A.D. by the philosopher Nagarjuna. It is an incontestably powerful theory, a system of particularly subtle and unusually bold dialectics, but one which has been very little understood in Europe, such is the difficulty of finding Western equivalents for Indian concepts. Nagarjuna's theory has consequently been labeled a nihilistic doctrine, a theory of "Emptiness and Nothingness." And the notion of *sunyata* to which the Indian sage reduces everything does indeed correspond to the idea of "voidness." But that is not to say that such a concept is purely negative; otherwise we should be forced to admit that it was possible for the most fervent mysticism and the most dauntless personal heroism to grant themselves upon a theory of Nothingness. No; in my opinion the teaching of Nagarjuna, as revived by modern Japanese commentators, is something entirely different, but in order to understand it we must first examine the intellectual currents which led up to it.

The first thing we must do is adopt the mentality of the Buddhist and of the Indian in general, for whom the object of philosophical inquiry is the attainment of salvation through the total purification of heart and mind. From the time of its foundation in the sixth century B.C. Buddhism had taught the purification of the heart by freeing it from all attachment to things; that, in fact, constitutes the whole of Buddhist ethics as subsequently developed in thousands upon thousands of texts. But in order for this setting-free to be complete it must also be extended to the things of the mind, for what is the detachment of the heart without mental detachment? After cutting the ties of feeling with the world and the self, the mind must become detached from all belief in the self and in things. And that is how the Madhyamika school came to create what we have called the metaphysics of Buddhism, which initially, seventeen centuries before Kant, was nothing more than a kind of critique of pure reason.

Dismantling the machinery of the categories of understanding in a discussion whose subtlety is not without a certain vigor, although perhaps occasionally somewhat disturbing, Nagarjuna demonstrates that the mind never attains, either through itself or through things, the substance of reality or divine "self" so dear to Brahminical thought—the *atman,* as the Indians called it. After that he had no trouble at all in pointing up the unreal and even to some extent contradictory character of the phenomenal world as such, reducing it to a merry-go-round of appearances of which it was possible to make neither head nor tail. Moreover the Indian philosopher appears to have been at particular pains to prevent the pure phenomenism thus established from turning into a kind of positivism where the world might, in the realm of facts, recover a certain solidity. It was with no less care that later masters of the doctrine attempted to stop it from evolving into an absolute idealism which (in Hiuan Tsang's case, for example) reconstituted the world within the mind and by this conjuring trick reinstated the whole of metaphysics. Having done battle with the idea of substance, then, Nagarjuna joined battle equally with the opposite thesis, fearing apparently lest the complete disappearance of the notion of substance should lend a positive character to phenomena themselves, unconsciously conferring on them a kind of substantiality.

With the heart freed from all attachment to things and to itself and the mind purified and liberated from belief in things and in itself, we are left with this negative concept of *sunyata* or "voidness," a notion which it is perhaps wrong to represent as a metaphysical concept and which could well be no more than simply a state of mind or manner of thinking. *Sunyata*—with respect to that theory of the world as will and representation to which all Buddhists subscribe—is the condition of the mind that is liberated from both representation and will.

And this is where the whole difference between the Indian and Western minds becomes apparent. In Western logic such an absolute simplification, going right down to the idea of emptiness, might indeed result in nihilism. The Indian, on the other hand, liberated both intellectually and morally from all attachment, purified alike in mind and senses, discovers in this affranchisement data for what we call reality, and finds in this condition of total deliverance the source of a tremendous mystical joy and the unleashing of a quite unsuspected vital impulse. The sage has descended to the bottom of his heart. There, anticipating our critiques of pure reason, he has seen the external world, in the phenomena of representation, taking form and waning away. He has seen all that can be called the self dissolve; the substantial essence because Buddhism denies it, the phenomenal self because its collapse ensues upon that of the external world. In place of this world of moral pain and material hindrance, of inner egotism and objective adversity, an apparently bottomless chasm opens up in the heart, a luminous, as it were submarine chasm, fathomless, full of ineffable beauty, fleeting depths, limpidities without end. On the surface of this void into which the eye plunges, dazzled with wonder, things play out their mirage of changing colors, but these things, he knows, "are no more than themselves-as-such"—*tathata*—and are thus as if they did not exist at all.

And, this mirage once dispelled, there in the inward contemplation of this bottomless, limitless depth, in the unequaled purity of this total void is every virtuality, every power. What is there to stop the heart now? It has broken its bonds and caused the world to disappear. What is to stop the mind now that it has freed itself not only from the world but from itself? By destroying its own lie it has triumphed over itself, and it returns from the unfathomable chasm victorious.

It is a doctrine of indubitable originality, obscure in many respects, but one which must on no account be overlooked, for whatever the application that subsequent schools made of the Madhyamika, its inward vision was the starting-point from which all their teachings were derived.

Thus, for example, the doctrine of the *Garland of Flowers* or *Avatamsaka Sutra,* a text written in India during the second or third centuries A.D., develops the mystical potential inherent in Nagarjuna's philosophy. Placing itself beneath the invocation of the Bodhisattva Mañjusri it plunges into the play of things within the void itself, a series of waves moving in everlasting succession upon the bottomless ocean, and discovers there the fundamental justification both for absolute idealism and radical positivism. In default of substance—that ancient Brahminical notion which Buddhism felt itself almost by definition obliged to refute—adherents of the *Garland of Flowers* were able at least to seize upon the "suchness" of things, the Sanskrit *tathata*. This "suchness" constituted a kind of divinity emerging from the very heart of Nagarjuna's *sunya* or void. From the point of view of sentiment if not from that of metaphysics it offered itself as an equivalent for the absolute, or perhaps better as an absolute that was no longer above phenomena but entirely inherent in them; the absolute as the very process of things. At the surface and in the interior of the unfathomable void, the bottomless ocean glimpsed by Nagarjuna, phenomena were the ocean considered as waves; "suchness" was the waves considered as ocean.

Mysticism was thus not exactly reinstated (it had never been absent from the Mahayana) but at least definitively confirmed. For this intuition of the "suchness" of things was henceforth, in the *Prajña Paramita* or *Perfection of Wisdom,* to become a kind of revelation of truth, or if you prefer of Holy Buddhist Wisdom, a veritable hypostasis which was prayed to and invoked and which communicated itself to the mind in an inexpressible communion.

Other schools of Buddhism in China, founded during the very period of Hiuan Tsang and Yi Tsing, developed these same principles and established two powerful sects. One of them, the Dhyana school or school of meditation (*Ch'en-na* in Chinese, *Zen* in Japanese), took as its objective the mystical communion of the mind with Supreme Wisdom, conceived as being synonymous with "suchness." And this communion, by means of which the mind adheres to the unique essence of things, makes it, in and through this sublime essence, master of things and of itself. Master of things: the Chinese Dhyanist gave himself out as a superman controlling the forces of nature. Absolute master of himself: the Zen masters of Japan, applying this radical doctrine to the training of *samurai,* drew from it lessons of unsuspected heroism. Once he has attained by the intuitive method this total purity of thought, the Japanese transposition of the Indian *sunyata,* the Zen follower can henceforth confront in all serenity and impassibility, as if he were playing a game, the innumerable vicissitudes of *samsara* or "life on earth."

Moreover, such are the secret processes of Buddhist thought, doctrines of intense life and boundless action were already potentially present in Nagarjuna's "void." Once delivered by this means from the chains of self and the world there was no limit of ecstasy or heroism which the Zen follower could not reach.

The same processes, resulting this time in a kind of mystical monism, can be seen at work in the doctrine of the Sino-Buddhist T'ien-t'ai school, which dates from shortly before Hiuan Tsang's time. A Chinese monk named Che-yi (531–97), having followed the teaching of the Dhyana school, and very much under the influence of the *Lotus of the Good Law,* the "Buddhist Fourth Gospel," founded this new sect around 575 together with a famous monastery on an extremely picturesque site of Mount T'ien-t'ai in Chö-kiang. Pushing the tendencies of the *Garland of Flowers* to the extreme the school took "suchness" or the essential nature of things, the *tathata* of the early masters, more or less without reservation as a kind of Buddhist equivalent of the Hindu *brahman,* or rather a *brahman* inherent in phenomena, which led moreover to the opinion that *samsara* is infused with *nirvana,* and that salvation is realizable immediately.

The T'ien-t'ai school was imported to Japan by the saintly Dengyo Daishi (d. 822) and there underwent fresh development. The Tendai, as it became known in Japan, together with the related Shingon sect founded by another Japanese saint Kobo Daishi (d. 835), elaborated on the pantheistic tendencies of earlier sects.

At the time of the Chinese pilgrims, however, much the most important school of Indian Buddhism and the one whose teachings Hiuan Tsang did more than anyone else to spread was the idealist or mystical school of the Vijñanavara or Yogachara (both terms are used indiscriminately) which it may be useful to go into in a little detail.

The idealist school, whose origins some have traced back to the philosophical works written by Ashvaghosha in the first century A.D., received its definitive form in the fifth century at the hands of two writers often eulogized in Hiuan Tsang's account of his travels, two brothers from the Peshawar region who spent part of their lives in

Oudh, namely Asanga and Vasubandhu. From these two thinkers, who finally gave Buddhism a true metaphysics, stemmed all the masters who made the monasteries of northern India famous over two centuries. Vasubandhu, in particular, counted among his disciples Dignaga, a metaphysician and logician who also lived in the fifth century, and Sthiramati,[1] the leader of another branch which several Japanese Sanskrit scholars consider the true heir of the two original masters. Dignaga taught Dharmapala, who must have lived between about 528 and 560, and he in turn taught Silabhadra who, as we have seen, became Hiuan Tsang's master.

What we shall summarize here is the idealist doctrine as expounded in the works of Asanga, Vasubandhu and Hiuan Tsang, to grasp which is to have grasped the essence of Buddhist thought.

One of the fundamental axioms laid down by Asanga was the old Buddhist thesis of the impermanence of things and the flow of phenomena, here taken to the point of utter instantaneity. "All that comes to pass is instantaneous," taught Asanga and Hiuan Tsang, going on to explain that each instant brings with it "something else" caused by what has preceded it, and that, just as the cause ceases to be the moment it has given rise to its effect, so that effect, after having become cause in its turn, itself immediately ceases to be. "But since this alteration is too subtle for definition one is inveigled into seeing only the resemblance between successive states of being." For example, to take Asanga's comparison, there is no discerning from one minute to the next the transformation of milk into butter. Asanga thus established that *samskaras* or the constituent elements of matter (*rupa*) are instantaneous, matter implying movement or something in a perpetual state of evolution. As we shall see he went on to try and demonstrate by the same reasoning that the constituent elements of the self are equally ephemeral, for mind is perpetual change or an endless series of instantaneous moments.

---

[1] The chronology of this author is uncertain but he is generally reckoned to have lived in the late fifth and into the sixth century. He appears to have still been alive at about 560.

The ultimate basis of things, what this school referred to as *alaya vijñana* ("the feeling of innermostness") was itself not exempt from this eternal instability. *"Alaya vijñana,"* said Vasubandhu, "proceeds in a continuous stream like the flow of a river." This kind of "universal subconscious," whose importance in the system we shall see later and which was the basis of all knowledge, was also referred to by Hiuan Tsang as a perpetual series: *"Alaya vijñana* has ever been born and perished at each moment, changing from before to after; it is cause and effect, birth and destruction." Some have read into it a transposition of *atman,* the psycho-ontological substance of Brahminism, but that would be to suppose a substance with neither permanence nor unity; the terms are too contradictory. However, if this "universal subconscious" is not permanent it is, by its very definition, continuous. Hiuan Tsang writes: "As the water of the stream flows in series, at all times, and with all it bears along, so *alaya vijñana,* at all times, being born and perishing, carrying with it *klesas* and actions, bears along being high and low, keeping being within existence." And he adds: "In the same way as the river, when the wind strikes it, gives birth to waves without its flow being interrupted, so does *alaya vijñana,* without a break in its perpetual flow, produce temporary thoughts. . . . Thus has *alaya vijñana* ever flowed, like a river, without a break." Dignaga says the same: "By virtue of the continuity with which cause and effect succeed each other without interruption, it can be said that time is without any beginning."

The world, then, in this system evolved by Asanga, Vasubandhu and Hiuan Tsang, comes down to a universal subconscious that is eternal, continuous and impermanent to the point of instantaneity, in short, to a perpetual series. And this, we have to admit, is no more than the philosophical formulation of the phenomenist tendencies of the early Buddhists.

Another point in the teaching of Asanga, Vasubandhu and Hiuan

Tsang is the unreality of the tangible world (*dharma nairatmya*), a thesis which is here taken to the lengths of the purest form of acosmism.

This thesis came into conflict with one of the principal Indo-Brahminical systems of the period, the Vaiseshika, which was entirely based on atomism. On this system our three metaphysicians declared bitter war, beginning with the destruction of the notion of the atom (*paramanu*). "The atom," writes Vasubandhu, "is not proven as such," nor *a fortiori* is the agglomeration of atoms which is an object. An object, he tells us, is either one or it is formed of a number of atoms or agglomerations of atoms. Now, the one is not an object because nowhere do we apprehend a whole which is other than its parts; and neither is the multiple an object since that object has not been apprehended in terms of its component atoms taken one by one. It will be seen that the Indian philosopher is here trying to break down the idea of the atom by means of a series of paradoxes: "If the atom," Vasubandhu continues, "is joined simultaneously with six other atoms, each atom will have six sides, six parts, for the place occupied by each atom is occupied by no other atom," which amounts to saying that atoms are not in fact atomic. If, on the other hand, to avoid dividing them spatially, the six atoms are given as being in the same place, they merge and become a single unit, in which case the agglomeration by means of which matter is created becomes impossible. Furthermore, Vasubandhu goes on to say, the very idea of the atom is contradictory: "That in which there is division into spatial parts (i.e., that which has extent) cannot anyhow be one. The part of the atom lying toward the east would be distinct from the part lying to the west. If the various parts of the atom are different, how can the atom which consists of them be one? If we do not admit this spatial division of the atom and if no atom possesses parts then where or at what point will an atom come into contact with another atom? And if there is no contact then all atoms occupy the same place and all agglomerations will merge to form a single atom. This is self-evident," concludes Vasubandhu, immediately drawing the consequence: "Since atoms are not proven, the objects of the senses (*artha*) are no more than idea (*vijñaptimatra*)."

Hiuan Tsang, in his treatise on absolute idealism, follows the example of his masters in refuting the atomic theory as elevated to the position of a dogma by the Brahminical Vaiseshika school. Even the Chinese philosopher's proof is the same as that of his Indian forebears: "If atoms possess extent they are divisible, like an army or a forest. If they do not possess extent, like mind and mental acts, then they do not partake of the nature of real entities as distinct from mind and mental acts. Moreover, having no extent they are incapable of agglomerating and matter does not exist." In other words, if atoms possess extent they are divisible and are no longer atoms. And if they are without extent they are still not atoms but "mental acts" and cannot produce matter.

Hiuan Tsang concludes as follows: "The Yogachara, using not a knife but thought, divides and redivides solid matter to the point at which it can no longer be apprehended. This ultimate fraction, the existence of which is entirely imaginary, they refer to as an atom. They believe moreover that the atom possesses extent and is susceptible of spatial division, yet that at the same time it cannot be divided for were one to attempt to do so the atom would appear as space or as gap (*akasa*) and could no longer be termed material. Wherefore it is said that the atom is the limit of matter. We conclude, therefore, that matter is an extension of mind and does not consist of atoms."

The school then went on to unravel the processes of the tangible world as created by the phenomenon of representation. The occasional inference tends to be on the feeble side: Asanga writes that *samskaras,* the psycho-physical components of reality, "since they are presided over by mind, are thus subject to it; hence they are the fruit of mind," but in the main the case is more tightly argued. And since the whole system of the school rests on this theory it will be as well if we give here some further quotations.

Let us look first of all at the formula of the system as stated by

Vasubandhu in his *Vimsakakarika Prakarana*: "The threefold world (*dhatu*) is no more than idea (*vijñaptimatra*) or mind (*cittamatra*). It is knowledge (*vijñana*) itself that appears as object . . . All that is no more than idea appearing in the form of objects which (in reality) do not exist." Farther on he writes: "It is idea that appears as visible, tangible." Or again: "Pure idea occurs as something visible." His disciple Dignaga, taking up the same theme, writes: "Knowledge occurs in the form of objects."

Hiuan Tsang, always the faithful commentator of his Indian masters, tells us similarly that knowledge (*vijñana*) appears to itself in two forms: picture-knowledge (*nimittabhaga*), which appears as external, and vision-knowledge (*darsanabhaga*) which operates on this artificial externality. In other words, "because mind fixes on itself it unfolds in the form of external things. These things, though seen, do not exist. There is only mind."

But, it may be said, if objects do not exist, what is it that "touches off" ideas? "Ideas are touched off by their action upon each other," is Vasubandhu's ingenious reply. Yet the objection remains a serious one: if the idea has no object it has neither occasion, place, time, nor differentiation. For example, if the idea of color occurs in the absence of an object, why is it that it occurs in such and such a place and at such and such a time, rather than everywhere all the time? Vasubandhu's reply to that is that in dream, too, mind has a local and temporal occasion and yet the dream is but a dream. This argument of dream-states and other delusions of the senses was invariably used by the school to deny the objective value of knowledge. The analogy of the picture, used by both Asanga and Vasubandhu, performs a similar office: "A picture painted according to the rules has neither concavity nor convexity, and yet these are seen; so there is never duality in the imagination, and yet duality is seen." By means of such analogies Asanga is able to prove that "thought is feeling and form"; mind, in other words, has become the cosmos.

One thing bothers Vasubandhu, however: if things (*dharma*) have no existence, how are we to establish (the existence of) pure idea, for that too does not exist. It is a weighty argument, particularly when we think that this was to be the great objection leveled against Yogachara idealism by the protagonists of Nagarjuna's absolute void. Vasubandhu, well aware of the threat it poses, replies with a formula of singular subtlety: "Doubtless things are unreal (*niratmanas*) in respect of that reality (*atman*) which consists in intrinsic nature, yet they are not without existence in respect of the ineffable manner of being which is the province of the Buddhas. . . ."

Asanga, too, was not so imprudent as to leave his acosmism vulnerable to the critical assaults of common sense. The shrewd metaphysician took his precautions in a somewhat curious piece of trimming: "The existence of things in the mirage of representation cannot properly be reduced to non-existence. Indeed insofar as we have the existence of such and such a figure, we cannot say that it absolutely does not exist. Yet it is not a real existence, any more than we can say that the (metaphysical) non-existence of objects is no existence at all. But the existence of such and such a figure in the mirage of representation is indeed the non-existence of the object, as the non-existence of the object implies a (relative) existence in the corresponding figures. We thus have duality in appearance but not in reality."

Like the external world the self, too, disappeared, for was it not the primary obstacle to salvation and as such the enemy of all Buddhists?

The school destroyed first of all the social and corporal self. In this we find no change from the position adopted by earlier writers, but the Mahayana brings to it a particularly urgent accent: "Look at this corpse," cries Santideva. "Why, dragged hither and thither by rapacious vultures, does it offer no resistance? Why, oh my heart, do you keep vigil over this clod, taking it to be yourself? And if it is distinct from yourself, of what consequence to you is its disappearance? You fool, you do not take a wooden doll to be yourself, and that at least is clean. Why take any thought for a machine that is doomed to decay? Remove then first with your mind this envelope of skin, and using the knife of intuition pare the flesh from its framework of bone; break the very bones themselves, look at the marrow that you find inside them, and tell me then what is essential. . . . Doubtless this wretched body serves man as a tool for action. But you tend it in vain; pitiless death will tear it from you and hurl it to the vultures. And what will you do then?" Having rejected this wretched body, this false illusion of self, the poet cries out in a transport of ecstasy: "When shall I go to that proper abode of the body, the charnel house, to bring my body that is vowed to corruption face to face with the corpses of others? Look at my body, see the putrid relic it will become; the smell of it will drive off even jack-als."

The dissociation of the psychological self in the teaching of Asanga, Vasubandhu and Hiuan Tsang is bound up with the dissociation of the external world. Nor should we forget that the negation of the self as a permanent metaphysical entity went right back to early Buddhism. Whereas the philosophy of Brahminism was based on the divination of the human soul (*brahman-atman*), Buddhism, adopting by a process of reaction the opposite position, began by denying the soul (*nairatmya*). The first properly philosophical text of the Buddhist church, the *Milinda-Panha,* which took the form of a discussion between the Indo-Greek king Menander and the monk Nagasena, was uniquely intended to demonstrate the substantial non-existence of the self, in this case conceived as a mere stream of phenomena. Nagarjuna, the patriarch of the Mahayana, founded the system of his Middle Path doctrine in the first century A.D. entirely on the basis of this concept. His critique of mind was intended solely to establish the unreality of any kind of psychological substratum or constant. As Chandrakirti, one of his later disciples, wrote: "Creatures are mobile and devoid of intrinsic nature, like the moon reflected in troubled water. Just as in very clear water which is disturbed by a violent wind the moon's reflection first appears and then immediately disappears at the same time as the ripple that gave it purchase, the intrinsic nature of both ripple and reflection being instantaneity and lack of substance, in the same way creatures are like a reflection upon the ocean of heresy that is the self."

Since Nagarjuna's time, however, between the first and fifth centuries A.D., the philosophical systems of Brahminism had undergone some development, and all of them were based upon the notion of *atman,* that is to say the soul or self endowed with the maximum ontological plenitude, substantial, eternal, universal, divine, and identical with the absolute. Consequently Hiuan Tsang devotes the early chapters of his treatise on radical idealism to demolishing the Brahminical systems on this point by attempting to compare them one with another. For example, if, as the Brahminical philosophers of the Vedanta school held, the *atman* is eternal, universal, omnipresent, and identical with the absolute, it is incapable of movement, so how does it operate? And if, as the philosophers of the Vaiseshika and Samkhya schools believed, it is a sort of spiritual atom, how is it able to actuate the immensity of extent? If it is intelligence it cannot be eternal, for Hiuan Tsang finds the mobility of intellectual phenomena to be in contradiction to the perenniality of substance. As for the direct perception of the *atman* in psychological consciousness, Hiuan Tsang feels that since the *atman* becomes in this case an object of perception it should be considered in the same way as any other object, not as substance any more but as a collection of phenomena.

With Asanga and Vasubandhu moreover the old Buddhist theory of the unreality of the self received fresh confirmation. The soul, the self, the moral personality and all the notions derived from it came under attack as never before. "The individual," write Asanga and Vasubandhu in formulating the doctrine of the school, "exists as notation (*prajñapti*), not as substance (*pudgala*)." They go on to explain that the idea of the self has its origins in the sight of the human body; but that sight, like all material perception, is spurious. At this point the school came up against the argument of common sense, elder and more lowly brother of the *Cogito ergo sum*: "The individual exists because it is he who feels, acts, experiences pleasure, knows, etc." And it replied:

"No, because in that case the individual would be the medium of thoughts and feelings both as encounter (= relationship) and as master (= substance). Now, if feeling is possible only through the encounter between two terms, this simple relationship cannot be the individual. And if the individual were 'master' (= substance), he could not as such, being permanent, operate the impermanent (i.e., the phenomenon of knowledge)." The individual is thus not he who sees, feels, etc., since he is neither permanent medium nor ephemeral function.

This doctrine of the unreality of the individual (*pudgala nairatmya*) was so dear to the hearts of Buddhists that it made them overlook what the Western mind would regard as a paradox. Indeed at the same time as they denied the soul they accepted as did every Indian the idea of moral responsibility, even, by virtue of the unquestioned dogma of transmigration, extending *ad infinitum* back into the past and forward into the future. Soul and the self do not exist and yet the human being transmigrates from reincarnation to reincarnation taking with it into each fresh existence the accumulated merit or demerit acquired during its previous existences with all their potential for reward or expiation. And we must bear this belief continually in mind when studying the Buddhist "dogma" of the non-existence of the self, for it is my opinion that it more than corrects and makes up on the practical side for the theoretical negations we have just been examining.

Leaving aside these requitals of the vital instinct we find that on this point as on every other Hiuan Tsang proves to be the obedient pupil of his Indian masters. In the light of absolute idealism he reconstitutes the origins of the self and of the external world. "By the power of (previous) impressions which have left in the mind the ideas of soul and world (*atman-dharma*) the mind begins from the moment of its birth to unfold in terms of souls and world. These images, although within the mind itself, yet appear through the power of false notions as if they were external. Hence have creatures ever perceived these images resembling soul and world as actually being soul and world. In fact soul and world do not possess absolute existence but only relative truth." Only mind exists, he adds, as manifesting itself in the semblance of self and in the semblance of world.

Taking his analysis still further Hiuan Tsang traces the origin of *atman,* that is to say of the notion of soul or self, back to the universal subconscious, *alaya vijñana* in Sanskrit, a term which has been variously translated as the "feeling of innermostness" and the "repository-mind." It is this feeling of universal psychological innermostness, when formulated in phenomenal consciousness, that gives rise there to the image of a real *atman.* The soul, as we shall see, is the way in which the cosmic subconscious sees itself.

There is no doubt that it represents a curious spectacle to our Western associations of ideas to see these idealist philosophers, these mystical poets, these pietist monks, hounding as a heresy all idea of soul. Of course one might point out that unconsciously they tended perhaps to reverse their own position. It has been suggested by some that while preserving the negative postulates of the old schools and remaining faithful to the letter of Buddhist positivism they found in notions like that of "repository-mind," the "feeling of innermostness," the "universal subconscious"—however we choose to render the term *alaya vijñana* —tangible equivalents of the notion of *atman.* "The *manas,*" writes Hiuan Tsang, to use his very terms, "or individual self clings to *alaya vijñana* as to its *atman.*" Yet despite this indirect and unconscious restoration, the condemnation of soul and self in the earliest sacred writings of Buddhism was clearly too categorical for the theoreticians of the Mahayana to override it. Our Western way of thinking must thus reconcile itself to the spectacle of deeply religious minds, idealists, mystics and pietists, locked in combat with any notion of soul and absolute.

These postulates once allowed, Hiuan Tsang held all the cards he needed to wreak havoc with the theses put forward by Brahminical philosophy, particularly that of the Samkhya system, regarding on the one hand the modalities or hypostases with which it endowed the absolute self and Nature, the "essential qualities" (*guna*) of Nature, and on the other hand the components of the psychological and social self, of the individual mind (*manas*) apparent at the surface of the universal subconscious. "These principles," Hiuan Tsang replies to the Brahminical philosophers, "consisting as they do in a multiplicity, cannot be real; they are fictitious, like an army or a forest." Elsewhere Hiuan Tsang asks how the coming together of these modalities, *guna* for Nature, faculties for the soul, can produce a single substance such as *atman* or the substance of the cosmos, and his witty and ingenious argument does the greatest credit to his dialectic abilities.

What exactly is the self, then, in the system of the idealist school? As we said a short while ago, it is the play of an illusion upon the surface of the mental ocean. Vasubandhu and Hiuan Tsang in fact reply in practically identical terms: "The thinking mind (*manas*) takes as its object the universal subconscious (*alaya vijñana*) by which it is upheld. It conceives the latter as 'I,' as its soul (*atman*), and conceives the phenomena associated with the subconscious as 'mine' (*atmiya*)." In other words the self is the aspect under which mind perceives its "innermostness," it being understood that this latter is in no way an onotological reality but simply an accumulation and also a ceaseless flow of phenomena.

Hiuan Tsang was meanwhile well aware of the difficulties which the anti-substantialist postulate of his doctrine let him in for. In the first place, if no permanent self exists, how do you account for memory, the perception of objects, feelings, etc.? The Chinese metaphysician gets out of that one by saying that every present thought implies a previous thought or "root-thought" (*mulavijñana*) which forms the basis of a homogeneous series and carries within it the seeds of all mental phenomena, which in turn produce other seeds, and so on. And there is no doubt that this does indeed constitute an admission of a psychological constant, though under another name. To the question of knowing what happens to the act when you suppress the agent, to the phenomenon of representation when you suppress the thinking subject, Hiuan Tsang's reply is to the effect that the *atman* put forward by his opponents, assuming that it is immutable, is incapable of being the seat of the act of representation which is by definition purely phenomenal. And he concludes, with the rest of his school: "The truth is that beings are corporeal and mental series (*samtana*) which act out their destinies by dint of the force of the passions and the weight of their previous sins. At length, tormented by suffering and weary of this endless cycle, they seek for and obtain *nirvana*."

The nihilist opponents of Asanga and Hiuan Tsang are surely not entirely wrong when they suggest that the idealism of these two masters attempts to demolish Brahminical animism only in order to replace it with tangible equivalents under another name.

That does not matter, though. From the point of view of the logic of the system the result is achieved. The non-self and the self have alike disappeared. The philosopher has forced mind into admitting that it and it alone is what clothes the appearance of duality, or as Asanga puts it the aspect of the receiver and the aspect of the receivable. The self and material phenomena have been driven into confessing that they are not in themselves real things but, as Hiuan Tsang says, "beings of reason." We have been shown that "internal mind unfolds to match external things," with the immediate rider that mind is not in fact internal *with respect to* anything. We now see that mind, as the only thing left afloat after the shipwreck of everything else, might for that reason find itself in a somewhat precarious position. Asanga is the first to recognize this (necessarily so, in order to ward off the attacks of the Madhyamika "voidists"): "As soon as the wise man," he writes, "has understood that there exist no receivable phenomena apart from mind, he realizes too that this Nothing-but-mind itself does not exist, for where there is nothing to be received there can be no receiver." Are we then to fall back with Nagarjuna and the Madhyamika school on universal emptiness? Vasubandhu gives us the answer in his famous formula: *"Cittamatra, the existence of pure idea, is established by our very awareness of the (substantial and objective) unreality of idea."* It is the Buddhist *Cogito ergo sum* again: pure idea corresponds to nothing real, pure idea is an illusion, therefore pure idea exists.

The reader will immediately appreciate the importance of this argument, which is indeed the turntable of the system, enabling us to pass from the universal emptiness or, if you prefer it, nihilism[2] of the Madhyamika to the absolute idealism of Hiuan Tsang.

At this point in the formulation of the system the horizon begins to clear.

On one side we have the debris; all that the Yogachara, in this respect a faithful heir to the Madhyamika, demolished. It demolished all duality in the phenomenon of representation. In Asanga's phrase there no longer exists either receiver or receivable, or as Hiuan Tsang puts it there is neither self (*atman*) nor phenomena (*dharma*). It demolished the self and the non-self, the soul and the world.

On the other side we have what the school puts up instead: the ideality of everything that in substance it has demolished. Indeed, the world and the self having been dissociated, evaporated, we are left with their memory and their ghost, Asanga's "Nothing-but-mind" (*cittamatra, vijñaptimatra*). We are left with the "Plane of Ideals" (*dharmadhatu*).

This whole dialectic of the Mahayana unfolds with such subtlety of nuance that before we go any further we must make one preliminary observation, to which we are invited by Hiuan Tsang. When the Yogachara philosopher puts things to us as being mind and nothing else (or better, as being the thought of them and nothing more), it is in order, as he points out to us, to compare the total unreality of things with the relatively greater reality of the thought of them. However, he adds immediately that even this thought does not exist substantially in itself, for to admit the absolute existence of thought would be to condemn, in a roundabout way, idealism itself. And whatever our opinion on the matter we cannot help but delight in the play of this subtle, soaring

---

[2] It is of course understood that I refer to the Madhyamika as "nihilistic" only in terms of its style, to borrow Fujishima's term. In fact as I have argued elsewhere I believe with Professor Yamaguchi that the Nagarjunian "void" or rather "non-substantiality" in no way implies nihilism.

dialectics, this fluent metaphysics which really and truly does flow into evanescence as one attempts to grasp it.

Ideals (*dharmas*), as put to us by Asanga, are simply, as he tells us himself, of the order of phenomena. Phenomena, as we have seen, combine together to give rise on the one hand to the illusion of self and on the other hand to the illusion of the external world. When the sage has exorcised this fallacious duality, when he has dispelled the magic of subject and object, of self and the world, he is left only with the act of knowing, functioning henceforth in a vacuum, what Asanga calls the mental word or, better still, with undifferentiated thought, indeterminate and virtual, anterior to subject, object, and the act of knowing. That, properly speaking, is what Asanga refers to as the "Plane of Ideals."

This impersonal and virtual knowing, this "Plane of Ideals," is capable of subliming in its turn. For if all is appearance—bodies, mind, differentiation—then ideals themselves are also appearances, imaginary things "like an optical illusion, like a dream, like a mirage, a shadow, an echo, like the moon reflected in the water." When all notion not only of substantial duality but also of mental plurality has been excluded we discover beneath ideals or rather within them the suchness or absolute nature of things (*tathata*) which is at the same time their total emptiness.

Here we come across one of the trickiest notions of the Mahayana philosophy. What exactly is this absolute nature of things, this *tathata,* that plays such a large part in the system? It is, beneath its apparent simplicity, an extraordinarily complex notion, one which is called upon to serve a radical positivism as an absolute and a ceaselessly flowing idealism as a permanent datum. It is an almost impossible notion to define. Hiuan Tsang makes a vain attempt to reach an approximation of absolute nature in his treatise on idealism by piling up opposites and weighing them against each other—being and non-being, ideality and reality, etc.—but really the only plausible definition is that it is ineffable, inexpressible. It cannot, moreover, be perceived in the full light of active intellectual understanding. Its apprehension is only possible through mystical communion in the darkness of the subconscious.

In this notion, however, lies the whole problem of transcendency in the Mahayana. Hiuan Tsang, trying to infuse in us a sense of the transcendency of *tathata,* tells us that it is above being and non-being alike. Asanga, in the early chapters of his *Sutralamkara,* similarly gives transcendency as an ineffable "non-duality" above both being and non-being. We may note in parentheses at this point that this definition of transcendency was to entail an entirely fresh conception of *nirvana*: "In the transcendent sense," writes Asanga, "there is no distinction between transmigration and *nirvana.*" Such a doctrine, as we shall see, placed salvation within the reach of everyone whose heart was pure.

At this level the saint attains knowledge without differentiation, a supernatural state in which the human being enjoys direct apprehension beyond self and non-self, transmigration and *nirvana,* being and non-being, and which Asanga appropriately calls a state of ecstasy.

Indeed, once the philosopher has reached this state of absolute mental purity his idealism gives way to mysticism. The *vijñanavadin* becomes a *yogachara.* Speaking of the Unique and the Ineffable, Asanga exclaims in lyric accents: "In truth there is nothing beside It and the whole world does not know It. What then is the origin of this extraordinary madness that makes the world cling obstinately to what does not exist (the self and the non-self) and neglect utterly that which does?" And he contrasts with this absolute nature, this "Plane of Ideals," secondary nature which is made up of a fallacious plurality, with its cardinal error of the imagined duality of subject and object. With absolute nature the mind of the sage at last reaches its longed-for landfall. There the saint, freed at one stroke from the double lie of self and the world, finds salvation, the mysterious Buddhahood.

CHAPTER 18

The Mystical Heavens
of Buddhism

Bʏ ᴍᴇᴀɴs ᴏғ this universal, synthetic understanding, this knowledge without differentiation, this direct communion with absolute nature, the sage acquires supernatural power (*prabhava*). Henceforth he is, to use Asanga's words, "perpetually in that condition which is Brahminical, holy, divine, incomparable, sublime. . . . The worlds with their creatures, creations and periodic destructions he sees without exception as an illusion, and he reveals them as he will, by various procedures, for he is in possession of Mastery. By emitting rays he translates to heaven those unfortunate ones who are languishing in hell. By purifying those who have gone to be reborn in hell he causes them to be reborn in heaven. By his supreme mastery he has conquered understanding and re-established his sway over a world that had lost control over itself. His one delight is to bring about the salvation of beings. He strides through his existences like a lion."

In language of great magnificence Asanga stresses the infinite joys of the Enlightenment and Buddhahood thus obtained: "By means of innumerable trials and innumerable accumulations of Good, total Understanding is attained. All obstacles stand aside and Buddhahood is revealed as a casket of precious stones; great is its power."

As was the case with the "absolute nature" of the foregoing chapter, no definition of Buddhahood is possible. It is ineffable; it can be glimpsed only through a succession of images. "Because it is the reason for the existence of the Jewels of the Ideal it has been compared to a gem-mine; because it is the token of the harvests of Good it has been likened to a cloud. All ideals are Buddhahood, since Buddhahood is inseparable from the Nature of Things . . . Buddhahood is the sum of all ideals."

The creature who attains this degree of perfect wisdom commands the world from above and feels compassion for it. "Once established there (in Buddhahood) he casts his eye over the world as if from the summit of a high mountain. And he has compassion on all beings." For all beings, declares Asanga, are susceptible of being raised up to the same heights: "The universality of Buddhahood in the multitudes of beings is established by the fact that it admits them all within itself. As space is universal in the multitude of forms so is Buddhahood universal in the multitude of beings." Though invisible in the majority of creatures it becomes suddenly apparent in the Buddhas: "Like music issuing from instruments which have not been struck, so does preaching emanate spontaneously from the Conquering One. Like a jewel which without effort pours forth its brightness, so do the Buddhas spontaneously unfold their activity."

We come now to the final notion of the doctrine, that of the essence of the Buddhas, the *raison d'être* and ultimate cause of all things. Here there is a question to be answered: in what does the personality of the Buddhas consist with respect to Buddhahood or the "supreme wisdom" which we have just evoked? Asanga replies magnificently, "Their personality consists of fundamental impersonality," adding moreover that this transcendent impersonality is none other than the absolute nature of things (*tathata*). Consequently, "although the Buddhas are innumerable they merge in a single activity." Certain later Japanese Buddhists like the followers of the Tendai school, restoring both in words and in their propensities the ontology of Brahminism, reached the conclusion that the soul of the Buddhas was universal soul.

Here Asanga comes face to face with one of the most difficult questions posed by the doctrine and one which is often asked by non-Buddhists as well as by Buddhists themselves: is Buddhahood plenitude of being or the complete waning-away of being? In other words is *nirvana,* the goal and reward of Buddhism, absolute or nothingness? Asanga refuses to give an opinion, replying like the fine metaphysician he is: "Buddhahood is neither existence nor non-existence. It is not existence since it is characterized by the non-existence of the individual and phenomenal, and since that is of its very essence. Nor can it be said to be non-existence since it exists in so far as its nature is the nature of things. Consequently to the question as to whether or not the Buddha exists no dogma has been formulated." Here we will simply point out the capital importance of this area of indecision and at the same time observe that Asanga and Hiuan Tsang place beside the ancient Hinayanist conception of *nirvana* as total cessation (*pratishthita*) a "*nirvana*-which-is-not-cessation" (*apratishthita*), which would seem clearly to reveal where their secret preferences lay. . . .

At times we have the impression that the Gandharan philosopher's thought is about to take a more precise turn. Buddhahood appears at a certain point in his argument to be almost a kind of Spinozan *natura naturans,* simultaneously animating and illuminating *natura naturata*: "The Being who is composed of Buddhahood sees now the Wheel of the Law through hundreds upon hundreds of openings, now complete Enlightenment, now *nirvana.* Yet he does not move from that spot and it is It that does everything." The miracle is made possible through a kind of pre-established harmony, for Asanga's Buddhahood in some respects resembles Aristotle's immobile and non-acting god: "The Buddhas do not say to themselves, 'Here is one that is ripe for me, here is one that I have brought to maturity.' But it is the multitude of beings which without any Operating Power is advancing to maturation through the Ideals of Good, perpetually, in all places everywhere. . . .'"

Another of Asanga's images shows us how Buddhahood reconciles within itself absolute unity and infinite plurality: the Buddhas, he says, are like sunbeams which mingle their activity and are both multiple and identical. Again: "As the world is lit by the beams thrown down together at one time by the brightness of the sun, so is the whole of the knowable illuminated together at one time by the understandings of the Buddhas. . . . By means of its bright, far-reaching beams the sun works without effort, everywhere and in all places, to bring the harvests to fruition; so does the sun of the Ideal, by means of the beams of the Ideals that ordain Peace, work everywhere and in all places to bring creatures to fruition."

To explain the relationship between Buddhahood and the world Asanga uses the theory, canonical in the Mahayana, of the Three Bodies of the Buddha: the Essential Body or "Plane of Ideals" (*dharmakaya*), undivided and common to all the Buddhas who are therein undifferentiated; the Personal Body, which varies according to the "planes" of the different Buddhas (*sembhogakaya*); and the metamorphic or magical body which alone is apparent in the incarnations of the various human Buddhas (*nirmatnakaya*).

Here we begin to catch a glimpse of the theological reasons underlying Asanga's transcendent idealism. The essential, undifferentiated and universal Buddha-body, the body which is also the "Plane of Ideals," is characterized by what the philosopher calls "mirror-knowledge," pure knowledge in which the knower sees himself as identical with the known, for it is "without self or the things of self," limitless and endless. It is in this pure and objectless knowledge that Buddhahood occurs. And since in Buddhism metaphysics is inseparable from ethics Asanga adds that this absolute knowledge finds immediate expression in infinite kindness and infinite compassion.

In the same spirit Asanga combats the theory of the unique Buddha and the theory of the primordial Buddha. "It is impossible," he writes, "for there to have been only one Buddha, for among all the Bodhisattvas should one alone attain Enlightenment to the exclusion of all the others? Why should that be? How should the merits of the Buddhas prove useless in promoting the other Bodhisattvas to the same rank? On the other hand we cannot imagine an original Buddha for it is impossible to become Buddha without the merits of another Buddha." Asanga adds, however, that if the idea of a single Buddha is absurd the hypothesis of a plurality of Buddhas is no less absurd since their ideal body or essential nature is undivided and held by all of them in common.

The Gandharan philosopher thus reduces the multitude of popular Buddhas to the metaphysical principle of Buddhahood alone. "The waters of the rivers," he writes in a poetic vein, "appear separate because of the multiplicity of the beds in which they flow, but once they reach the ocean they have no more than the one bed and form but one mass of water. It is the same with the wise once they have entered their common Buddhahood." Such a system, in so far as its shifting outlines allow us to form a precise idea of it, appears to come very close to a kind of monism which is both mystical and without substance.

The nature of this *tathata,* so fluctuating and almost disturbing to our minds, is well indicated by Asanga when he says with infinite refinement: "In Suchness are contained the non-existence of all Ideals, which are imaginary, and also their existence, for this exists by virtue of the very fact of their non-existence. Existence and non-existence are alike undivided. *Tathata* is both defiled by virtue of incidental subdefilements and also by nature entirely pure. It is differentiated and without differentiation since it is beyond the reach of all differentiation," etc.

This identity of opposites entails at least one fortunate result, for at this point the Bodhisattva no longer makes a distinction between himself and creatures: "When through the impersonality of Ideals he has partaken of equality (identity) with them he always entertains with regard to all beings the same thought as he has for himself. He no longer distinguishes between self and others. He desires with equal force the cessation of pain for himself and for others. Nor does he take any more account of a return payment whether coming from himself or from others."

We now come to the mystical relationship between the Bodhisattva and the believer. In stanzas of quite remarkable spirituality Asanga celebrates the flight of creatures toward the ideal of Buddhahood on the wings of Enlightenment: "The multitude, attracted by Ideals, is drawn on by the Compassionate Ones (the Buddhas) who act upon them by means of fascination, as serpents do." Elsewhere, in an image of almost biblical vehemence, he shows us the sage being "thrust forward by the Buddhas. It is they who set him up in the mouth of the Ideal; taking him as it were by the hair they drag him out of the cave of error and plant him forcibly in Enlightenment." And then the believer, too, "having entirely overcome the world, illumines it like a great sun from the topmost heights."

The poet-philosopher then continues in a different tone, telling us in stanzas of infinite sweetness the tender feelings of the Bodhisattvas toward created things, and their sublime and total charity: "The Bodhisattva feels in the very marrow of his bones a love for creatures as great as a parent's love for an only son. As the dove cares for her little ones to hatch them out, so are the feelings of the Compassionate One toward the creatures who are his children." And elsewhere he writes: "The world is incapable of bearing its own pain. How much less can it bear the pain of all others together! The Bodhisattva is quite the opposite for he is able to bear the pain of all creatures together, as many as may be in the world. His fondness for creatures is the supreme marvel of the worlds, and yet it is not, since for him others and self are identical, and creatures are as himself."

What a stream of images Asanga uses to celebrate the mystical heights thus attained! For this metaphysician was also a magnificent poet. The supreme initiation to which he has pointed the way is for him the "unction of the consecration." And the mystical union reached at the last is the "union that is like the Diamond," since, as with the diamond, no duality can invade it.

We now see what a primary role the notion of the Bodhisattva plays in the doctrine of the school. The Bodhisattvas or "Beings of Wisdom," candidates for total Buddhahood and, until that time, intermediaries between Buddhahood and the world, were, if we may use the expression, the keystone of the whole system. And here the purely abstract metaphysics of the Mahayana abruptly betrays a sentiment which is frankly pietist.

The idea of the Compassionate One undoubtedly arose because it answered to a need of the human heart. The preparing of individual salvation with which the original Order had been content and with which the Hinayanists—the "Probationers," as Hiuan Tsang disdainfully called them—were still content was no longer capable of satisfying the aspirations of all the faithful. To posit the intervention of the Buddha himself might appear illogical to some since he had once and for all attained *nirvana*. But the Bodhisattvas were always there and always within reach. These heroes of sancity were waiting for and earning, by keeping watch over the world, the moment when they in turn would attain final Enlightenment. Avalokitesvara, "He who looks down from on high," Maitreya, "descended from the luminous Mitra" and destined to be the Buddha of the days to come, Bhaishajyaguru, saviour of the sick, Kshitigarbha, the ever-merciful judge of souls, Mañjusri who with his flaming sword cuts down demons and rescues the prisoners from hell—all of them stooped down toward the distress of humanity in order to bring it Buddhism's very *raison d'être*: refuge.

"The Bodhisattva," writes Asanga, "would like at every instant and for every creature to create worlds as numerous as there are grains of sand in the Ganges, fill them with the Seven Jewels, and offer them to all creatures as a gift. For the Bodhisattva's inclination to give is insatiable. And the Bodhisattva is happier in the giving than are creatures in the receiving." The poet-philosopher emphasizes this point: "This inclination of the Bodhisattva is his joyful inclination to give. And the Bodhisattva regards the creatures to whom he thus does service by his gift as being more beneficent than himself, for he says to himself that they are the framework of all-perfect and unexcelled Enlightenment."

At about the time when Hiuan Tsang was completing his treatise on absolute idealism another Buddhist saint, Santideva, gave expression to the mysticism of the Mahayana in a magnificent poem. Hiuan Tsang may have met this young man during his travels through eastern India for Santideva was the son of a king of Saurashtra, roughly corresponding to the present-day Gujarat, and he flourished in the reign of Sila, Emperor Harsha's son. On the day appointed for his coronation he was visited in a dream by the Bodhisattva Mañjusri, the same as once appeared to Hiuan Tsang near Nalanda. Obeying this vision he renounced all honors and fled into the jungle to embrace the monastic life. None has ever evoked the mystical heavens of Buddhism as he did. Take, for example, this hymn which is like the vocational summons of the Buddhas-to-be:

"May I become for all beings He who assuages suffering!

"May I be for the sick their cure, their doctor, their nurse and at the last the disappearance of their sickness!

"May I allay by showers of food and drink the torments of hunger and thirst, and in times of famine become myself both drink and food.

"May I be for the poor a store-house of inexhaustible wealth!

"All my incarnations to come, all my goods, all my past, present and future merit—I renounce all with indifference if the goal of all beings may but be attained.

"I give up my body for all beings to do with it what they will. Let them beat it without ceasing, insult it and cover it with dust. Let them treat my body as a toy and as an object of derision and amusement. I have given my body to them. What is it to me! Let them make it perform all the acts it may please them to see it perform. If their hearts are angry and bear me ill-will, may that assist me to realize the goal of all! May those who slander and harm and mock me and may all others too attain Bodhi!

"May I be the protector of them that are abandoned and the guide of them that trudge upon their way, and for them that yearn for the Other Bank may I be boat and causeway and bridge! I would be the lamp of them that are in need of a lamp, the bed of them that are in need of a bed, slave to them that need a slave! I would be the Miracle Stone, the Healing Plant, the Wishing Tree, the Cow of Desire!"

We come across flights of similar feeling in Asanga's work as well, for example in this definition of the Bodhisattva's pity: "The Compassionate One suffers as he reflects that the world is all suffering and pain. He suffers and has pity. He knows exactly what this means; he knows exactly what pain is and how to cause it to cease . . . The water that waters his compassion is kindness . . . Through compassion the Bodhisattva suffers the pain of others. How then should he be happy unless he bestows his happiness upon creatures? Hence the Bodhisattva creates his own happiness by bestowing his happiness upon others . . . The pleasure-seeker feels less satisfaction in pleasure than the Compassionate One experiences in his lavishness, his heart being swollen with the three blessings."

Here we have the very essence of Buddhism: compassion even above justice. "Compassion for the wretched," exclaims Asanga in a splendid litany, "compassion for the enraged, compassion for the choleric, compassion for the heedless, compassion for the servants of matter, compassion for stubborn persistence in the ways of error!"

In his *Training for Enlightenment* Santideva magnificently expounds a similar thought: "The author of the most hideous crimes escapes their consequences in the instant that he leans upon Bodhi, just as the intervention of a hero might rescue one from some great danger.

Like the fire of the end of the world it consumes the greatest sins in a moment . . . Men throw themselves into suffering in order to find refuge from suffering; their desire for happiness leads them foolishly to destroy their happiness as if they were their own enemies. They are starved of happiness and tormented in a thousand ways. Someone who will satisfy them with every blessing, who will cut short their torments and put an end to their foolishness—where shall be found a man so good, where such a friend, such merit? We praise a man who rewards one service with another; what shall we say of the Bodhisattva whose generosity needs no asking? . . . I pay tribute to the bodies of the Bodhisattvas and take my refuge in those mines of happiness which it is impossible even to insult without obtaining some reward."

And I cannot refrain from quoting here the magnificent hymn to the Bodhisattva with which Asanga brings his work to a close:

"You are freed from every hindrance, you are superior to the whole world, you fill all that is knowable with your Knowledge. Your mind is untrammeled. To you be homage!

"You possess impassibility, no ties bind you, you are in mystical union (*samadhi*). To you be homage!

"All beings acknowledge when they have seen you that you are true man! The mere sight of you brings clearness of vision. To you be homage!

"Day and night you keep watch over the world. Diligently you practice the Great Compassion. You seek nothing but Salvation. To you be homage!

"You have perfected the sense of transcendency. You have emerged from the whole earth and become the chief among all beings, you are the Liberator of all beings!

"Diligent in all inexhaustible and unparalleled virtues you manifest your presence in the worlds and in the circles of heaven, and yet you remain as invisible to the gods as to men!"

What do the doctrine's metaphysical negations matter now? Such a pitch of religious feeling raised the soul above itself and truly transformed the initial idealism of Asanga and Hiuan Tsang into an ardent mysticism. Moreover, whether this was the desired result or no, Buddhahood here assumed the role of the Divine. Present in the hearts of all men and common to them all it united them among themselves in an ineffable communion.

Notice the extent to which the charitable impulse in Buddhism received confirmation from such conceptions as these. For the logical result of this mysticism was a thirst for charity of unquenched ardor, as celebrated by Santideva in these burning stanzas:

"This remarkable fragment which inspires in us the virtues of a Buddha is present in all creatures, and it is on account of this Presence that all creatures ought to be honored.

"And what other means have we of doing our duty toward the Buddhas, our sincere friends and matchless benefactors, than to give pleasure to creatures?

"For the benefit of creatures they lacerate their bodies and plunge down into hell. Whatever we may do for creatures we do also for them. We must thus do good even to our worst enemies.

"When our masters themselves sacrifice themselves without reserve for their children how then shall I show pride before these sons of our masters rather than the humility of a slave? . . .

"From today onward, then, to please the Buddhas I make myself with all my heart the servant of the world. May the multitude of men tread upon my head and kill me, and may the Protector of the world be content!

"To serve creatures is to serve the Buddhas, to fulfil my purpose and to remove suffering from the world; this is the vow under which I place myself!"

And to round off, this almost Christian thought: "If the suffering of the many is to end through the suffering of one alone, then he ought to bring about that end out of compassion for others and for himself."

And so, by the terrestrial paths of the great pilgrimages and by the spiritual ways of mysticism and art, the sages of the Far East wended their way toward the land of their dreams, whence they heard this mysterious summons:

"For the caravan of humanity as it follows the road of life, yearning after happiness, here is prepared the banquet of happiness at which all who arrive may partake of their fill."

With these lines of Santideva we may bring our brief account to a close. It is not our business here to pass judgment on the doctrine of the Mahayana from the point of view of its philosophical or religious value. But at the very least we may agree that it inspired the most sublime devotion, that it created some wonderful images, and that as art and history bear witness it propagated goodness and beauty in the very highest degree.

We have besides a further token of this, and one which is perhaps of even greater value than that of the thinkers and poets. It is that of the humble men and women who found in the promises of Buddhism a measure of consolation and hope, and whose voices reach us out of the depths of the past on the Chinese funeral steles, memorial statues and *ex-votos* of the Wei and T'ang eras.

On a carved stone bearing a Buddha between two Bodhisattvas we read: "I, Ts'ui Cahn-tö, servant of the Buddha, for long abandoned myself to lonely grieving for my dead parents. Before a tree shaken by the wind I thought long of them and I questioned heaven without receiving an answer. I desired to place myself in the hands of the spirits that they might draw me out of this solitary way. I then donated my family's wealth to have respectfully erected this stele with its images. I have had carved on the front the image of Maitreya (Mi-lo-fo) and behind that of Kshitigarbha (Ti-tsang). It is my hope that happiness may spread among the living and among the dead, and that animals and sentient beings alike shall all attain the fruit (of the Bodhisattva's merits)." This melancholy and touching prayer was written in the first year of the Hien-heng period (670) "by grandfather Ts-ui Fa-ying and his whole family."

Or this: "Under the great T'ang dynasty, the eighth day of the eighth month of the second year of the Ch'ui-kong period (686). The Dark Door (i.e., Buddhism) is profound and solitary. Its teaching is unique and expressed in subtle words, and the principles of its Law are as deep as the Void. . . . The Buddhist Yang Che-yuan and his sister have, for the benefit of their deceased aunt, respectfully caused to be made a stone image of the Buddha, that all their family may serve the Buddha wholeheartedly."

Could there be any more moving testimony than that of these humble voices confiding in us their anguish and their hope down the long centuries beyond the tomb? Voices raised in prayer for that Refuge, confirming how deeply the mysticism of Asanga and Hiuan Tsang corresponded to the invincible need for consolation that lies latent in the depths of the human heart. Voices raised in prayer out of the distant past, poor human voices, the voices of our brothers. . . .

CHAPTER 19

The Apocalypse
of the
Indian Aesthetic

THE METAPHYSICS of the Mahayana had created a new vision of things.

The external world had vanished like a dream. It barely more than hovered now before the eyes of the sage like the veil of mist or sea of cloud that blurs objects and dims the horizons of the tinted drawings of the Sung period. The essence of the universe, the ultimate reality itself, now found form only in a kind of dream vision, like the abrupt mountains in the landscapes of Hia Kwui or Ma Lin which loom up at an indeterminate range in great, ideal lines against the unreal distances.

Against this background of distances and mists in which the materiality of the world dissolves into a nebulous ideality we see in the foreground some sage absorbed in lonely contemplation. His face appears to express indifference, and playing across it is the half-smile of supreme wisdom before the vanity of all things. His gaze with its intense inner life is as it were lost in the vastness of the airy depths and void of all material content. For, like the face of the world, the sage's soul has emptied itself of all concrete reality. His ephemeral personality, freed from its attachment to self, has dissolved away or rather become depersonalized, and the pure ideals into which it has melted have become one with the ideality of the universe.

What then remains of the world and of the human soul? We find ourselves, as regards both, in the midst of that ocean of cloud which the traveler points out to us from the summit of some Himalayan peak, swirling away to infinity above the valleys of Kashmir.

But suddenly the mists clear. Their grey, insubstantial fluidity takes on, under the magical influence of the sun, a brightness and color such as the world of concrete forms can never know. And the universe that comes to fabulous life up there beyond the last ridges and peaks is a more beautiful universe than our own. Thus was the idealism of the Mahayana transformed by the advent of the Bodhisattvas.

Everything else is mere semblance and dream, but they, a dream more beautiful than any other, they abide. In the dissolution of the world and of self their appearance abruptly takes on a supernatural brightness. What does it matter that everything has disappeared since they are there to bring consolation to the soul? Or rather, as the Buddhists would say, all the better since it is the disappearance of things that has given birth and form to their image. These wonderful, loving figures, whose brightness the world of concrete forms entirely obscured, now in this sublimated atmosphere shine out radiantly and the whole conception of beauty is transformed by their presence.

Let us listen again to Santideva: "All flowers and fruit and herbs, all the treasures of the universe, the pure and sweet waters, mountains made of precious stones, woodland solitudes, bright creepers decked with blossom, trees with their boughs bent beneath the weight of their fruit, the perfumes of the divine and human worlds, the wishing trees and the gem trees, lakes with their decoration of lotus and their embellishment of swans, wild plants and cultivated plants and all the thousand adornments scattered throughout the vastness of space, all these things that belong to no one I gather up in spirit and present to the Great Saints and their Sons. May they who are worthy of the finest offerings accept these gifts, and may They, the Great Compassionate Ones, have pity upon me. . . .

"In perfumed bathrooms that enchant the eye with columns gleaming with precious stones, dazzling curtains embroidered with pearls, pavements of pure and brilliant crystal, with many urns encrusted with a thousand gems and filled with flowers and scented water prepare I the baths of the Buddhas and their Sons to the sound of singing and instruments of music.

"I wipe their bodies dry with matchless fabrics steeped in incense and washed clean of every stain, and I dress them in fragrant, gleaming robes.

"Samantabhadra, Mañjusri, Avalokitesvara, Kshitigarbha and the other Bodhisattvas I deck out in smooth, fine, dazzling and celestial garments and ornaments of diverse kinds.

"With exquisite perfumes whose aroma permeates the vastness of the universe anoint I the bodies of the Buddhas until they gleam like fine gold when it is polished and burnished.

"I give them torches, and jewels laid out on golden lotus blossoms, and along the perfume-soaked pavement I strew a carpet of pleasing flowers.

"I give to these Merciful Ones a multitude of aerial chapels festooned with pearls and echoing to melodious hymns. . . . I present the Great Saints with tall, bejeweled parasols with sticks of gold, rich in form and of radiant brightness. . . .

"Formed in the heart of the great lotus so perfumed and fresh, the

Bodhisattvas unfold their shining bodies and emerge from the chalices spread open to the rays of the Blessed One and are born beneath his gaze in their perfect beauty. . . .

"See them now, the damned, lifting their eyes toward the blazing Vajrapani as he stands in the sky, feeling themselves delivered from their sins, and flying up with joyous haste to join him.

"See the rain of lotus blossom mingled with perfumed water. Oh happy they as they see the fires of hell extinguished beneath its waves.

34. Bodhisattva, from Ajanta. (*Musée Guimet*)

What is this? ask the damned of each other, suddenly suffused with pleasure. It is the apparition of Padmapani!—oh that it may become visible to them!

"Brothers, they cry, we are summoned to life. See, there comes a young prince with fillets about his brow (this is Mañjusri) bringing peace to hell. Behold him! The crowns of hundreds of prostrate gods glitter beneath his lotus-feet; his eyes are moist with compassion; a rain of flowers descends upon his head from the charming palaces resounding to the song of myriad *apsaras* proclaiming his praises. . . ."

The Buddhist poet's stanzas might serve as a commentary on the frescoes of Ajanta, a parallel which is further justified by the fact that Santideva was a native of Valabhi, not far distant from the Maratha country where these famous caves were hewn from the rock, and was very likely a contemporary of the unknown masters who painted there the wonderful Bodhisattvas of Cave I.

For is not the Mañjusri evoked by Santideva the same as the "Beautiful Bodhisattva" we find on the left on the back wall? There behind him are the tiers of "aerial chapels" glimpsed by the author of the *Training for Enlightenment,* delicately colonnetted pavilions rising amid elegant palms; and farther on are other enchanted buildings and huge, stylized, almost geometrical rocks "forming as it were corbels and shadowy niches in which spirits of all kinds are disporting themselves, joined by loving couples." Against this dream landscape we see the figure of the Bodhisattva. His head is crowned with a *kirita-mukuta,* a tall, tiara-shaped headdress of gold filigree work. A pearl necklace hangs at his throat, his forearm is adorned with a bracelet of ribbons and he wears a striped loin-cloth about his hips. The shoulders of Olympian breadth, the long, slender, flawless torso, the Apollonian nobility and serenity of the face all bespeak the "Conqueror" in the fullness of his power. There is something of the Prince Charming too, of the hero of a Hindu folk-tale, in the sovereign elegance of his gestures: the right hand delicately holding up the symbolic blue lotus, the left arm hanging straight down with the hand resting lightly on the hip. His solemn, searching countenance is imbued with infinite gentleness. His eyelids are half-closed and his gaze curiously distant, turned upon the world's sufferings. The head is tilted slightly toward the right shoulder and the face is inclined in an attitude of mercy and tenderness. Lastly the mouth, clearly and firmly drawn, presents an expression of great complexity, ranging from divine serenity to human sadness before all the suffering glimpsed by the eyes, the overall impression remaining one of immense pity. This is truly the "hero clothed in modesty and virility" of whom we read in Asanga, and indeed were all the scriptures of the Mahayana to disappear this pleasing, manly figure would suffice to bring back to us the spirit of those distant times and the great compassion of Buddhist teaching.

The graceful creatures surrounding the Bodhisattva of Cave I participate in his atmosphere. The young princess, no doubt his wife, whom we see on the right, naked to the waist and crowned like him with the royal tiara, offers the same smoothness of line and the same pensive attitude. Even the pairs of spirits seated two by two in the background in the posture of the Siva and Parvati of Ellora breathe the same religious feeling in the tender inclination of their bodies. The gentleness of their caresses resolves itself into gestures of a mystical quality, so deeply are they imbued with meditation and silence.

And that is only one of the twenty visions depicted in the first cave. We turn from the "Beautiful Bodhisattva" to the large figure adorning the rear wall of the main room to the right of the vestibule. Whether, as I believe, this represents a Bodhisattva or whether it is a simple *danapati* wearing the richly worked gold *mukuta* of royalty, we cannot, once we have set eyes on it, ever forget this conception which has for thirteen hundred years pursued its silent life, so strange and so intense, in the darkness of Ajanta. The eyelids are half-closed beneath the firmament of the vast forehead, crossed by a kind of celestial arch in the great meditative furrow above the brows. Thus shielded, his gaze appears to be plunged into the inner essence, into ineffable Buddhahood; it is a gaze that sees beyond, a haunting gaze, charged with all the metaphysical thought of the Mahayana, a look of burning steadiness bearing all the virtualities of the cosmic game and disappearing within in the emptiness of all substance.

The art of Ajanta thus presents itself to us as the very illustration of the mysticism of the Mahayana. And everywhere the Mahayana went it took with it the same aesthetic, so that today, at Borobudur, at Tunhuang, at Lung-men and at Nara, it is the ideal of the Great Vehicle, the dream of Asanga and Hiuan Tsang, that is conjured up before us by the painters and sculptors of the past.

Nor need we be surprised at this immense artistic effulgence when we recall the close relations established across half of Asia by Buddhist pilgrims. The travels and accounts of Hiuan Tsang and Yi Tsing have shown us how easy it was to move about between China and India at that time, whether overland or by sea. And on the other hand the testimony of both pilgrims confirms the importance which they and their brethren attached to works of art. Their great concern, apart from bringing back Sanskrit texts, was to carry home with them Indian sculptures and paintings.

We have seen particularly the important place occupied in Yi Tsing's account of his travels by the Sumatro-Javanese kingdom of Sri Vijaya, the capital of which corresponds to the present-day Palembang. It was a kind of second India where the Chinese pilgrims stopped on their way out and on their way home in order to improve their Sanskrit or to translate the texts they had brought back from the Ganges. So we should not be surprised to find, in the eighth and ninth century reliefs of Borobudur, the same inspiration, the same atmosphere and the same figures as appeared a century earlier on the frescoes of Ajanta. The reader will find hundreds of the Borobudur reliefs with their many figures of Bodhisattvas reproduced in the volumes published by Krom. Lithe-limbed, elegant, elongated figures crowned with the tall royal tiara, performing graceful gestures of gentle tenderness and seated "Indian-style" in nonchalant poses among daises and cushions,

35. Scenes from the life of the Buddha, from Borobudur. (*Roger-Viollet*)

these Sons of the Buddhas are indeed very like those of Ajanta. Their flawless Indo-European nobility occasionally has a slightly disenchanted air, as if they were weary of their own perfection and yearned only to stoop down to the sufferings of created beings. Around them, sunk in a similar contemplation which is here preserved even in the tender attitudes of love, are the same retinues of women as we see at Ajanta, elongated nudes leaning in postures of dreamy gracefulness, performing the same ardent, lovely gestures. And in the background are the same somewhat unreal structures where the stone, worked in

36. Scenes from the life of the Buddha, from Borobudur. (*Roger-Viollet*)

Gothic fashion almost like lace, contrives to produce the same "aerial" effects as in the fabulous palaces of the Ajanta frescoes.

The same figures were evoked again at Tun-huang on China's northwestern border. There has been too much talk of the paintings from these famous caves as being the work of artisans. In fact the banners and frescoes brought back by the Pelliot and Sir Aurel Stein expeditions include some very noble works of art. It is impossible not to be moved at the sight of these late T'ang Bodhisattvas, and though clearly

37. Scenes from the life of the Buddha, from Borobudur. (*Roger-Viollet*)

glimpsed by Santideva and Hiuan Tsang. In the Pelliot expedition's "Paradise of Avalokitesvara," for example, in the Musée Guimet, Paris, the whole dream of the monks of old comes to life again before our eyes. We see the Bodhisattva in all his glory, an irradiation of faded gold in which the faithful might catch a glimpse, through the forty arms bearing the forty attributes of the Compassionate One, of the everlasting miracle of his providence. At the foot of the mystic lotus from which the Bodhisattva is emerging is a *preta* or damned soul receiving, just as in Santideva's poem, the saving drop of dew. And all around the

38. Scenes from the life of the Buddha, from Borobudur. (*Roger-Viollet*)

inferior to the paintings of Ajanta and Nara they nonetheless constitute invaluable historical witnesses. I am thinking particularly of the still purely Indian figure of Samantabhadra with his naked torso draped in dull green and pale yellow scarves, and of Kshitigarbha with the Pearl, already more Chinese but still what elegance in that classical drapery with its lively reds. Before these works of faith the pilgrims of old doubtless sat and meditated; perhaps, who knows, they even pronounced before them the fervent invocations of Santideva. . . .

And even more evocative, here we see unfolding the very paradises immense halo that surrounds the "Being of Wisdom" crowd the saints and gods and spirits. At the top, with the Buddhas of the Five Regions, is the fairy Apsaras, who has made the journey from Vedic India to the threshold of medieval Kansu there to don the red costume of the young Chinese beauty. Lower down to left and right are the Indian gods Brahma, Indra and Siva, their physical type and costume combining remembered Indian elements with the first beginnings of Sinicization. Then comes Maitreya, the Buddha-to-be, a handsome, gentle young Chinese bonze shown with hands together, wearing a red and

39. The Avalokitesvara miracle. (*Musée Guimet*)

white sash and set against a halo of garnet-red. Next we see the saintly monk Vasubandhu, the father of Mahayana idealism, here depicted as a kindly old man in Indian dress kneeling with hands together close beside the Bodhisattva on his left. In the two bottom corners are two Vajrapanis, protectors of the Law, struggling in a tall red flame with two little demons (quite charming, however), one with the head of an elephant and the other with the head of a boar. In the lower part on the right we have the monk Tao-ming worshipping a friendly-looking Kshitigarbha dressed in a green and red robe with the Golden Lion at his feet. On the left is the donor of the picture, a fine Chinese mandarin of the year 981 carrying his offertory incense-burner and (this frontier post being somewhat behind in fashion) still wearing the costume of the T'ang period.

We find the same mystical visions in the paradises of Avalokitesvara in the British Museum, brought back by Sir Aurel Stein. One of them in particular, dating from 864, is pure enchantment. Within a vast circle of old pink the Bodhisattva is enthroned upon the lotus, a starry halo about his head; his face, still Indo-European, radiates an impression of truly supernatural serenity and solemnity. The naked trunk and upper body preserve a flawless smoothness; the flesh is a dull amber shading into brown. The legs, arranged in the so-called "lotus position" (*Padmasana*), are draped in a bluish-purple robe. Above the Bodhisattva to right and left, set in two discs, one a pink sun drawn by horses, the other a yellow moon carried by birds we find the delightful naked torsos of two charming divinities. Likewise below on either side, set in lotuses, we find two further characters, one of them an ascetic; his face shines with a strange spirituality and his right arm is raised toward the Compassionate One in a gesture of adoration. These wonderful, tender images in their irradiation of old gold and pink still have the power to move us after all this time. We can imagine what impression they made in the centuries of faith upon the ardent souls of the readers of Santideva, Yi Tsing and Hiuan Tsang. . . .

Following in the wake of Dosho and the other pious pilgrims who bore with them homeward across the sea from China to the Japanese Archipelago the teachings of Hiuan Tsang and the cult of the Mahayana, we find again, on the frescoes of the Kondo or Golden Temple of Horyuji at Nara, the same supernatural figures as at Ajanta.

Superhumanly beautiful beneath the immense halo encircling their faces and the Hindu tiara of chiseled gold or the flower-decked *mukuta,* these heroes of holiness retain that inexpressible gracefulness which is their heritage from the soil of India. As with their brothers at Ajanta their Apollonian nobility of feature and mild, sedate expressions

40. Frescoes of Kondo Horyuji, in Nara. (*Mitauo Nitta*)

rob them of none of their Olympian power. They remain, like Saky-muni, their common spiritual father, "Lions of Men." Possibly Japan has even stressed, along with the Aryan purity of their features, their voluptuous "Prince Charming" solemnity. What magnificent elegance there is in their Indian postures and in the richness of the necklaces and bracelets playing against the dullness of the skin. What manly tender-ness is expressed in these naked shoulders, busts and torsos, occasionally less lithe, perhaps, than those of Ajanta, but even more harmonious.

One notices above all how in the handsome bodies, at once haughty and tender, of these Olympians of idealism the pride of eternal youth is so imbued with intellectual seriousness, so permeated with an awareness of the vanity of all things and so matured with religious feel-ing and ardent mysticism as occasionally to give the impression of be-ing almost weary of life. The generous line of the eyebrows forming, as at Ajanta, a contemplative arch across the forehead appears to give soar-ing wing to all the problems of metaphysics. And again recalling Ajanta, what inner mystery is concealed beneath these slightly lowered eyebrows which yet give passage to the eyes' unfathomable gaze? What is the word which has just died on those lips that know the vanity of everything and maintain a silence of expectation and tender compas-sion?

Their gestures, finally, what mysticity still vibrates in their graceful movements, almost haughty for being so pure! The long line of a slen-der arm with the hand held delicately open at the hip, holding a single, immense stem of flowering lotus. Gestures of "fearlessness," gestures of "reassurance" which, on these superhuman figures worthy of Leonardo himself, are so intensely significant of salvation and refuge. Lastly the hands in prayer, not properly joined together as in the Christian art of the West nor simply placed palm to palm as in the *añjali mudra* of India but, in this final rest, with only the very tips of the fingers inter-laced with infinite delicacy. These gestures of Horyuji and Ajanta, ges-tures of contemplation, detachment, fondness and faith, are instinct with the very soul of the long centuries of the Mahayana.

41. Eighth century Chinese head of Bodhisattva. (*Giraudon*)

Leaving these visions of the beyond and turning to the Sino-Japanese Buddhist sculpture of the T'ang period is rather like coming back down to earth. And yet how profoundly the statuary of Lung-men and Nara harmonizes with the thought of that great epoch.

There is no denying that the T'ang art of Lung-men is in terms of spirituality inferior to that of the Wei dynasty, and yet what beauty there still is in those crowned Bodhisattva heads from the Chinese eighth century in the Stoclet and Doucet collections. In their pure, simple, powerful lines are they unworthy of the Ajanta ideal? Is the arch of the stylized eyebrows any different from what we find at Horyuji? Are their still lips and half-closed eyes any less eloquent of the sublime meditations of the Mahayana? And do they not, in the slightly cold nobility

42. Sangatsudo Bonten, from Nara.

and serenity of their features combined with the unparalleled sweetness of their expressions, symbolize as vividly the match between the tenderness of early Buddhism and the transcendency of the new metaphysics of the Mahayana?

Take the "Monk with a *Patra*," for example, a sandstone sculpture in the former Golowbew Collection and a work as simple, direct, fervent and unpolished as a Gothic statuette; surely there could be no

43. Miroku Bosatsu, from the Chuguji at the Horyuji.

more complete expression of the ardent enthusiasm of the great pilgrims whose travels we have just evoked? Indeed one evening as I was
turning Hiuan Tsang's journey over in my mind I actually saw the
Master of the Law in the guise of this tall monk.

We might go further and cite as a symbol of the almost excessive
idealist constructions of the Mahayana the "Colossal Buddha" of Lung-
men, which dates from the very period with which we have been deal-

ing (672–6). In the vast halo of flame around the head, in the forehead penetrating far beyond human things, in the eyes, which in this case are no longer lowered to look upon creatures but gaze out beyond the world, beyond the self, into the unfathomable inner and cosmic void, the whole of the Mahayana has found expression, a Mahayana which, even at this lofty height, has almost ceased to be specifically Buddhist and has become universal. . . .

Even the crudest of terra cottas sometimes takes on unsuspected spiritual life for us when we read on the pedestal the *ex voto* inscription: "Under the dynasty of the great T'ang this image was modeled out of the bountiful earth as if the beauty of the Buddha enveloped it."

The fact remains, however, that the realism of the T'ang period, fruit of an epic century and legacy of a warlike and victorious society had an unfavorable influence on Buddhist sculpture. There too, as in the case of painting, it is to Japan that we must turn to find the true masterpieces of religious art. We need only mention by way of example the "Bon-ten," a dry lacquer sculpture in the Sangatsudo at Nara, with its contemplative face, its joined hands and its drapery which, like the character itself, is all purity, simplicity and gentleness, the very soul of prayer.

Or, to take another example of even greater spirituality, the "Miroku Bosatsu," a seventh-century sculpture in wood in the Chuguji at Horyuji. The naked bust so smooth and pure as to be almost immaterial; the rounded folds of the robe over the leg so stylized that they give an impression of fluidity; one leg crossed over the other and the left hand resting on it; the right hand supporting the head; the eyes half-closed in a distant dream completing this tableau of meditation.

Moreover this great tradition of Mahayana art continued in Java right up until the eve of the Moslem period, and from thirteenth-century Singhasari we have that magnificent statue in the Leyden Museum representing the *Prajña Paramita* or "Perfection of Wisdom," a work whose doctrinal power, elegant simplicity, spiritual vigor and also, despite its gentleness, somewhat cold beauty put us in mind once again of a kind of Oriental Gothic. It is as if the vision of Asanga, Vasubandhu and Hiuan Tsang had arisen once more on the threshold of the new age to tell a forgetful world of the greatness of the Buddhist Middle Ages.

INDEX

This book has been composed by H. Wolff Book Manufacturing Company, New York City, and has been printed and bound by Halliday Lithograph Corp. of West Hanover, Massachusetts. The text has been set in Granjon with Garamond used for display. The index was prepared by Dr. Morris Rosenblum. The design is by Jacqueline Schuman.